Nagaland

Nagaland

A Journey to India's Forgotten Frontier

JONATHAN GLANCEY

faber and faber

First published in 2011
by Faber and Faber Ltd
Bloomsbury House
74–77 Great Russell Street
London WC1B 3DA

Typeset by RefineCatch Limited, Bungay, Suffolk
Printed in England by CPI Mackays, Chatham

A CIP record for this book
is available from the British Library

ISBN   978-0-571-22148-6

1 2 3 4 5 6 7 8 9 10

For Laura

Contents

'People should develop along the lines of their own genius and the imposition of alien values should be avoided.'

Jawaharlal Nehru

'The worst sin against our fellow human beings is not to hate them but to be indifferent toward them; that is the essence of man's inhumanity to man.'

George Bernard Shaw

List of Illustrations

Acknowledgements

This book has taken some while to write, on and off over several years. Sarah Chalfant at the Wylie Agency suggested it to Julian Loose, my supremely patient commissioning editor at Faber. I would like to thank them both very much indeed. Thanks, too, to Kate Murray-Browne for guiding the book through the production process and to Trevor Horwood for his meticulous copy-editing and many useful suggestions. Peter van Ham and the late Jamie Saul travelled extensively through Nagaland between 1996 and 2006, their journeys overlapping my own. Peter has kindly provided his and other photographs of rural Nagaland together with images from the extensive Macfarlane Archive of which he, as chairman of the Society for the Preservation and Promotion of Naga Heritage in Frankfurt, is custodian. Jamie died in the Burmese Naga Hills in 2006. Their book, *Expedition Naga* is a beautifully illustrated and revelatory travelogue following in the remote footsteps of the European district officers and anthropologists of the 1920s and 1930s. I am indebted to them both. Above all, my thanks are to the people of the Naga Hills who have let me see so much of their beautiful, if challenging, country. Their names are mostly left unrecorded. This, however flawed, is their story.

While acknowledging new names for cities and countries, I have in most instances used, for clarity's sake, those best known over the centuries to Nagas, Indians, Burmese and British alike.

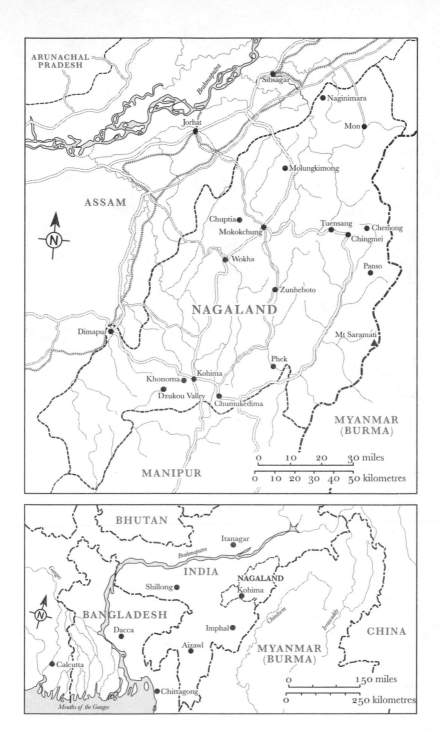

Introduction

Landlocked, and largely inaccessible to foreigners, Nagaland is one of the youngest and certainly the most hidden state of modern India. Cut off from the rest of the world at the eastern hem of the Himalayas, it is home to nearly two million people from some sixteen Tibetan-Burmese tribes who have been fighting a remote and rarely reported war for independence from India, on and off, since the early 1950s. The fighting continues sporadically, skirmishes between rival independence movements and against Indian armed forces undermining fragile treaties while tourists, some apparently unaware of the struggle being fought around them, continue to enjoy the more peaceful areas of the state.

Nagaland is tucked into the far north-eastern corner of India. It borders the states of Assam, Manipur and Arunachal Pradesh and, across an international frontier, the Union of Myanmar, once known as Burma. But up to a further two million Nagas live outside the state's borders. For many of them Nagaland, which has existed as a state only since 1963, is an Indian fabrication that fails to recognise their nationhood: a fragmentation of their natural homeland by politically expedient boundaries. What Naga independence movements and guerrilla armies have been fighting for over several decades is the dream of 'Nagalim', or a Greater Nagaland, an independent country that would unite all the tribes in a land of their own. As this book hopes to explain, their dream remains just that, and may do for many generations to come.

Here is a remarkable place – Shangri-La through a glass darkly – a people, and a war without end, largely unheard of outside the Indian subcontinent, and not much known even within it. Nagaland is a place of stunning beauty, a once-flourishing secret garden blighted by war and effectively cordoned off from the rest of the world. More than 200,000 people have died here in seven decades of brutal conflict while its political masters, despite numerous short-lived peace settlements over the years, maintain a heavy-duty military presence in the region. The Nagas, however, remain unwilling to settle for anything less than a much greater degree of freedom than the government of India is ever likely to sanction.

I had wanted to visit this high and haunting land since I was a small boy. My father, Clifford George Glancey, a child of the Raj born in Lahore, and my grandfather, George Alexander Glancey, an Anglo-Irish Indian Army general, knew Nagaland well. It was then the partly unexplored Naga Hills district of Assam, the great tea-growing region, where my uncle Reg, a future Eighth Army officer, was a planter. He spoke fondly of the Naga people. They were, he said, headhunters. But they were also hospitable, loyal, brave and passionately fond of music, dancing, hunting and extravagant costumes. They lived in remote regions of lush hills and valleys patrolled by tigers, and across the Burmese border in self-governing highland villages.

My father returned to the region with the RAF in 1944, when Commonwealth forces and Naga warriors loyal to the British drove the Japanese back from the Indian border to Burma and the tropical seas. The Japanese had hoped to reach Calcutta (now Kolkata) and Delhi through the Naga Hills. Had they done so, they would have broken the back of colonial India and of the British Empire itself.

My father said I would enjoy a trek to Burma from India through Assam and the Naga Hills. This, tricky enough in his day, is more easily said than done in mine. For many years Nagaland has remained a dream destination, much as Kafiristan had been for Brothers Daniel Dravot and Peachey Carnehan, Freemasons and soldiers of fortune, in Kipling's 'The Man Who Would Be King', a short story that I read over and over again as a boy. In 1975 it was made into an equally enjoyable and compelling film, directed by John Huston and starring Sean Connery and Michael Caine, renewing my enthusiasm for some unknown, mythical Asian world beyond established frontiers.

What few written references I came across to Nagaland as a boy were, however, hardly encouraging. I remember buying a second-hand paperback copy of H. E. Bates's *The Jacaranda Tree* at a time when this author was best known for his frightfully English novels *Love for Lydia* and *The Darling Buds of May*, but not for the stories he wrote as 'Flying Officer X' for the RAF during the Second World War. Bates developed one of these into *The Jacaranda Tree*, published in 1949. It tells the story of English settlers in Burma making a tragic escape to India with the Japanese army in hot pursuit. Led by Paterson, manager of a rice mill, their route would take them north . . . through Naga territory:

> The hills might be tough, but he knew the road, if you could call it a road, for about a hundred and twenty miles north-westward, roughly in the direction of Naga country, but beyond that he did not know it and there were few who did. He could only guess what lay there. Soon the scraped-out terraces of blistered rice-field would give way to the wretched fields where nothing grew but the thinnest sesasum and millet where in harvest the flocks of raiding paroquets were like hordes of banana-green locusts ravaging the seed. It had always been a country of continual exodus up there: a wandering from place to place by thin cattle, lean men, sore-eyed children, women with faces of teak-wood, an endless search for the hills' less bitter places. And soon all that would go, to be replaced by the folded parallels of forested rock, basaltic, bitter, waterless, like hills of iron veiled with minutest

3

cracks of sand scorched to whiteness by the long dry season, mockingly like rivers between the great sunless towers of forest and bamboo . . . It was not the things that lay behind that troubled him . . . but the things that lay in front of him. If he feared anything at all it was that the road might die up there, somewhere in the high jungle, between the foothills where they now were and the far tea country of Assam.

Bates's Paterson and his fellow escapees are left at the end of the book as they cross a bridge into these darkly haunting hills, although not before they have encountered at least a few Nagas on the way, written off here as 'the eaters of opium, the head-hunters', forever squatting, spitting chewed betel nut and waiting silently for nothing.

Undeterred by this hardly enticing advertisement, in time I got to Nagaland, and have returned several times since, not always in possession of the correct visas, yet with good grace and in hock to no party, faction, media, military or business interest. I have trekked through its eleven districts – Dimapur, Kiphire, Kohima, Longleng, Mokokchung, Mon, Peren, Phek, Tuensang, Wokha and Zunheboto. I have crossed the high and slippery eastern and southern mountain borders into Burma, where the eastern Nagas live in a world that has changed little since my grandfather's day, or even for centuries before that. Sometimes it has been a very cold place to be, at others baking hot or, all too often, sopping wet. Walking in Nagaland is rarely easy, and walking is usually the only way to travel in the saw-toothed Naga Hills, though the flora and wildlife, hunted to near extinction in parts, have provided ample and very beautiful reward. I have seen leopards and elephants on hilltops. I have watched and listened in mute amazement to striped laughing thrushes and other stunning birds competing with the extraordinary nightingale-like songs of flying lizards. I have brushed my way through a wild proliferation of rhododendrons, orchids and bright mountain flowers while eating as many wild

4

cherries, mangoes and figs as I have been able to pick. And while the area has few conventional buildings of note, the state's natural architecture of densely crumpled and deep green landscapes crowned with traditional thatched hilltop villages remains imprinted and reprinted in my mind's eye. The Naga Hills have indeed been my secret garden.

The beauty of this mesmeric landscape is only the more haunting because of the sorry state of Nagaland's volatile politics. A tourist visa will grant access to the main approved visitor sites and nature reserves, and seeing them will be memorable experiences, yet, without understanding the story of the Nagas and their country, such trips are like travelling around England ignorant of the fact that it is a monarchy and the cradle of modern democracy, however imperfect.

The politics of Nagaland are arcane and understood by all too few people even in India, many of whom still look down on their 'primitive' countryfolk with a condescension that recalls the views of British imperialists a century and more ago. A report I watched on India's NDTV in October 2007 on the problem of Delhi's ever-increasing monkey population encouraged viewers to suggest what might be done with these cheeky, and sometimes aggressive, simians. 'They can be sent to Nagaland, where the local people have no problem dealing with monkeys: they will eat them,' was one suggestion. Presumably while swinging naked through the trees between bouts of headhunting.

My own experience of the Nagas is of open, friendly, funny and protective people, despite tribal differences and bloody rivalries between their well-armed guerrilla armies. No Naga has ever threatened me. Perhaps, I have been lucky; perhaps the place has been kind to someone who wanted to see it so much and who has no axe to grind. What I have learned, though, is that the story of Nagaland, all too rarely written, is as rich as it is uncertain and even baffling. This is a land of myths and an unfathomable ancient history, of deep valley shadows and long-buried secrets. Despite many changes of lifestyle here since the

British left the Naga Hills in 1947, the intense and even spiritual relationship between the Nagas and the mist-shrouded land they dream of being wholly theirs again one day is both compelling and tragic.

This is a small corner of the world. The stunningly beautiful Naga Hills are the backbone both of the state and of this book; at their greatest extent they cover an area about one hundred and fifty miles by seventy. The highest peak, Saramati, rises some 12,500ft above the precipitous valleys carved by the Dhansiri, Doyang, Dikhu, Milak, Zungki and Tizu rivers. Yet this geographically impractical landlocked hillscape has been fought over by some of the greatest military powers and the most formidable political regimes of the past century. Astonishingly, the story of Nagaland has touched the lives of families in the depths of rural England, Germany, Japan, China and the United States. When the British stepped foot here in the nineteenth century, they drew the eyes of the burgeoning imperial world to the blue-tinged Naga Hills – an area that, until then, had been isolated for hundreds of years.

The British first gazed out over this vertiginous, semi-tropical landscape in the 1820s when driving out the Burmese, who had been there since the thirteenth century. They found fierce 'Stone Age' peoples living according to the tenets of an age-old animist religion. Despite a nominal conversion of many lowland Nagas to Christianity, these highlanders were not ready to be pacified. In 1880 the British signed a treaty under which the Nagas allowed Indian Army bases to be set up in the hills; in return, Naga tribes retained many of their old freedoms. Civil and criminal administration remained in Naga hands in areas of no immediate interest to the British.

Nearly seventy years later, on the day before Nagaland was due to be incorporated into a newly independent India in 1947, the tribes declared their own independence. Although Mahatma Gandhi had given the Naga people his reluctant blessing to follow their own destiny, Pandit Jawaharlal Nehru, India's first prime minister, most certainly had not. Seven years of fruitless negotiation followed until, in 1954, India invaded with an army 100,000 strong. Tens of thousands of Nagas were herded into fifty-nine makeshift concentration camps, where many died either from starvation or after drinking contaminated water. A 'shoot to kill' order from Delhi caused the bloody deaths of countless Nagas, combatants and civilians alike.

In 1964 a ceasefire was announced, by which time Nagaland had been declared a state of India. Fighting soon broke out again, with atrocities committed on both sides. The conflict polarised political stances. The National Socialist Council of Nagaland (NSCN), a Maoist-Christian revolutionary force, was founded in 1980. Fighting for a socialist state, and for Jesus Christ, the NSCN has battled on, in various guises, against both the modern Indian Army and breakaway factions in its own ranks up to the present day.

Although increasingly represented in the wider world – there are many Naga doctors and university professors in North America as well as mainland India – all Nagas remain, at heart and in their bones, antipathetic to their powerful and hugely populated neighbour. Most Nagas certainly live very differently from those in the rest of India. Nagaland remains a rural state. More than four-fifths of the population lives in small, isolated villages. Built on the most prominent points along the ridges of the hills, green in the day, blue and then purple as the sun drops behind them, traditional villages remain stockaded with massive wooden gates approached by narrow, sunken paths, just as they were centuries ago. Even by Indian standards, Nagas are very poor: the official per capita income of Nagaland, although reliable figures are hard to come by, is something like £75 ($120) a year, although those living in the most inaccessible valleys earn, if anything, considerably less.

And, however modern some Nagas might appear in the few towns worthy of the name, dressed in jeans, trainers and even high heels, and with mobile phones glued to their ears, tribal loyalties bind them together with ties a first-time visitor would find hard to discern. Between them, Nagas speak at least seventeen distinct languages, including Angami, Ao, Chang, Konyak, Lhota, Sangtam, Sema and English. And, of course, there are countless dialects. What Nagas will not speak, except when careermongering or working in shops and the new service industries in Dimapur, the ramshackle border town that acts as the principal gateway to Nagaland, is Hindi, the official language of India. Away from the few main towns and despite a slow invasion by global capitalism, and even a visit by the television celebrity chef Gordon Ramsay in 2009, Naga culture remains remarkably intact.

Protected and largely left alone by the British, the Naga tribes had little or no inkling that theirs was to be the country through which the Japanese Imperial Army would try to hack on its supposedly triumphal way to Calcutta, and what Tokyo believed would be the fall of the Raj in 1944. Nor would they have imagined that the communist Chinese would threaten to come this way less than twenty years later in their war with India. By default, this isolated corner of the world, inhabited by tribes whose way of life had changed remarkably little over hundreds of years, became an unlikely hub of international ambition, an improbable junction of global importance.

To me, this is one of the most extraordinary things about Nagaland. Some of the greatest political ructions and military campaigns within living memory took place here in jungles and valleys thousands of miles from the mechanised capitals of Great Britain, Italy, Germany and Japan. In my story we will meet a host of characters to whom the Naga Hills would have meant precisely nothing until political ambitions, Eastern and Western, became the stuff of global strategies and rainforest tactics.

Because Nagaland became such a slippery meeting point of global powers between the 1940s and 1970s, the Indian government has tried to keep the tightest of grips on this, its geographic Achilles heel. The tricky thing, though, is that the

Naga tribes want as little to do with India as possible. Sixty years on, independence is still little more than a dream, and the fight for the Naga Hills and for Nagalim continues, together with its attendant atrocities. (I narrowly missed being blown up myself one day walking through the Hong Kong market alongside Dimapur Junction.)

Well before I was born, Nagaland had been sealed off from the rest of world. During the days of the Raj, visitors to the Naga Hills required special internal visas to travel east of Dimapur Junction. The British reasoned that they were protecting the tribes from both Indian and modern culture. From the 1960s, Delhi went further, and made it all but impossible for anyone to enter Nagaland, including Indian citizens.

The situation is exacerbated by the fact that Nagaland itself is demographically fragmented. Its people adopt different stances on their nation and its awkward relationship with India and the world beyond. Some Nagas, especially those in Burma, live almost wholly remote from the modern world while others serve guerrilla armies equipped with modern weapons, laptops and satellite phones. Some want Nagaland to revert to the state of freedom, if not innocence, that prevailed before the British first turned up in the 1820s. Many, probably most, support separation from India whatever the consequences, and a Greater Nagaland that will encompass all Naga tribes in the region. There are those, too, who want to live a more or less wholly modern life, and others who have already emigrated in search of one.

Delhi is keen to point out that an independent Nagaland would be economically weak as well as prey to neighbouring powers, China chief among them. India needs Nagaland as a buffer to protect its north-eastern border. A slowly increasing trickle of tourists over the past decade see an ideal Nagaland as a happy marriage of environmentally friendly nature reserves and unchanged traditions. As for me, I simply do not have an answer. I can only say that I grew up with a dream of a Lost Kingdom that I hoped I would find in Nagaland. Now that I understand this uncomfortably fabricated state, and its people's aspirations, a little better, I know that the Shangri-Las we carry in our mental rucksacks can only ever be the products of yearning or wandering minds. But the disappointment of discovering that utopias exist only in the stories of ancient Tibetan mystics, Thomas More, Jonathan Swift or James Hilton, author of the curious novel *Lost Horizon*, is offset by the fact that, in reality, their supposed locations can be richer and more moving, even if in disquieting ways, than we had ever expected them to be.

My enduring relationship with Nagaland has matched and mirrored my own path through life. My story begins with the Nagaland of my childhood, experienced from another continent only through the writing, maps, photographs and researches of long-dead soldiers, anthropologists, missionaries and colonial officers. Without them, I would never have been inspired to see for myself, nor would I have met those Nagas whose voices and histories emerge as my story unfolds. Initially, this is a tale told through British eyes; as it develops, the Nagas find their own voice and their story becomes their own.

1

The Naked Nagas

The first port of call in my quest as a student to learn something more about Nagaland than I had as a child was Professor Christoph von Fürer-Haimendorf at the School of Oriental and African Studies (SOAS), a few minutes' walk from the British Museum in central London. Until remarkably recently, studies of Nagaland were the preserve of anthropologists, often with names as exotic as Nagaland itself. They seemed to hold the key to the gate of my far-off secret garden.

I must have been ten or eleven when I first tried to read von Fürer-Haimendorf's *The Naked Nagas*, a book published in 1939. This, I hasten to add, was not some half-cloaked volume of prurient Victorian pornography, full of pictures focused all too closely on the shapely figures of its unclothed subjects, but a serious early anthropological study of what, to me, were the utterly mysterious and magnetically appealing Naga tribespeople.

The subtitle of the book was 'Head Hunters of Assam in Peace and War'. What could possibly be more bewitching to a boy brought up on a heady mixture of tales from the furthest corners of the Raj: visits from Catholic missionaries bearing spears, feather headdresses and poison darts and a dream of finding his own special, wild place somewhere far away from a London – also special in its own way – of groomed red buses, polished black cabs, crested school uniforms and Underground trains that ran like clockwork?

One of the pictures I enjoyed most in *The Naked Nagas* was captioned 'Procession led by Mills going into Thenizumi village'.

Here was the khaki-clad Mills (whoever he was), striding purposefully under the brim of a sola topee into a thatched village very unlike those of the plains of India, much less those of the English Home Counties. The houses, rising from a moist tropical hillside, boasted wild and magnificently carved timber entrances adorned with crossed buffalo horns. With their untrimmed roofs, they seemed to be all but alive, more beings than bungalows. Behind Mills trailed a crocodile of local tribesmen, one of whom had turned to stare at the camera. The photographer was the twenty-six-year-old von Fürer-Haimendorf. How I wanted to be in this picture, in Mills's boots perhaps. Before you judge me too harshly, remember how old I was, and my background. I had no idea of the reality of these colonial-era journeys.

When I sat with the professor in Bloomsbury, forty-six years after he had taken that picture, I finally learned something of the mysterious Mills. It mattered to me to get to know something of men like him, because it was they who framed the mirror through which for many years the Nagas were seen by the few people in the outside world who cared to look.

James Philip Mills was born in 1890 and educated at Winchester School and Corpus Christi College, Oxford. In 1913, a year after my father was born in the eastern Punjab, Mills joined the Indian Civil Service. For the next thirty-four years he made his career in north-east India. He was a sub-divisional officer at Mokokchung in the Naga Hills from 1917 to 1924, and then deputy commissioner at Kohima, that narrow defile where the Japanese made their push on India in 1944 (and where my father, with suds in his eyes, once mistook a poisonous snake for a shower hose).

It was Mills who gave permission for von Fürer-Haimendorf to visit the Naga Hills district in 1936–7, by which time this young colonial officer had written three studies of Naga tribes – *The Lhota Nagas* (1922), *The Ao Nagas* (1926) and *The Regma Nagas* (1937), all dutifully published by the Government of Assam. In 1943 Mills was given overall responsibility for tribal matters in the north-east.

Leaving his beloved Naga Hills with reluctance in 1947, Mills sailed to England, where the following year he became Reader in Language and Culture with special reference to South-East Asia at the School of Oriental and African Studies. Between 1951 and 1953 he was president of the Royal Anthropological Institute. Ill health forced him to give up work in 1954. He died in 1960.

Professor von Fürer-Haimendorf was keen to stress how annoyed it made him to hear modern left-wing British academics and their even hotter-headed Indian peers portraying officers of the Raj in wilfully simplistic terms, as boorish, whisky-soaked racists who felt nothing but contempt for India and her people. Men like Mills, he emphasised, were far from rare. They loved India in their particular ways, and they did their best, given their backgrounds, to help those in their care, especially in tribal regions. Von Fürer-Haimendorf was not, I think, a sentimentalist. An eagle-eyed academic, ambitious explorer and sharp judge of character, he was one of many intelligent people whose fascination with India was cautioned, and hurt, by the ways in which this often great democracy had treated peoples on its margins, and especially the Nagas, since the end of the Raj. In his view the British, for all their faults and despite the necessity and rightness of Indian independence, had been far better protectors of the Nagas than their own countrymen – a view shared, as I was to discover, by many Nagas today.

The professor also told me some delightfully hair-raising stories of his first trip to the Naga Hills with Mills. They had been accompanied by several hundred Naga 'coolies' through wholly ungoverned areas on what turned out to be a punitive raid against hostile tribes by two platoons of the Assam Rifles. At one point the expedition was ambushed by hostile Nagas. After a fierce fight the victorious troop returned to base camp complete with a catch of fresh human heads, much to the delight of friendly Nagas and the horror of the Europeans.

The Nagas, as the British knew well, and as the Japanese and Indian armies soon learned, were enthusiastic headhunters. Although the practice was criminalised by the British sometime in the 1920s, the Nagas were unable to give up the habit of many lifetimes. Headhunting was still rife in the 1960s, and examples I have seen proudly on display from the 1980s onwards have sometimes seemed too fresh for comfort. Although the Nagas' main battles in recent decades have been with Delhi and the Indian Army, they continue, as they have done through the centuries, to fight among their own.

As for the professor, he quickly learned to speak Nagalese (or Nagamese), a patchwork language most Nagas understand, and, after a break back home in Vienna to write up his research notes, he returned to the Naga Hills just before the outbreak of the Second World War. Although Austrian, since the Anschluss of 1938 he had been a citizen of the Third Reich, and on the outbreak of war he was arrested by the British authorities and interned as an enemy alien under the jurisdiction of the Nizam of Hyderabad. This was a happy break. Here, von Fürer-Haimendorf was able to spend time with such tribes as the hunting-gathering Chenchu and the fierce Apa Tanis of Arunachal Pradesh. Appointed Advisor for Tribes and Backward Classes to the Hyderabad government in 1945, von Fürer-Haimendorf did his best to set up institutions that would safeguard tribal life in the India of the future.

Returning to England, and to the SOAS, in 1949, von Fürer-Haimendorf went on to write such fine studies as *The Sherpas of Nepal* (1964), and, in 1982, his incisive and moving *The Tribes of India: Struggle for Survival*. Although published a quarter of a century ago, the conclusions of this meticulously researched book are as relevant now as they were then. Take this passage from the final chapter:

During the last years of British rule in India there raged a passionate controversy about the policy to be adopted vis-à-vis the aboriginal tribes. While anthropologically-minded administrators advocated a policy of protection, which in specific cases involved even a measure of seclusion, Indian politicians attacked the idea of segregation and seclusion on the grounds that it threatened to deepen and perpetuate divisions within the Indian nation, and delayed the aboriginals' integration into the rest of the population.

The difficulty faced by the Indian politicians, however, was one that strikes anyone lucky enough to visit Nagaland today: the Paleao-Mongoloid Naga tribes have almost nothing in common with the great mass of Indians on the great plains stretching from below the Himalayas all the way down to the Bay of Bengal. They are different in appearance, culture, custom and religion.

Indian governments have sometimes been far too determinedly Hindu for their own country's good, attempting to turn this vast and hugely varied subcontinent, with a population of some forty million aboriginal tribespeople, into a homogeneous and Hindi-speaking nation. Chauvinism aside, popular acceptance of such policies may have a lot to do with the fact that the vast majority of Indians have never ventured into the far corners of their own country. And, as it has been all but impossible for them to obtain visas for Nagaland itself, how are they to know just how special this part of their own world is?

Until very recently, India's national newspapers had few or no correspondents in Nagaland. News would be filtered through desk-bound journalists in Calcutta. For many Indians, Nagaland, and all the far-flung north-eastern states, known like some galactic constellation as the 'Seven Sisters', are indeed as distant as Alpha Centauri. As for the world beyond India, Nagaland remains little more than a name. Ask most people where it is and they'll probably say central Africa. True, an increasing number of Hindi Indians work in Dimapur and Kohima. True, it is now possible to buy global consumer goods in these places, log on to the internet and watch reality television (Nagaland TV even has its own *I'm a Celebrity*-type game shows). Yet the region remains essentially remote. And, should you manage to travel beyond Nagaland's few main towns and approved villages, where life is played out like a colourful stage show by well-rehearsed local performers, you will see that this land is truly as distant from Delhi as it is from Derby or Dar es Salaam.

Von Fürer-Haimendorf summed up the view from Delhi in *The Tribes of India*:

> While many [educated Indians] concede that there is a need for some special protection [of Indian tribes], there is also a widespread feeling that any privileges enjoyed by tribes [would be] required only for a period of transition, and that within a span of ten or twenty years the integration of the tribes within the mainstream of the population should be completed, whereupon there would be no more justification for the continuation of scheduled areas and privileges for scheduled tribes.

Significantly, and for all the measured nature of his scholarly prose, von Fürer-Haimendorf prefaced the final chapter of his last book with a quote from Nirad Chaudhuri's *The Continent of Circe* (1965):

> In an industrialised India the destruction of the aboriginal's life is as inevitable as the submergence of the temples caused by the dams of the Nile . . . as things are going there can be no grandeur in the primitive's end. It will not be even simple extinction, which is not the worst of human destinies. It is to be feared that the aboriginal's last act will be squalid, instead of being tragic. What will be seen with most regret will be, not his disappearance, but his enslavement and degradation.

Since 2000 it has been possible for small groups, usually of exactly four people, to cross the border from Dimapur into Nagaland. There are even wondrous official websites dedicated to tourism in Nagaland that make this state look like an adventurer's heaven, all sunshine, exotic wildlife and happy, smiling locals dressed in feathered costumes. 'Come to sunny Nagaland,' they seem to say, 'and see paradise on earth.' Not so long ago, when I felt more or less ready to try to write this book, a foreign correspondent from the BBC told me that my trail-blazing efforts would be wasted, as it was clear from the web that any Tom, Dick or Jonathan could get into Nagaland today.

Strictly speaking, that is true. The present situation is that tourist visas are more or less easily obtained to visit 'protected areas' within officially defined 'tour circuits' with 'definite entry and exit permits'. The Government of Nagaland's policy is to 'monitor the movement of foreign tourists'. What all this means is that outsiders are relatively free to explore the areas around Dimapur, Kohima, Mokokchung and Wokha, without being escorted by state or even federal officials. These are all special places, so no holidaymaker would ever feel cheated. But what they may not do is to continue up into the heights and depths of the Naga Hills, in the footsteps of Mills and others, where the borders disperse into surrounding states and countries and traditional village life continues alongside Naga warriors dressed in battle fatigues and armed with American Bibles and Chinese rifles.

In truth, the Indian government has little to fear from curious foreigners. Aside from a few arms and drug smugglers, and a small number of ideological foreigners wanting to fight, Che Guevara-style, for the independence of a faraway people of whom they know little, most who come this way are either academically minded anthropologists or Christian missionaries. Some, like me, simply find locked doors a challenge, secret gardens alluring and the idea of mysterious tribes, imagined since childhood, intriguing. In any case, what few roads there are through the forbidden highlands are largely impassible even by Jeep or Land Rover when the rains fall – eighty inches a year, mostly during a five-month period – and they become rivers and even landslides of mud. Somewhere in the high tree canopy that still covers much of Nagaland, monkeys seem to howl with mocking laughter.

I went to see Michael Palin, the globe-trotting television presenter, author and former member of Monty Python's Flying Circus, at his office in Covent Garden. He told me that his visit to Nagaland for his BBC television series on the Himalayas was very much as I have described. He needed to complete his journey from one side of the great mountain range to the other, and to include Nagaland.

When I mentioned I was going there, friends and colleagues thought I was saying 'Lagerland'. I'd made a comedy series in the mid-seventies for the BBC with Terry Jones called *Ripping Yarns*. These were silly send-ups of *Boy's Own*-style tales of Victorian derring-do during the days of the British Empire, with one silly chump battling up the Andes with a party of frogs and another being struck down by some ancient curse made by the god of the tribesmen in the Naga Hills. We knew nothing really about the Naga Hills, but the name sounded wonderful, full of the mysteries of the colonial East. When I finally got there for the Himalayas series, I was quite aware that we were only being tolerated by the authorities, and that the true Nagaland lay somewhere up muddy tracks in those misty hills. Even the mighty BBC couldn't take us to where very few Indians have ever stepped foot.

To have travelled through Nagaland at any time over the past half-century has taken determination and no little imagination. Crossing the borders is possible, but the problem for the curious traveller, the perils of uncharted forest treks aside, is that the Indian authorities tend to view the motives of anyone wishing to travel this way outside a package tour as suspect. This is a sad state of affairs. They seem to find it hard to understand why anyone with a love of India should also have a romantic interest in the Naga Hills, or why simple curiosity might drive a traveller higher and deeper into this enticing region.

Of course, India worries. A confusing and divided independence movement appears to have been funded at various times by Pakistan, or Pakistani interests. It has been funded to some unfathomable extent by Beijing, too. Naga insurgents, meanwhile, have been trained both in China and in Vietnam during the years of US military intervention. Rival Naga armies may well have been fuelled at times by profits from extortion and the international drug trade. In any case, the authorities are understandably wary of foreigners becoming involved in the daily doings of a state that remains violent, often corrupt and generally injurious to India's self-image. Nor, of course, would it ever want journalists investigating atrocities once committed by Indian soldiers as Delhi tried to impose order on Nagaland in the face of an increasingly well-armed Naga resistance.

The cause of would-be independent visitors has not been helped by well-attested stories of Europeans posing as BBC journalists when they have been no such thing, although at least one of these stories, told in this book, is an extraordinary and moving one. Meanwhile, insurgency movements in the north-east of India as a whole have multiplied over the years. The seven new states created from the eastern recesses of Assam and the former North-East Frontier Agency in an attempt to control their destinies – Arunachal Pradesh, Assam, Manipur, Meghalaya, Mizoram, Nagaland and Tripura – have all been up in arms one way or another in recent years. A train ride through Assam along the plains of the Brahmaputra, a pleasant diversion in the days when Uncle Reg planted tea here in the 1930s, can be a dangerous experience today.

Despite these concerns, it is just about possible to make forays deep into Nagaland, to discover and understand this haunting place for yourself, as I have tried to do in this book. How strange that a land once the preserve of pith-helmeted colonial administrators and anthropologists, and little more than a curious cul-de-sac on the global map, has played a key role in the geopolitics of recent times.

And when you learn that a pan-Asian highway is planned that will link Beijing to Bengal via Nagaland, and that there seems to be oil in these virginal hills, then you might have to agree with me – or, if not with me, then with such informed observers as J. P. Mills and Christoph von Fürer-Haimendorf – that even if Nagaland were to become independent, the forces of globalisation might be too great for the dream of an undisturbed homeland ever to be made real.

My journeys to Nagaland have been an attempt to learn more about a mysterious, largely unknown and frequently misunderstood corner of the world. They have taken me well away from my early childhood view of some magical green mountain kingdom, and away, too, from the picture of Naga tribes painted with imperial European brushes by well-meaning academics and district officers. While researching this book I watched a film of von Fürer-Haimendorf revisiting Nagaland in the 1970s. Whatever his motives and interests, he seemed every inch the model of a pre-war European anthropologist patting the heads of fascinating natives. Even so, such men helped to unlock the gate to a hitherto hidden region and a people who were only just learning to make their own story known to an outside world they found difficult to come to terms with. Today's travellers are more inclined to accept the people they meet, however different, on equal terms, though it remains all too easy to over-romanticise and view those living close to nature as somehow always on the side of the angels. In my most recent travels, I have tried to put aside such distorting attitudes and instead view the country through a freshly ground lens of twenty-first-century objectivity. I hope I have succeeded.

2

Train to Shangri-La

Settled down with 'very hot' tea, a bag of mangos, a tin-foil carton of fish curry, the *Statesman*, the Gideon and King James Bibles, Khushwant Singh's *Train to Pakistan* and James Hilton's *Lost Horizon*, I began to drift in and out of sleep almost as soon as the long and heavily laden Kamrup Express departed promptly from platform 9 of Calcutta's Howrah station early one evening behind a pair of growling diesels under low clouds threatening seasonal rain.

This 2004 trip was the latest and most comfortable of the four journeys I had made since the early 1980s to India's north-east, through to what were once the loosely governed lands of the Naga Hills and, beyond them, Manipur, Burma and the North-East Frontier Agency (Arunachal Pradesh). I have travelled into and out of Howrah many times, on teeming local trains rumbling alongside platforms thick-strewn with beggars who have long made this magnificent red-brick Edwardian terminus their home, and very public washroom.

Calcutta's busiest station was given a good wash and brush-up for its centenary late in 2005, even though Halsey Ralph Ricardo's magisterial design was only finally completed, to its original plans drawn up in a studio in London's Bedford Square in 1911, the year the newly crowned King-Emperor, George V, announced that New Delhi was to replace Calcutta as the first city of the Raj. At the time of my trip the station, although undeniably grand, was decidedly grubby. Its twenty-four platforms heaved with twenty-four-hour life. The sight, though, of this great, Romanesque-style station set on the west bank of the Hooghly glimpsed through the heaving traffic grinding over Howrah Bridge as a blood-red sun sinks beyond the ever-growing sprawl of Calcutta is never less than stirring; for this is the gateway from the great plains of India, and the steaming heat of Bengal, to the fractious, stirring and largely forgotten north-east. To Nagaland.

Today, most foreigners alight at Siliguri, four hundred miles north of Calcutta, or, if they have taken the Kamrup Express, at New Jalpaiguri Junction (change for Siliguri Town). From here, tourists and railway enthusiasts head for the bright blue 'toy trains' that wind up, in improbable spirals and puffs of hazy steam, to Darjeeling and the blissful coolness of the foothills of the Himalayas. I have been one of them.

A smaller number of long-distance passengers head east for the rest of the next day in the company of Bengali bureaucrats, army officers, businessmen and migrant workers from the north-eastern states heading home, some from the coalfields east of Calcutta, as the train rumbles at a more or less steady 50mph through the pinch-point of the Siliguri Corridor. Then on along the banks of the Brahmaputra, for centuries the only more or less reliable way of travelling in this area, towards tea plantations and Guwahati, the furthest navigable point up this daunting river. And so to the fringe of Nagaland, where the train slows to a steady, station-to-station crawl, picking up and dropping off local traffic.

A deep part of my own imagination, and of my desire to travel to parts of the world that had become virtually inaccessible, was nurtured here, at this point where the great plains of India are pinched into the tea plantations of Assam and finger out into the eastern reaches of the Himalayas and the distant blue hills that lead on, through tigerish jungle, into Burma, Mongolia, Tibet, China and, perhaps, to some lost world still awaiting discovery. This is where the certainties of the civilised world crumble into unchartered waters, forests and hills of tribal territories. Where architecture becomes vernacular building. Where scrubbed and starched underwear is replaced with loincloths. Repeating rifles with bows and arrows. The honk of motorised traffic with the screech of hidden monkeys.

My father, an impeccably dressed and beautifully spoken young man, rode the overnight trains from Calcutta to reach Darjeeling by teatime the following day many times as a boy and as a young man. Noël Coward might have sung 'Although the English are effete, They are impervious to heat' in 'Mad Dogs and Englishmen', yet, in truth, anyone who was anybody on the imperial payroll, British or otherwise, could be found on those trains steaming north from Calcutta when the summer heat began to blister the stucco facades of handsome neoclassical villas leading off the Lower Circular Road and the smart southern enclaves of the Empire's 'second city' – London, of course, being the first – where my father was brought up. That Calcutta, a British foundation, was a curious mirror image of London was as true then as it is now. I cannot imagine a Londoner born and bred not taking to Calcutta like a barge to the Thames.

Making for Howrah station, carrying a sola topee and pressed into the lightest of crisp white linen suits, even the healthiest young Englishman – or Anglo-Irishman in my father's case – would be pining for Darjeeling and its promise of cool Himalayan air as the great city began to sweat beneath the burden of a Bengal summer it carried on its neoclassical shoulders. On my way to Howrah to board the Kamrup Express, on a day of simmering heat and threatening rains, I had walked from the Tollygunge Club, some five miles south of the city centre, as far as the Victoria Memorial before tumbling, broiled if not charred, into a cab for the rest of the way.

My walk was not simply a diversion but a voyage, as it were, around my father's youth. These streets, his old school, the cathedral where he'd sung in the choir, the park where he'd played cricket, the race track he'd frequented, brought to life the extraordinary difference between the form of civilisation nurtured by the British in the Indian mainland and life far beyond in the north-east. When the British came to India they brought something of – indeed, much of – the home country with them. Not just uniforms, guns and sola topees but the very streets and buildings they were familiar with and that would make them feel as if the centre of Calcutta was just a tightly rolled umbrella's stroll from Regent's Park and the Hooghly was the Thames. And since, despite the climate, colour and customs of the local people, British India really could look like this, the Naga Hills must have seemed as far away to British families in Bengal as they would have done to those at home in Buckinghamshire. Relatively few of the British stationed or settled in Calcutta ventured very far into Assam. What was to become Nagaland would have been a mystery to them. When they escaped, it was to Darjeeling. And when they travelled it was across the plains of India, or home, by white-painted liners from Calcutta Docks to Blighty. They knew of heroic military deeds performed along and over the North-West Frontier, but of the north-east . . . ? Precious little.

My walk through Calcutta, the last I would take on pavements for some weeks, took me along streets and avenues that once really did resemble those around Regent's Park in London. They made me think of how these views of India, through family photographs, old travel books, diaries, memoirs and my own youthful researches, were my very first. It was this dream of Calcutta, and the train rides north to Siliguri and Darjeeling, that first encouraged me to travel to India by myself.

Since then, I have travelled extensively there, and like so many British people with roots of a kind in the country, I have become inordinately fond of her. The stucco cocoon of what had been imperial Calcutta had also given me the confidence to look for an India beyond its Hindu and Muslim heritage, an India beyond the plains and into the hills where disaffected tribes led a very different life and for whom the Calcutta of the 1920s and 30s, and even of the 1980s and 90s, might well have seemed as distant as Calcutta is from London. Calcutta was my stepping-stone, as it had been for my father, grandfather and other half-recalled relatives to the frontiers, north-west, north-east and on to the Naga Hills.

*

Calcutta was founded on the banks of the River Hooghly in the late 1680s. By the early twentieth century it had been transformed into a great trading centre adorned with an extraordinary wealth of grand, and grandiloquent, Palladian, neoclassical, Gothic and Indo-Saracenic buildings. It was as if the best of London had been transported to Bengal via ancient Rome, medieval Europe and even Rajastan. It was also as if its grand facades and avenues had been designed to impress Western civilisation on a land surrounded on all sides by the threat of the unfamiliar and the unknown.

Although a number of Calcutta's imperial villas survive, some hidden behind gloriously garish Bollywood film hoardings, others botched and battered beyond easy recognition, it seems significant that many were once coated in gleaming white stucco. In the terrible heat and humidity of Calcutta, this began to peel almost as soon as it was applied; it was as if the process of instant decay was saying, 'Remember, Raj, that thou art dust and unto dust thou shalt return.' All empires, as history teaches us, rise, crumble and fall and, for all its architectural splendour, Calcutta must have always had the look of a city struggling with sickness, change and decay.

On a good day, though, and if you happened to be a dashing young man about town in the 1920s and 30s, Calcutta must have been a delight – as long, that is, as you kept yourself busy within limited confines. From my father's home it was a short walk in the cool of the morning, beneath skies whirling with scavenging kites, to his school, La Martiniere, described as 'East of Eton' by Delhi-based travel writer William Dalrymple in *The Age of Kali* (1998), set on what had once been immaculate lawns along Loudon Street and housed in Regency splendour. Today, an unsightly modern building, all dripping air-conditioning units and stained concrete, lurks next to the main school building like some local guttersnipe spitting a gob of energetically chewed betel nut at an elegantly dressed, and foreign, passer by.

The school on Loudon Street was one of several founded in Calcutta, Lucknow and his native Lyon by the parvenu French imperial adventurer Major General Claude Martin, a soldier who switched his allegiance to the British after being captured at Pondicherry in 1761. Amassing a fortune serving, at first, the East India Company and then the Nawab of Oud over the ensuing thirty years, Martin became variously a dilettante surveyor, balloonist, gunsmith, watchmaker, cartographer, diplomat and soldier. An educationalist and an architect, too. Today, this engagingly picaresque eighteenth-century adventurer is best remembered for the grand and successful schools that bear his name.

Although Martin was not responsible for the design of La Martiniere boys' school in Calcutta – he was long in his mausoleum by then – the main building dating from 1835–6, all Ionic columns and white stucco, by J. P. Parker and Captain Hutchinson, a military engineer, might be easily mistaken for a grand architectural refugee from Regent's Park. The last time I walked into the grounds and entered the chapel, some things had clearly remained unchanged since my father was a pupil here in the 1920s. Inside the Ionic chapel, immaculately uniformed schoolboys and their teachers in gowns were singing one of my favourite hymns:

> Immortal, invisible, God only wise,
> In light inaccessible hid from our eyes

This superb hymn, its opening couplet based on 1 Timothy 1.17 and written in 1867 by Walter C. Smith, a Scottish clergyman, ends with the transcendental lines:

Great Father of glory, pure Father of light,
Thine angels adore Thee, all veiling their sight;
All laud we would render; O help us to see,
'Tis only the splendour of light hideth thee.

Imagine singing this on a day of blinding Calcutta light. I can hear my father humming the lovely Welsh air that accompanies Smith's lyrics, and standing in that chapel that morning I could picture him there, a young suntanned Western face in the choir stalls among today's Indian pupils. My father had left La Martiniere before its doors were opened to pupils of other colours and religions in 1934. It remains one of India's top schools.

As I left, I listened to the boys sing their school song, noting down the rousing chorus in memory of an eighteenth-century French soldier of fortune written by Frederick James Rowe, an assistant teacher here, so a plaque tells me, in the late 1860s:

Faithful may we ever be
Followers of his constancy,
Firm of hand against our foe,
Soft of heart to succour woe,
This then our song shall be
As we chant his eulogy –
May our Founder's name endure,
Ever spotless ever pure!

That hymn, this song, both express a desire for purity, light, right, order, endurance and cleanliness that anyone brought up in Calcutta, whether in the eighteenth century, the 1920s or today, would understand. On a good day, years ago, the city shone in its imperial splendour, and yet its facades were always crumbling, while poverty, chaos, disease and death lurked at every door. My father was not a man given to odd habits, but he used to wash his hands more often than seemed necessary. It was

27

as important to keep clean in Calcutta as it was to dress immaculately, and preferably in whiter-than-white clothes. As with architecture, so with dress.

I imagine my father so attired just down the road from La Martiniere attending services and functions at St Paul's Cathedral, built between 1839 and 1847 to an airy Gothic design by Colonel, later Major General, William Nairn Forbes. For a strange moment, its 201ft bell tower could be mistaken for that of Canterbury Cathedral, despite the fact that it rises above a choir of swaying palms. This is a mistake even the most august historian might make on a sweltering Calcutta afternoon. The tower of St Paul's is indeed modelled on Canterbury's superb late-fifteenth-century 'Bell Harry' Tower, yet dates from only the mid-1930s. In 1934 an earthquake caused the original tower, modelled on that of Norwich cathedral, to collapse. It was already truncated, the spire that had once adorned it toppled by an earlier earthquake in 1897. The British desire for permanence was, it seems, constantly undermined. Nature was never spent here, and the call of the wild could be heard if anyone in this great city devoted to the world of getting and spending cared to listen.

St Paul's, however, still stands proudly and continues its gracious episcopal ministry. Inside, whirling ceiling fans cool its aisleless interior while, from richly carved choir stalls, selections from *Hymns Ancient and Modern*, accompanied by a mighty Willis organ, rise, in the cool of mornings and calm of evenings, to the glory of the invisible Christian God. Here there is a richly coloured Burne-Jones west window, there an alabaster reredos by Arthur Blomfield inlaid with Florentine mosaic. In such a setting, the Naga Hills might never have existed. During the heat of days that could never resemble Canterbury at any time of the year, the doors of this immaculately mopped cathedral are kept firmly closed.

I made two more turns around my father's formative years in Calcutta before hailing a cab for Howrah and trying to avoid the evening rush when the entire population of India appears to be intent on crossing Howrah Bridge. Although officially renamed the Ranbindra Setu in 1965 in honour of the poet Rabindranath Tagore, India's first Nobel laureate, pretty much everyone calls this magnificent 1,500ft-long suspension bridge by its original, workaday name. When declared open in 1943, Howrah Bridge was instantly busier than old London Bridge. Today it bears the weight of more than four million pedestrians a day as well as oily clouds of motorised traffic.

I paid a call at the city's racetrack, founded by the Royal Calcutta Turf Club in 1820. This would have been a natural stamping ground for my father, a fine horseman in his day. The track runs around the southern end of the Maidan ('open space'), the great Calcutta park laid out along the banks of the Hooghly. Originally a parade ground for the British military, the Maidan has long been Calcutta's 'lung' or green playground. It is modelled on London's Hyde Park. Today is it home to sporting clubs, fairs, statues of Indian luminaries, including several who despised the Raj and all its works, and, most notably, to one of the grandest of all British Indian buildings, the Victoria Memorial.

My father loved this building. I can see why. A British version of the Taj Mahal, clad in the same Makrana marble as Shah Jahan's deeply moving and brilliant memorial to his beloved wife, the Victoria Memorial was declared open by Edward, Prince of Wales, in December 1921. It was a symbol of all the British had done, or had tried to do, in Calcutta and India as a whole over three centuries. Indian nationalists would understandably have seen this great domed Indo-Saracenic building as one almighty offence, and yet it was commissioned, designed and built more as a vast marble love letter to India than a symbol of crushing imperial power. The occasion for its construction was, of course, the death of the Queen-Empress in 1901. The inspiration came from Lord Curzon, Governor General and Viceroy of India from 1899 to 1905, those curious years when the British Empire, although soon to implode, was at its epic and mythical peak.

Curzon imagined a kind of Anglo-Indian Valhalla, a treasury of the historical, cultural and artistic wealth of the past three hundred years. This was to be housed in ambitious galleries set around echoing courtyards and a vast central domed hall in which a statue of the young Queen Victoria would stand serenely for ever. Curzon's pantheon is a remarkable creation. The design, though, by William Emerson, who had spent much time working in India as a young architect, assisted on the spot by Vincent J. Esch, a brilliant British-born Indian railway engineer-turned-architect, is, it must be said, a little staid. Although a play of sorts on the plan and spirit of the Taj Mahal – which was restored by Curzon – the Victoria Memorial is stiff, formal and chaste. It certainly lacks the genius of that greatest of all Anglo-Indian monuments, the Viceroy's House in Delhi designed some years later by Edwin Lutyens; then again, Lutyens was one of the finest of all twentieth-century architects and the Viceroy's House, now the Rashtrapati Bhavan, or Presidential Palace, one of the world's very best buildings of any regime, period or style.

The Lutyens building is the crowning glory of Delhi, the city of grand avenues that replaced Calcutta as the capital of British India. This decision had been announced on the day of the coronation of George V in December 1911. This momentous decision meant that Curzon's Victoria Memorial would no longer be the architectural and cultural focal point of the Raj it was intended to be. Nevertheless, building work continued slowly and steadily, and today the Victoria Memorial, although less than ninety years old, appears as solidly rooted in Calcutta as any of the celebrated Mughal monuments or ancient Hindu temples to be found elsewhere in India.

After a slightly patchy post-independence history, the building is now well cared for once again and home to a richly diverting collection of Anglo-Indian, Western, Mughal and Indian paintings, sculptures, armour, manuscripts, furniture, and much else besides. Grand portraits of Anglo-Indian nabobs, once neglected, are slowly coming back to life. There may well still be some energetic, if ageing, nationalists in Calcutta who despise anything remotely British, yet the times really have been changing. For most young Indians today, the history of British India is happily just that: history. Something to be understood and not despised; to be curated, exhibited and even relished and enjoyed. The Victoria Memorial was paid for entirely by public subscription. Indians gave generously to a building that since 1947 has, in any case, been theirs.

*

On a fine morning or in a ruby sunset, the Victoria Memorial does look rather splendid, especially seen from the lakeside, with light glowing and reflections of water rippling gently across its blue-tinged marble walls. Nothing, meanwhile, and certainly no building on the subcontinent could be more different in spirit, either then or now, from life in the Naga Hills.

For my father, the appeal of the north-east must have grown as he made his first well-heeled steps away from the roundelay of imperial British life in Calcutta. His elder sister Kitty married a rugged young tea-planter from Upper Assam, Reginald Knowles, who later served with distinction in North Africa as a major in the Eighth Army. Uncle Reg had first-hand experience of meeting and dealing with local tribesmen. Gradually, my father came to know these areas, these people, and especially so as he fought and served with the RAF in Burma, Manipur and the Naga Hills in 1944–5. I cherish a photograph of him cradling a tiny Naga baby in some remote village in northern Burma. He never had a bad word to say about the people he fought for and with in this remote corner of the world.

There is in many of us a desire to both live a civilised life and experience, if only temporarily, a wilder, less-controlled world. The tricky thing is that to do so we need to step into other people's everyday lives. And such trespasses tend to expose our dreams as just that: dreams. Nevertheless, the reality of such

31

places, even if so very different from the stuff of our expectations, has the power to make us think differently about the 'civilised' world we return to. Certainly my own journeys into the Naga Hills have only encouraged me to think that so much of what we in the West build and uphold in the name of culture and civilisation is vacuous bunkum – all the getting and spending stuff – and yet the very dashing of those romantic preconceptions has helped me to understand, at first hand, an equally important concept: there are no Shangri-Las in this world, and the wild places that do exist, the landscapes and cultures we long to find and to experience, are frighteningly fragile. Of course, beautiful and even numinous landscapes remain – the high altars of desert, the dense chantries of jungle – yet humans have the unwavering ability to desecrate them all. What I have found, though, as my dreams have been pricked by sharp reality, are peoples and stories that, although far from innocent, spell out loud and clear, in word and deed, just how hard it is to maintain traditional life when faced with the lure of 'civilisation'.

Passing through the Siliguri Corridor, India's 'chicken neck', on the train from Calcutta is certainly a defining experience, although only by keeping one eye on a map and one on the passing scenery (glimpsed, in my case, through a rain-splattered window) is it possible to realise that this is truly the end of readily knowable India. Flanked by Bhutan and Meghalaya to the north, and Bangladesh to the south, the Kamrup Express snakes it way along an improbable stretch of India never more than a dozen or so miles wide into Assam. Look at the map. The seven north-eastern states might be another country, almost entirely separate from the rest of India. They balloon out from the far end of the improbably narrow Siliguri Corridor as if they were some political and geographical afterthought. And, even though Hindu nationalists and Indian politicians will take umbrage at me for saying this, perhaps that is what they are.

At New Boigaigaon the Kamrup Express turns abruptly south and crosses the Brahmaputra between Jogighopa and

Pancharatna, and then skirts the border of Meghalaya as the evening closes in. And then it stops and starts on the long crawl along the flanks of the Naga Hills. When I first came this way by train, the transition from 'mainland' India to the north-east was made graphically clear by the switch of track gauges. The broad-gauge main line ended at New Boigaigaon, and trains heading deeper into Assam ran on narrow-gauge tracks. Conversion to broad gauge took place between 1984 and 1997 as the Indian government tried to improve the infrastructure of the north-eastern states in an effort to undermine insurgency in Nagaland and elsewhere by economic means.

My first railway journeys here were not only on narrow-gauge tracks, but steam-hauled. This section of line has never been smooth railroading, however, either then or now. Not only is the number of derailments along its length something of a regional scandal reported religiously in the pages of Calcutta's *Statesman* newspaper, but the Kamrup Express has also been held up at gunpoint on several occasions in recent years, and even bombed.

Fortunately, my journey on this occasion produced no such drama, and at getting on for one in the morning, and nine hundred miles from Calcutta, the Kamrup Express bore me slowly into Dimapur Junction, the one and only railway station in Nagaland. (There is talk of a new line to Kohima, the state capital, fifty miles distant, but this, I think, is a project that will remain on the drawing board for very many years yet.) In the dark and driving rain, and amid a clamour for luggage, for documents, for taxis, for hotels, Dimapur seemed a very poor reintroduction to the land of my childhood dreams.

*

I had last come this way ten years earlier, and then twice before that in the early 1980s. Well, not quite this way. The problem of obtaining a visas for Nagaland is an age-old one; British citizens were not free to travel here during the long years of the Raj. And for all my love of the place, and of India, no exception had ever been made for me. I had wasted much time, albeit perfectly pleasantly, drinking tea and munching biscuits at the Indian High Commission and elsewhere in London, leaving with a promise that an official visa for independent travel would definitely be coming ... but always sometime in the future. Official procrastination, although wrapped in charm ('my dear Mr Glancey ...') and ever more cups of tea ('won't you take some sugar?') and biscuits, was leading nowhere. So, I became, for a while at least a would-be Baptist missionary. This is why I was carrying a Gideon Bible, a volume whose inescapable association with the top drawers of bedside cabinets in characterless hotels worldwide began when the very first batch of their kind was slipped into the bedrooms of the Superior Hotel in Superior, Montana, in 1908. More relevantly, though, it also happens to be one of the editions preferred by Naga Christians, although the King James version and translations into Naga languages appear to be equally popular. Officially, 90 per cent of Nagas are baptised Christians, and of these pretty well all are Baptists. Hindus account for an official 7.7 per cent of the population, and Muslims 1.8 per cent. Most of the tribes living in Burma still practise their age-old animist rites. Their world has barely changed since the British first came their way.

Nagaland's Baptist chapels, however, are cavernous places of worship, some crowned with lofty towers and spires and seating up to three thousand worshippers. They are certainly well financed; all parishioners are required to pay a tithe, or 10 per cent of their income or produce, to their churches. So pastors live well, and, in any case, there is clearly money winging its way from overseas, especially from Baptist congregations in the United States. Inside these barn-like modern churches, the singing on Sundays is loud and clear. As Dr Vito Aomi, principal of the Baptist College of Nagaland at Dimapur, proclaims, 'Jesus is the God of the valleys, and the God of the mountains.' You would be hard pressed to meet Ganesh, Vishnu or Kali in the Naga Hills. Naga guerrillas carry copies of the Gideon Bible with them at all times, its precious pages between camouflage covers custom made by the US publishers. Onward Christian soldiers, indeed.

When I discovered that my 'Naked Nagas' were mostly Baptists I was, to say the least, surprised. To me this was like stumbling across some lost tribe of Israel in the Brazilian rainforest or discovering an outpost of recusant Catholics attending Mass in some voluptuous Baroque shrine dedicated to the Virgin Mary in Djenne or Timbuktu. If anything, surely, the sixteen tribes living in Nagaland might have converted to Hinduism or Buddhism rather than the Baptist version of Christianity? Either would make some sense, given the state's borders with Assam and Burma. Still, as a temporary missionary, Bible in hand, I have been able to move through Nagaland quite freely.

My first visit in the early 1980s involved a long, arduous winter trek through Bhutan and Arunachal Pradesh and so across the north-eastern border. That was an adventure and made for its own sake through magnificent wild landscapes, but it was a very inefficient means of getting to the Naga Hills. If only the Indian government had been able to tell the difference between those intent on innocent travel and those bent on trade, trafficking and trouble.

My destination in sight, I walked down to the banks of Brahmaputra, fresh from visiting the then brand-new and thrilling tiger reserve at Namdapha and finding the strangely mutilated Second World War military cemetery in the jungle close to Jairampur (brought to the attention of the world in 1997 when it was officially 'discovered' by a team led by Tage Tada, Director of Research of the Arunachal Pradesh government. I had stumbled across it long before then, of course, and it must have long been known to the locals, but who had defaced this sacrosanct place?) Fishermen told me that there was a railway across the river that would take me into Nagaland, which I found puzzling. I'm good on railways and was sure that there was no line in Nagaland itself. I was wrong. Ferried into neighbouring Assam across the muscular river, in one of its gentler moods and in fine weather, I was dropped off at Dikhomukh. Here innumerable tributaries flow into the Brahmaputra. One of these is the River Dikhu, and while I was climbing up its banks the better to watch its progress through a deep and winding gorge I was approached by a slight, wiry, long-haired young man of about my own age, dressed in sawn-off jeans, his bare chest and shoulders draped in necklaces made of beads, animal teeth, tiny fur-lined paws, small gold and silver coins and, intriguingly, a Second World War Burma Star. This was 'Ngangshi' – a nickname taken from the fine cloths his family wove. He was the first Naga I had met outside London, and I was the first Englishman he had met in his life.

We sat by the river, plopping and rippling with hidden fish. Ngangshi had learned English at school. We swapped our stories, and I told Ngangshi, a Konyak Naga, of my plan to walk through Nagaland as best I could without a permit. 'They will not give you one?' No. 'My family is in Naginimara, uphill; I'll take you there.' By train? Ngangshi laughed. 'The train is not working.' So there was a railway line? And indeed there was, although some way upriver from a junction with the old Assam–Bengal Railway at Simaluguri. This had been built in 1917 to carry tea, coal, timber and stone up to the Naga Hills from the Brahmaputra valley. Now it was run down and there were no trains to be seen, though there has been talk of reviving the line ever since it closed. Not that I could have travelled by train even if there had been one, tempting though that would have been. I would have been asked to show my papers in order to buy a ticket and permit. I had none.

Ngangshi led me to a little faded-blue putt-putt boat tied to a tree on a bank, and with my one bag and his knapsack on board we set off into the shadowy riverine landscape. So low were we that not until the following morning, having scrambled up a steep bank, did I catch sight of the Naga Hills for the very first time. It really was like a glimpse of Switzerland

seen through a tropical filter. I knew my decision to come
here, however secret and strenuous the journey, had been the
right one. How those hills glistened! The pastures and paddies
leading up to them were adorned in alpine-like flora. How the
birds sang, while monkeys chattered and jeered. Up in that
beckoning green citadel was a part of my own history as well
as that of a people who had, to date, barely divulged a word
of theirs.

The journey up to Naginimara – a little over a thousand feet
above sea level – didn't look far on my out-of-date map, and
yet it took the best part of three long days. We had to abandon
the boat when we came across a string of barges carrying
some heavy-duty and well-guarded construction equipment –
something to do, I think, with a dam and a future hydro-
electricity project that, to my uncertain knowledge, has never
come about. In any case, we thought it best for me to avoid
officious-looking Indians and proceeded on foot. The road
alongside the river led through a canopy of high trees to the
old railhead at Simaluguri. Here, various of Ngangshi's relatives
fed and watered us in their tin-walled thatched hut. On
the verandah, bright insects clattered around oil lamps in the
dusk.

Fuel for the lamps came from River Dikhu itself, where
Ngangshi had shown me the sudden natural eruptions of crude
oil that formed slicks on the water. No wonder officials had
seemed so intent on development here, and yet how wonderful it
was, and I hope it still is, for local people with precious little
money to light their lamps for free.

In the morning we walked up by the old railway track and, as
the path steepened, arrived at the rickety wooden settlement of
Naginimara. I was in the Naga Hills at last. And, from here, and
with new-found friends and by tracks that could defeat a less
than hardy goat, I got about the country. I was lithe, light and
very fit back then, so the terrain held no challenge in terms of
contours, but as for leeches, sand flies, mosquitoes and other

biting, snapping tormentors, I found the going as hard as anyone else who has come this far from its few metalled roads and even fewer railways. Even the narrow-gauge locos of Wales would run out of steam in a landscape that can make Snowdonia seem little more than a rock garden.

On that first trek into Nagaland from the north through Arunachal Pradesh, I must have somehow strolled right by Shangri-La itself, and missed it. On my latest journey by train, I had been reading James Hilton's *Lost Horizon*. This is the novel that introduced us all to the dream of 'Shangri-La', a magic, peaceful land set somewhere, in Hilton's book and our collective imagination, in a lush, snow-capped Himalayan Valley. Cut off from the rest of the world, Hilton's mystical landscape was rooted, as much by accident on the part of the English novelist and screenwriter as by design, in the mythical city of 'Shambhala', a citadel of faith and dreams in the Tibetan Buddhist tradition mentioned in such ancient texts as the Kalachakra Tantra. The tradition, though, dates back even further than this, long before the emergence of Buddhism to the Zhang Zhung culture of western Tibet which located Shambhala in the Sutlej valley of what is now Himachal Pradesh.

Because Tibet was as remote and as mysterious to previous generations of travellers as Nagaland was to me as a boy growing up in England in the 1960s, Shambhala haunted the imagination of those who trekked this way in the late nineteenth and early twentieth centuries. Heinrich Himmler's bizarre belief that there existed in Tibet an Aryan master race, or something akin to one, led to seven Nazi-funded expeditions in search of both it and Shambhala, the best known led by Ernst Schafer in 1938–9. A Soviet agent, Yakov Blumkin, had led an earlier abortive expedition to discover Shambhala in the late 1920s.

He was hardly the first. Europeans had been looking for an earthly Shambhala since at least the early seventeenth century, when the Portuguese Jesuit missionary and explorer Estêvão Cacella told of his visit to the mystical city. He had certainly travelled into Tibet, where he died on some high and freezing plateau, having made the long trek from his Jesuit base in tropical Kerala. In 1833 the Transylvanian philologist and orientalist Alexander Csoma de Koros offered the precise location of Shambhala, 'a fabulous country in the north . . . situated between 45° and 50° north latitude'. Like Cacella, Csoma de Koros had also ventured into Tibet. He spent his last years writing up some of the first scholarly accounts of Tibetan culture, sponsored by the British, in Calcutta, where this 'father of Tibetology' died.

And yet, as the present Dalai Lama has made clear, Shambhala is not a city of bricks and stones: 'Although those with special affiliation may actually be able to go there through their karmic connection, nevertheless it is not a physical place we can actually find,' he told Buddhist monks during an initiation ceremony in Bodhgaya in 1985. 'We can only say that it is a pure land . . . and unless one has the merit and the actual karmic association, one cannot actually arrive there.'

The far hills of Nagaland, meanwhile, can only be visited openly with a hard-to-get visa, while Hugh Conway, Hilton's main protagonist, tells the tale, between bouts of amnesia, of his accidental journey to the secret lamasery of Shangri-La. There could never have been an easy or obvious way to reach such a mythical place. Unlike Himmler, Schafer, Cacella or Csoma de Koros, Conway had not been on a quest to discover some oriental Holy Grail. The aircraft evacuating him and his staff from the British Consulate in Baskul to Peshawar at the time of a local uprising had crashed beyond the Himalayas, somewhere in Tibet. Before the pilot died, he told Conway, in Chinese, to seek refuge in a place called Shangri-La.

The lamasery, set beneath the 28,000ft Blue Mountain, proved to be a very handy refuge indeed. Not only were there bathrooms with all modern conveniences, and central heating, but there was also a well-stocked library, a music room with a grand piano, wonderful fresh food fetched up from the fertile valley below, and, most remarkably of all, an atmosphere so tranquil that time itself had been slowed to walking pace. People grew old only very slowly in Shangri-La.

Hilton is said to have based his novel partly on articles published in *National Geographic* by the Austrian-born American ethnologist and botanist Joseph Rock. Whatever its inspiration, *Lost Horizon* was a great, and immediate, success. The name 'Shangri-La' caught on in Britain and the United States. President F. D. Roosevelt gave the name to his Maryland retreat, as did the English owners of many a Crittall-windowed southern seaside bungalow and glum north-western boarding house – no singing in the bath, no hot water after 5 p.m.

By association, 'Shangri-La' came to mean any far-off and imaginary utopia, or place of escape, as different as possible from the grim reality of the Europe and United States of the depressed 1930s. The word roosted in the Western imagination. And, perhaps, as the possibility of world travel opened up to ever more people with the advent of affordable air travel, so ever more people dreamed of their own, personal Shangri-Las, away from the madding crowds of their homeland. I was well aware as I grew up that the more people went in search of a real, geographical Shangri-La, the less likely it was that one would ever be discovered.

*

'Where are the wild places?' I asked Wilfred Thesiger over a very English meat-and-potatoes lunch at the genteel Surrey care home where this legendary traveller and writer was to die some months later.

'Wherever there are no motor cars,' he answered. 'Wherever people still walk.'

Most of us carry a wild place, a Shangri-La of one sort or another, in our hearts and dreams. The railway enthusiast in me had singled out India as one such long before I walked the hills of Nagaland, where no trains now run beyond Dimapur. Here was a country whose length and breadth I could travel behind exquisitely decorated Pacific-class steam locomotives. I wrote up one trip, a footplate ride made on a WP Pacific from Old Delhi to Chandigarh, the capital of the East Punjab planned by Le Corbusier, for Ian Jack, then the steam-loving India editor of the *Independent on Sunday.*

The footplate of a big steam locomotive, cramped by the sweaty industry of three firemen shovelling cheap, dusty coal, running at 60mph for several hours across the scorching plains of the Punjab, might not be everyone's idea of Shangri-La, but, for me at least, it was one of the truly wild places to be in the late 1980s.

Even then, that story was the result of a happy accident: the line to Chandigarh had been electrified, but something had gone wrong with the power cables that day and steam had come to the rescue. A mere two decades later, in July 2006, the Chinese National Railways opened its new, 713-mile line from Golmud on the Sino-Tibetan border to Lhasa, the capital of Tibet. Since then, officials and politicians from Beijing have been able to ride in luxurious Canadian-built coaches hauled by General Electric diesel locomotives made in Pennsylvania to the very heart of Tibet. Dangerous treks across a land that was once so very mythic and mystical to romantically inclined outsiders had become a thing of the distant past.

I rode one of the new trains. Its air-conditioned dining car, equipped with a well-stocked bar, boasted digital electronic read-outs giving continual updates of our speed, the outside temperature (inside, bottles of Tsingtao beer, originally brewed in China by Germans for German soldiers stationed there, was nicely chilled) and our altitude. A mind-numbing 600 miles of the new railway runs above 13,200ft. Trains climb to a peak of 16,740ft as they glide over the Tanggula Pass. Oxygen is provided under passengers' seats. Unarguably, this is a stupendous feat of engineering, but the Tibetans who have lived under the yoke of Beijing since the ruthless Chinese invasion of 1951 watch the trains thunder over tracks laid on permafrost and tell you, quietly and without obvious emotion, that the railway has been designed to accelerate the Han settlement of Tibet, and to allow the easy movement of troops and weapons.

Once upon a time, in days when something like Shangri-La might have existed, the Tibetans had invaded China, seized its capital (Ch'ang-an, modern-day Xian) and appointed an emperor of their own choosing. This, though, was in 763, during the rule of the Tibetan king Trisong Detsen. But life, like the express from Beijing to Lhasa, rolls on. Today the trains of the new Qingzang railway thunder through Tibet at 75mph, and even if their well-fed passengers could glimpse the faintest shadow of Shangri-La, it would be out of sight and mind in the wink of an eye, an imperious blare of air-horns and a thin, high trail of diesel exhaust. The dream destination for seekers of Shangri-La can no longer be occupied, mapped, militarised and railroaded Tibet, but rather a secret world that they alone might hold the key to, and which they might call their very own.

Wilfred Thesiger's name will forever be associated with the marshes of southern Iraq, largely drained by Saddam Hussein since his sojourns here, and perhaps even more so with the 'empty quarter' of Saudi Arabia. Born in 1910, Thesiger was the first Westerner to cross the all but lifeless Rub al-Khali desert. This represents a formidable challenge even by Jeep or Land Rover today, but Thesiger went on foot. His belief was that such basic, unaided exploration was the only way to penetrate those isolated corners of the world unmentioned by guide books, whether in Arabia or the borders of Pakistan and Afghanistan, where life remains untainted by modern technology (including, of course, the motor car). The travel writer Jan Morris described him to me some years ago as a 'remote hero, a distant figure in a far and vanishing landscape'.

Such landscapes are even rarer now. Who today can find a truly wild place of their own? Who can live out Thesiger's dreams? Of course, such sentiments are seen by many as old-fashioned today, naive and out of tune with politically correct global thinking. My experiences of Nagaland have certainly lifted me a long way from my cherished childhood dream. I might have found my own Shangri-La, but it was hardly the utopia I'd been expecting.

3

Crossing the Border

Dimapur is where most visitors to Nagaland enter the state. This rapidly growing and increasingly cosmopolitan town is just inside the border with Assam. It is where trains from what Nagas describe as the 'mainland' call on their way to and from Bengal, and to the furthest reaches of India's east. Beyond the station compound, often heaving with police and military patrols, a quarter of a million people drawn from across India and beyond its borders make some sort of living. Here are Tibetans, Bangladeshis, Hindus, Muslims, salarymen in suits. Vast Baptist churches towering over makeshift shops. Open-air food markets. A huge hospital. An airfield. Military barracks. It looks like a town thrown together from scraps and distant memories of what a town here ought to be.

This, though, is most visitors' first experience of Nagaland. Returning for the first time in some years, it reminded me of how one can travel so very far seeking somewhere special only to feel you have barely left home. A question anyone arriving at Dimapur might innocently ask is, 'Where are the Nagas?'

They are here. They just happen to look more or less like everyone else in Dimapur, a town that, superficially, nods more to the world outside than to the mist-shrouded hills that rise high and far beyond its municipal borders. But Dimapur is not Nagaland. Nagaland is still some way off, up roads bustling with 4x4s, minibuses and military convoys lumbering onwards and upwards to ever more remote villages, most of them out of bounds to foreigners and Indians alike. There is only one reliably

44

metalled road through Nagaland; it leads from Dimapur to Kohima, the state capital, and on down south across the Burmese border to Manipur. Other roads vanish in the monsoons. They turn from negotiable tracks, tricky at the best of times, into flowing channels, tributaries and even rivers of mud. They seem to be saying, 'Turn back; there is no easy way up into these hills.'

On its western flank, along and above the Brahmaputra valley, Nagaland rises to little more than 2,000ft. As you trek south-east from Dimapur, though, and on towards the Burmese border, the land climbs to an average of around 6,000ft, rising to 12,552ft at the peak of Mt Saramati high above the orchids and rhododendrons. It is notoriously hard to get above the brooding, hail-filled clouds that wreath the Naga Hills in the long months of the monsoon, yet when the clouds lift, views of Nagaland from these crests, peaks and ridges, whether at 2,000 or 12,000ft, are utterly sublime. For mile after mile a densely green landscape rises from leech-infested, mosquito-haunted tropical jungle before plunging down the next ravine to deeply shadowed rivers snaking through hills. Ravine follows ravine in apparently ever-closer succession until the greenery blurs into one under peerless blue skies. In spring, the hills are a mass of alpine flowers. This might be Switzerland or Austria. You could almost break into song. And perhaps you should, now that Dimapur is a distant memory.

This deep valley landscape means that travel through Nagaland can only ever be difficult. It is easy to see, though, why Dimapur, back across the border with Assam and with its semblance of modernity and lack of hills, attracts a growing number of settlers. Nagas love to tell tales, as the vast vermilion sun sets over the hills and the skies turn the deepest, star-studded black, of wandering souls in their forests – forests so dense that getting lost, with the possibility of never being discovered, is a genuine concern. Nagas have told me that skeletons and ghosts of wartime British and Japanese pilots haunt the jungle, as do prowling weretigers and even Shaitan himself, a demonic giant

45

who threatens hills and valleys after dark. And if the supernatural doesn't bother you then cobras, venomous insects, enormous leeches and other hidden, creeping things are dangers real enough. No wonder most rural Nagas are in bed soon after dark.

There is little in the way of grassland or, despite the alpine flowers, easy walking meadows in the hills. When you do come across anything resembling a flat stretch of ground it is far more likely to be clothed in razor-sharp elephant grass than anything found in the manicured lawns of Surrey and Sussex where so many British colonial officers chose to retire in bungalows named 'Dunroamin' or even 'Shangri-La'. Little in the way of pastureland, too, although here and there you will come across mithun, massive indigenous cattle, bred for their milk and for their horns, which have long been used to decorate the formidable entrances of Naga village houses.

Traditionally, hill people walk. The Nagas have little choice. Even the toughest 4x4 can get to the more remote villages only between October and mid-May. Walking, for a foreigner, means trekking through a jungle cathedral: great naves, transepts and aisles of palms, bamboo, rattan and mahogany. Temperatures in summer can rise to 105 °F, falling to close to zero at the top of the hills in winter. Nagas are no stranger to frost as well as sweltering heat and driving rain. They are compelled to hardiness.

Whether or not they are still headhunters is another question altogether. Some travellers, such as the contemporary German-born Peter van Ham, who has produced several beautiful pictorial books on the region, believes they are. In the first of my journeys to Nagaland I met many chiefs who had been celebrated headhunters in their younger days. They were adorned with tattoos and, on high days and holidays, sported wonderful fur or feathered hats from which sprouted the horns of wild boar. I was shown a stack of skulls in a chief's house in a village in one of the valley folds that squeeze the landscape into an improbably deep concertina between Tuensang, a hill town, and the Burmese border. I spent the night there, looked after by Sevi, a Sangtam Naga, and her family after a trek to the top of Mt Saramati.

That evening there was a wild party in the village and the men, dressed in battle gear, set off into the misty hills and folds with whoops and songs. Sevi led me out of the village late that night, saying that soldiers were on patrol close by, and took me up and up to the decidedly wobbly road that winds its often hopeless way up to Tuensang. I should stay here, she said, until it was all clear. To this day I have the haunting feeling that the village men had been on a head hunt. Perhaps I am wrong, but why else would they dress up so and, armed with their flashing daos (short-bladed swords), vanish into the night and towards Burmese villages they said they were in dispute with? Missionaries, of whom there are very many real ones, and beaming government officials like to tell visitors how all the nastier old customs have gone and how progressive Nagaland is today. Yet, in the villages that line Nagaland's long border with Burma and where families are lucky to have the equivalent of £22 ($35) a year to spend, life is still a case of subsistence farming, old stories and songs around fires, the haunted jungle and old rivalries, too.

Those dense jungles are certainly alive at all times of day and night. Zoologists and botanists describe Nagaland as a 'biodiversity hotspot'. The wealth of plants, flowers, birds and animals here is stunning. Pangolins, porcupines, barking deer and buffalo share forests, clearings and river beds with monkeys, wild dogs, elephants and at least forty different types of snake, several of them poisonous. There are bears in the higher hills, leopards too, and, best of all, tigers. This reminds me of the pocket survival guide my father and his RAF colleagues carried during the Burmese campaign that took them up as far north as Kohima. This spells out the best course of action upon encountering various breeds of potentially dangerous animal. The entry for 'Tiger' reads 'Pray'.

And, of course, living for the most part in villages high in the hills with magnificent views all around them, there are the people, including former headhunters, packaged anew for the trickle of tourists who make it here today. A website created by the National Informatics Centre of the Nagaland State Centre in Kohima under the direction of the Ministry of Communications and Information Technology has this to say about the Naga tribes:

[Their] people belong to the Indo-Mongoloid stock, whose ancestors lived off nature's abundant gifts, blessed with sturdy formidable dispositions. Above all, the people here are warmhearted and extremely hospitable! You will feel it in the air!

The Nagas with their joie de vivre, dance and songs are a part and parcel of all their festivities. Most of their dances are performed with a robust rhythm.

Here, music is an integral part of life; folk songs eulogising ancestors, the brave deeds of warriors and traditional heroes; poetic love songs immortalising ancient tragic love stories; Gospel songs that touch your soul (should you have a religious bend of mind) or the modern tunes rendered exquisitely to set your feet a-tapping.

The present generation of Nagas have ventured into fashion designing in a big way, reproducing fabrics that represent the ancestral motifs blended with modern appeal. Indeed, it is a beautiful mix of the past with the present . . . a paradise for those who are into fashion designing. This is an affluent fashion station of the East.

Nagaland is blessed with salubrious climate throughout the year and one can visit it anytime. If one is looking for a quiet getaway, from the hustle and bustle of city life, it provides the right ambience; as life here is laidback and slow – providing a tension free life.

Nature could not have been kinder to Nagaland, sometimes referred to as the Switzerland of the East; the exquisitely picturesque landscapes, the vibrantly colourful sunrise and sunset, lush and verdant flora . . . this is a land that represents unimaginable beauty, moulded perfectly for a breathtaking experience.

And so to their conclusion:

Nagas, by nature, are lovers of fun and frolic, and here life is one long festival.

I have no idea exactly where this Nagaland is. Certainly not in Kohima, much less in far-flung hilltop villages to the north or east along and across the Burmese border. It lies somewhere, perhaps, in the mind of Indian advertising agencies or government departments in Delhi. It is deeply rooted in the virtual, topsy-turvy jungle of the internet. Like most advertising copy, it is simplistic at best, pure and utter nonsense at worst. An official tourist brochure I picked up in Dimapur on my last visit told me, 'The Nagas are a handsome and friendly people. In colourful tribal outfits, with bamboo shields sheathed in bearskin and decorated spears, the Nagas are simple people, almost entirely tribal.'

Do they shine shoes, too? Have they got natural rhythm? Do they excel at sports? Such patronising representations of 'native' people will be familiar to any American or European. It seems as if the Indian authorities are as casually racist as the British had often been during the long years of the Raj. Nagas are hard-pressed people who have been fighting a war against India, and among themselves, for more than half a century. For the record, they do not spend their lives dressed in colourful traditional costumes and dancing for visiting post-colonial nabobs up from Calcutta and Delhi together with the occasional passing troupe of tourists. It is, though, rather amusing to see myths perpetuated. Here is a quote from a Burmese-based travel company specialising in exotic overland tours: 'Naga men generally go almost naked except for a small loincloth. Men's tattoos are a form of identity signifying his village or tribe. Women usually go bear breasted and wear tattoos from the time they are children as a sign to the gods.' I hope those who pay good money for such tours are not disappointed.

If you do take an officially approved tour of Nagaland – the only kind possible unless you want to risk running into trouble – you will see Nagas wearing jeans in Kohima and Dimapur. You will be able to read the latest international celebrity gossip in the *Nagaland Post*. You will be able to buy custard creams, digestive biscuits and Snickers bars in all-purpose corner shops. Tapes and CDs of the latest Western chart music. Here you will find the excess as well as the detritus of modern global civilisation. And yet, far up in the eastern and northern hills, there are Nagas, some of them admittedly dressed in jungle green battle fatigues, others resplendent in traditional costumes, still preserving or simply living the old life. In the far north-east and south, and especially along and across the Burmese border, where no tourist is permitted, the old rites and religions are still practised. Here are villages, largely unknown to British empire makers and almost wholly unknown to contemporary Indians, that make Dimapur and Kohima seem like New York and London. Here, there is no attempt to entertain what are, for the most part, decent and well-meaning middle-class Westerners in search of a holiday with a difference.

On festival days, of which, happily, there are many, Nagas dress up for their own delight in gorgeous and even outlandish costumes, rivalling those of the Rio Carnival. My friend Charity, a Sema Naga, spent many days introducing me to the real crafts and costumes of Nagaland. A careful trawl of Naga markets will still uncover superb woven baskets and mats, bamboo mugs and tuneful bamboo flutes together with some of the most stunning fabrics and headdresses to be found anywhere in the world. For anyone with the energy, a book on Naga fabrics would be a wondrous thing to research, write and design.

The rest of the time, however, the majority of Nagas are busy in rice-fields and terraces, or hard at work cultivating corn, millet, pulses, tea, tobacco, ginger, linseed, potatoes, rubber, tomatoes and sugar cane. Some tend cattle. Forestry is a major industry. Grim mines, well away from the tourist circuit, yield low-grade coal, chromium, nickel, cobalt and iron ore. Limestone is quarried. Mobile phone masts have begun to appear above treetops as modern commerce and communications gain ground. There is oil in the Wokha district, so expect Britain and the United States, as well as Delhi, to take a renewed political and military interest in the region in coming years.

Modern industry and ways of life have certainly been making inroads into Nagaland. This appears to be inevitable as the tentacles of global economy grip more and more of the world and its ways, both untrammelled and well trodden. Televisions are made in Dimapur while computer-based industries are springing up in the back streets of the town. Up in the hills, the national liberation armies produce highly professional websites. Laptops and mobile phones are as familiar here as they are in many parts of the developed world.

What Indian tourist brochures describe as 'simple people', living a laid-back life of dressing up and dancing, are, in fact, a people trying to find a way of being themselves in an increasingly homogeneous society. Contact with the outside world has been made possible in the past decade, but not especially because of roads, railways and airlines. There is only that one main road worthy of the name in Nagaland: National Highway 39, which begins in Assam, enters the state at Dimapur and heads south-east to Kohima and on down to Imphal in Manipur. This is the road to Burma. On many stretches it is pot-holed, monsoon-swept and downright dangerous. Lorry drivers refuse to make long journeys south of Kohima. If you look at the map of Nagaland, you will see that the road describes a small arc across the south of the state. The rest of Nagaland is effectively road free for much of the year. I can hear Wilfred Thesiger giving three throaty cheers from his grave.

The railway line from Dimapur to Kohima is unlikely to be laid for many years. Spoken about in eulogistic terms by Indian Railways and the Department of Transport, it would be difficult to build, unprofitable, probably blown up occasionally, and almost certainly washed away by the rain at other times. As for air travel, most civil aircraft that fly to Dimapur are the preserve of Calcutta-based officials and business executives. In late 2007 internal helicopter flights were introduced for the benefit of politicians, business executives and a few wealthy tourists and game hunters. No international carrier flies there.

Sporadic violence, endemic corruption among politicians and civil servants, extortion-style local tax gathering by Naga liberation armies, poor roads, unreliable electricity supplies and a general lack of modern infrastructure all give the lie to Nagaland as the 'Switzerland of the East'. That said, where in the Alps can you pick your own bananas, oranges, plums, pears, pineapples, passion fruit, figs, mangos and jackfruit? (Picking a jackfruit, by the way, is not so easy as it sounds: the largest of all fruits in the world, they can grow to three feet. They are best cooked and served like a vegetable – boiled or fried – although in Malaysia I have eaten them as a delicious pudding served 'à la mode'.)

There remains enough accessible and approved Nagaland to keep the tourists happy: beautiful landscapes, Kohima, festivals, wrestling contests, folk dancing and dazzling traditional costumes. Are they aware that their movements are monitored, and that they are being moved around an officially sanctioned 'tour circuit'? Perhaps; perhaps, not. And maybe it hardly matters. Nagaland is still far enough off the beaten tourist track for its allure to excite anyone who dreams of experiencing a largely forgotten land. Some first-time visitors have spoken to me of their excitement at being the very first foreigners to enter such and such a village since the British left in 1947. (Or so Nagas tell them, while keeping a straight face.) Of being feted and dined in communal village halls. Of being asked to attend ancient rituals denied other outsiders. So far, so package tour.

No one can say that Nagas lack a sense of dry, or sly, humour. They are, like other essentially poor people, making their way in the modern world, increasingly well aware of how to entertain tourists. I have seen much the same thing in different parts of the world. In the Tiwi Islands, north of Darwin, I watched aboriginals perform mysterious rituals, ate an indigestible lunch cooked over a mean open fire, washed down with horrid bush tea, and went to look at some painted poles in a wood that may or may not have had something to do with ancestor worship. Journalistic licence allowed me to stay overnight. Usually tourists are allowed only day trips to these otherwise strictly native-only islands.

Once the evening plane had whirred off into the Australian sunset with its complement of contented visitors from Sydney and Melbourne, off came the face paint and the tribal costumes. I sat down to watch a football match, drinking cold beer with the locals at their clubhouse. How was Manchester United doing, they wanted to know. What news of Arsenal? Supper was burger and chips. Cheery calls were made to fellow members of the tribe, and to relatives in New South Wales, on mobile phones. There was an electric kettle, instant coffee, toast and Vegemite to hand. Two well-fingered laptops sat open on a trestle table alongside some recent copies of popular magazines.

When I visited Petra a few days after the al-Qaeda attack on the twin towers of the World Trade Center, I had the run of the once-secret rose-red city. This tourist magnet was almost empty. The Arab world had become a terrifying place to international tourists. They had abandoned Petra as if it had been visited by all the plagues God sent to smite his many enemies in the Old Testament. The guides were left playing dice games with pebbles in the sand. They looked the part, as if they might have been there since 1812 when Johannes Burckhardt, a Swiss geographer and adventurer, stole through the narrow defile in the rocks leading to the wonder of Petra disguised as an Arab pilgrim, the first Westerner to set eyes on the fabled Nabatean city. The guides waved me hello, offered God's blessings and glasses of sweet mint tea. Had I seen the monuments? I had. Then what about joining them for lunch, as nothing else was going on? So I rode my horse and they rode their camels along the steep tracks leading up and out of the ancient city until we arrived at their caravan park, all gleaming mobile homes and chrome-plated 4x4s, and shared a fresh meal over a prolific display of the very latest cellphones. 'I have three with me always,' said one guide as he stepped out of his caravan dressed in Calvin Klein jeans, Gucci loafers, gold chains and baseball cap. 'One for calling family. One for friends. And ... one for mistress!' Cue, uproarious laughter.

On that same trip I asked guides in Wadi Rhum if they could help me organise an overnight trip into the desert, just so I could sleep under the stars and enjoy a Lawrence of Arabia moment. A price was agreed. Within two hours, well-groomed camels had been tethered to the back of gleaming 4x4 pick-ups. Cool boxes were filled and stowed. Tents furled and loaded. With cries of 'Yellah! Yellah!' and air-horns blaring 'Colonel Bogey', we headed off to what travellers in love with the desert have called the High Altar of God.

I did not get my camel ride. Our food, however, was delicious. The cool night did shine with stars, so many of them that the universe seemed too small to contain them. As for silence, and the distant voice of the God of the desert, these were drowned out by one mobile call after another all night long. I hadn't known there were so many different ring tones. I did, though, like the one of a digital muezzin calling the faithful to prayer.

My night trip in the desert was great fun, but hardly the venture I had been dreaming of. Our romantic dreams are often set obstinately in pre-modern worlds and peopled by characters from *Ali Baba* or *Just So* stories in a pantomime of our own making. The reality is usually far more prosaic.

Naga elders, as well as smart young men and women with access to mobile phones and the broadband internet, are good at telling tales tourists want to hear. All you can be certain of is that you will not be the first foreigner to visit any village on an officially approved tourist route.

In Khonoma, the village where the Nagas made their last stand against British invaders in 1879, Kitovi, a young guide affecting to be a medical student from a far-off hill family, tried to tell me exactly this. I told him that my grandfather came here as a young boy shortly after the battle. 'I don't believe you,' said Kitovi. 'You can't be old enough to have a grandfather alive then.' 'Well,' I replied, 'I don't believe I'm the only foreigner to have come here since 1947.' Kitovi laughed. 'OK, but no more tales about your ancient grandfather.' I agreed, although my story was true.

My grandfather came this way again as an Indian Army officer, based in Calcutta, as did my father years later with the RAF. A particular type of Indian Army officer tended to travel greatly before settling down and breeding late in the day. A number of them loved these hills, their flora, fauna and the fierce warriors who guarded them. After decades of sporadic fighting, from the 1820s a regard of sorts grew up between many of the British who served here and the Naga tribes. Here, in part, was a friendship between very different peoples that was to pay off handsomely in the late stages of the Second World War, much to the annoyance of Indian nationalists frustrated by the fact that the majority of Nagas proved to be pro-British when the Japanese clawed their way into their hills.

Whatever tall tales Nagas might tell you, their tradition of hospitality, like that of Bedouins, is as genuine as it is unaffected.

And the 'tourist circuit' of Nagaland can only be a delightful experience for travellers temporarily exhausted by the crowds, beggars and unmitigated bustle of central India, despite its many wonders. They are very unlikely to encounter Naga insurgents, although in Dimapur and Kohima, at least, they will probably be aware of an extensive Indian military presence.

Mostly, they will head off to Kohima, the state capital, 'a pretty town', says the official brochure, 'situated at 1,444.12 metres above sea-level. It is endearingly unspoiled, tranquil and immersed in history.' The third of these claims is undeniably true. Kohima, as we will see, has claims to be, along with Thermopylae and Stalingrad, one of the great turning points of military history and global politics. The other two claims are simply potty. Kohima has never been a dream Indian hill resort like Simla, Darjeeling, 'Ooty' or Shillong. It has always lacked handsome villas with verandahs adorned with imaginatively carved woodwork. It has no pink-gin 'n' polo clubs. No public gardens. No charmed circle.

The journey up to Kohima from Dimapur, although less than fifty miles, can take up to three hours even in a bravely driven Hindustan Ambassador taxi. The road twists and turns some miles out of Dimapur and, like any main road in the Indian subcontinent, can be a bit of a challenge. Roadside signs proclaim, 'Be Gentle with My Curves' and 'Be Patient, not a Patient'. Luckily, in the dry months, the main road is lined at comfortable intervals with stalls selling tea, snacks and, if you're lucky, delicious fresh pineapple lollies. In any case, Nagaland is no place to hurry. An attentive driver will point out the ruined fort of the Kachari and Ahom kings. Built, probably, in the thirteenth century, the fort was fed by water from enormous tanks, or reservoirs. In front of the fort there are sixty-four menhirs in four rows of sixteen. Highly decorated, and looking like a cross between giants' penises and mushrooms from outer space, some of these standing stones must be very nearly twenty feet high. They have long attracted archaeologists and anthropologists as well as the kind of Victorian clergyman in danger of being defrocked. They are certainly meant to have a phallic force, proof perhaps that Dimapur was the centre of a once-virile civilisation of which we truly know very little. Neglected for centuries, the stones were restored by order of Lord Curzon, Viceroy of India from 1899 to 1905. In his youth he had been a tireless explorer. Today, some of the menhirs are battered and chipped, while others have fallen over.

Thinking of food rather than menhirs, on my last visit to Kohima market I looked with resigned sadness at what was on offer on its scattered stalls. Skinned dogs. A capuchin monkey which I hoped was not the one offered to me for sale as a pet the previous day as I ambled through Kohima cemetery. And, along with perfectly acceptable eels and interesting beetles, pickled or otherwise, wriggling red worms, writhing white grubs and live rats tied by their tails to wooden posts, there were dozens of birds. Many of these bright and beautiful creatures offered little more than a mouthful apiece, and some were so rare that they were in danger of extinction after lunch. Nagas eat them mostly because they are poor. The books I have of the birds of Nagaland date back a long way. With the sole exception, I think, of the diligent Anwaruddin Choudhury, they are all by British authors, most of them long in their graves.

Nagas have long killed birds in their flock-loads to make beautiful headdresses, as well as for the cooking pot. Nagaland is host to four or five hundred species of bird. Some are as rare as hens' teeth. I have seen an endangered Blyth's tragopan – a red-breasted pheasant – and think I've glimpsed a wedge-billed wren babbler, if not the elusive brown hornbill. Here, though, early in the morning at Kohima market, I found myself staring queasily at a clutch of tiny scarlet finches for sale on a crude wooden bench, along with a nest of yellow-throated laughing thrushes, a brace of Mrs Hume's pheasants, a large-billed crow in a paper bag and even the sorry corpse of a great hornbill. The great hornbill happens to be the national bird of Nagaland; this, though, does not stop it from being served up as a tasty dish at supper. For me, this is like a US President tucking into a barbecued bald eagle.

Nagas will munch away happily on pretty much anything that flies and can be shot, strung up, netted, skinned, butchered or roasted. On previous visits I have been offered a grass owl and a brace of red junglefowl. If nothing quite like the unmitigated horror of its Chinese counterparts, Kohima market is not recommended for anyone with a queasy stomach or a love of animals. The Nagas are equally careless with their flora, employing slash-and-burn tactics in their forests to grow rice and other crops. Where the trees have been cleared to form rice terraces, the results can be rather beautiful, but mostly the natural landscape has been treated in a rough and ready way. Such cutting, slashing and burning is known as jhum cultivation. Bit by bit, it is destroying the very land that feeds the people of Nagaland.

When I first began reading about Nagaland in some detail as a schoolboy, I learned that 42.8 per cent of the state, officially speaking, was covered by forest. By the time I'd reached my twenties the figure was 29.8 per cent. This had fallen to less than 20 per cent in 2000. Because Nagaland is sparsely populated, the negative human effect on the natural environment has, until very recently, passed relatively unnoticed.

A tourist will still be largely unaware of the destruction being visited on the natural fabric of Nagaland. There is so much beauty to go round that the rape of the landscape, whether by traditional or modern industrial means, can be easily ignored. And there are, in any case, just enough familiar moments, certainly for British visitors, to make a trip to Nagaland a curiously comforting mix of the exotic and the everyday. The English language (of course). Cups of tea (naturally). And, here, in Kohima, the War Cemetery, a pine-fringed corner of a foreign field that is for ever England (and Scotland, Northern Ireland and Wales. India and Africa, too). Young, computer-literate clerks from government offices sit eating lunch and chatting on the short-back-and-sides grass, among the rose bushes of this gentle hillside site overlooking Kohima's tin-crowned houses, the pitched roofs of the vast new Catholic cathedral and the hideous new domed police headquarters, designed as if to say, 'Watch it, because we're watching you!'

Occasionally a party of veteran servicemen turns up in blazers and berets, sunglasses and eye-patches, to do what the locals don't: study the names on the 1,378 immaculately scrubbed white stone markers recording the death dates and ages of those who fell here, whether blown to pieces or succumbing to dreadful wounds and infection in the long weeks after the Battle of Kohima in 1944. A separate monument records the 917 Hindu and Sikh soldiers of the Indian Army who perished similarly, their ashes scattered on the terraces of the cemetery. A central cross marks the site of the former deputy commissioner's bungalow that was at the very heart of the three-month engagement that cost so many lives on both the Allied and Japanese sides; it stands at the edge of what had been the deputy commissioner's tennis court; the markings of the court have been picked out in stone.

Those who lie here are the unsung heroes of one of the most important, though largely forgotten, battles of the twentieth century. Here, among so very many, I jotted down the details of

Trooper Arthur Hillard, 7th Battalion, King's Own Yorkshire Light Infantry, 28 April 1944–20.
Private Donald Bush, 2nd Battalion, Royal Norfolk Regiment, 4 May 1944–25.
Corporal Jack Ramm, 2nd Battalion, Royal Suffolk Regiment, 4 May 1944–24.
Lt James Edward Vincent, Royal Engineers, 2 January 1945–23.

Some of the inscriptions on the gravestones are enough to bring even the most stalwart visitor close to tears. 'A very parfit gentle Knight.' 'Our only beloved son, who died that freedom might live.' 'Beatae memoriae quis nos separabit?' 'Good-night, Daddy.'

One marker honours what are thought to be the remains of Private Thomas Collins, 21, from Barkingside in Essex. The fighting at Kohima was so intense that bits of bodies were mixed into a mash of bloody tropical ooze. It seems not only sad that a life such as that of Private Collins should have been blasted from him at such a tender age, but also somehow almost ineffably strange that this young lad from just outside London should have died here in the Naga Hills. I mean, this was very probably his first trip abroad. One moment his big adventure would have been to take a steam-hauled train up to the Smoke from Barkingside station, a handsome brick building topped with an exotic cupola, and designed by the Great Eastern Railway's architect W. N. Ashbee. The next moment, drilled, dressed in khaki, Lee-Enfield .303 over his shoulder, Collins was packed off not to sexy France or Italy, nor even to exotic North Africa or Iraq, but to this utterly remote and godforsaken corner of the British Empire. I can almost hear him now: '*Nagaland?* Where the bloody 'ell's that, then, Sarge?'

I sat by Private Collins's grave and tried to imagine what he might have made of his improbable fate. The train to the docks in an uncomfortable and doubtless ill-fitting uniform, the long and increasingly sticky voyage out from Southampton on a crowded troop ship stinking of coal dust, young men, dreadful food and unwashed socks all the way to Bombay or Calcutta. The slow and sooty train ride up and through Assam. Marches in the rain through a landscape and among peoples utterly alien to most Englishmen, a land that, a decade after Collins's death, was to be sealed off from the rest of the world. Everyone Collins mucked in with spoke English, of course, and – would you Adam and Eve it? – so did the blinking natives. That would have been something to write home about. But, still, how peculiar to have ended up on your first trip overseas in an uncertain grave in Kohima.

Kohima's military cemetery was designed by Colin St Clair Oakes, an architect I know only for the design of this and other military cemeteries in south-east Asia, and for a historically minded block of polite stone-fronted shops, with flats above, in the centre of Cambridge; this is where you will find Boots the Chemist. I do not know how many times St Clair Oakes journeyed out to the Naga Hills, although he did display a sensitive drawing of his design for the cemetery in the Royal Academy's 1947 Summer Show. Again, this makes me think of just how strange and distant what was to become Nagaland must have seemed to people in Britain before Indian independence. What could those who made their way by trolleybus and Underground to that RA Summer Show have made of events in Kohima in 1944, of those who died defending it, of the Nagas themselves and of the bitter and violent politics that went hand-on-detonator with Indian independence? St Clair Oakes's terraced cemetery remains, though – all 36 tons of cement, 200 pine trees, 1,378 graves and 50,000 rupees' worth of it – a lovely place to sit and rest with the shambles of Kohima spread below, and the glistening green hills beyond.

What else can tourists see here? The zoo, perhaps. Best, though, that they give this a miss. I suppose there must be worse zoos in the world, yet this is a truly awful place. Maddened by its cruelly exposed cage and with nowhere to hide, a bear paws constantly at the iron bars framing his ragged black body; he bangs his great head against them. Monkeys next door are covered in sores. Birds lack feathers. Stones and scraps of food are thrown at these luckless prisoners. Cages are cleaned only very occasionally by skinny keepers who sleep in huts and lean-tos behind their hungry and stir-crazed charges. No, forget the zoo.

Try the museum instead, with its sad and dusty dioramas of native life complete with rather shabby and disturbingly unnatural looking mannequins. The Government Sales Emporium is hardly gleaming, although here tourists can at least stock up on examples of Naga craft. Some of this is even worth having. Woollen Naga shawls and blankets are lovely things, although I have a feeling that the best are packed off to the big government emporium in Delhi, the one that offers something special from each of India's twenty-eight states.

What else? There is that massive Catholic cathedral with its cuckoo-clock architecture of uncertain parentage, where you can meet American Jesuits, a change from the American Baptists endemic elsewhere in Nagaland. And, you can visit Kohima Village, the original Naga settlement here. This has become rather like one of those Great Exhibition villages found in Barcelona and elsewhere, depicting the life, culture and architecture of a country on an enclosed and Toytown scale. I was once shown a baboon skull here and told that it was the shrunken head of an old tribal enemy. When I laughed, the village trickster laughed with me. There are, though, especially in the villages north of the line where British governance effectively ended, and the Indian Army fears to tread today, plenty of human skulls on display. This area comprises no less than 70 per cent of Nagaland. The British had long given up trying to control tribes in the highest hills before the Queen-Empress Victoria died in 1901. The new imperialists, the Indians, like the idea of being in control of that difficult two-thirds of Nagaland, but they aren't really.

In December, the peak month for Nagaland's few foreign visitors, Kohima hosts the Hornbill Festival. Organised jointly by government, various non-government organisations and the Nagas themselves, this is the kind of slickly organised and sickly patronising event that makes me want to leap head-first through the open window of the nearest bus and head for the hills. My reaction is possibly peevish, perhaps even a bit aloof. Here, those in search of the exotic, yet unwilling, unable or forbidden to travel deeper into Nagaland, will find plenty of feather headdresses, bone jewellery, traditional dancing and wrestling, carefully edited local cuisine – no dog, not too many bugs – and clothes and faces that would be the toast of fashion magazines in the West.

When they have exhausted Kohima, tourists can take a bus ride of some twelve miles to Khonoma. When the rains set in, a 4x4 might just manage the trip, assuming that the tank has been filled with unadulterated diesel, which is not always the case. This is a beautiful place set around with rice terraces and famous for its graceful trees. It is also a village pumped with money from central government, for Khonoma is important to Delhi. This is where the great hero of Naga independence, Angami Zapu Phizo, was born, and this is where the Nagas made one of their last defiant stands against the invading British in 1879. A monument here records the deaths of British soldiers including one Lt H. H. Forbes, whose portrait I found, by chance, in an old copy of the *Illustrated London News* left unopened for decades in the cellars of my house in Suffolk. 'Killed by Naga People', reads the caption. This copy of the *ILN* was published on 14 February 1880. Valentine's Day. The British fought with breech-loading .45-calibre Martini-Henry rifles, pistols and either 7-pounder or brand-new 2.5-inch artillery pieces. Doubtless, they fought bravely.

Captain Richard Ridgeway (1848–1924), an Anglo-Irish officer of the Bengal Staff Corps, won the Victoria Cross for his single-handed attack while severely wounded on a Naga barricade while 'under fire'. From spears and rocks, I would imagine, unless they had managed to capture guns, learned to fire them and found a stash of bullets, for the Nagas of the day usually fought Bronze-Age wars. Right up until the age of AK-47 assault rifles, grenades and hand-held rocket launchers, their most effective weapon was the dao, a cross between a short-handled sword and an axe. Deadly, but hardly a match for British guns. The source of most British casualties however was usually contaminated water, dehydration or disease.

Khonoma was also attacked by the Indian Army during the early fight for independence in the early 1950s, and with full force in 1956. If Khonoma can be happily neutered, the thinking went, perhaps all of Nagaland might fall into well-ordered place. Instead of a nation of fierce, independently minded warrior tribes, Nagaland might become a land of latter-day lotus eaters. Government propaganda, in the form of tourist brochures and websites, does tend to prattle on about the peace-loving ways of the Nagas for whom life is one long festival-cum-siesta. But while Nagas can be as relaxed and as friendly as any people you might shake hands with around the globe, it is worth remembering that they have always fought among one another as well as against the British, the Japanese and the Indians.

Young people especially in Khonoma are being encouraged to develop their village along very friendly lines indeed. Which socially concerned, liberal minded and generally decent visitor to such a place would fail to be impressed by the attempt to turn this village into the very model of a modern sustainable tourist resort? Developed along such lines, this could surely be an idyllic place to stay, sunk in a deckchair at sunset listening to monkeys howl and watching stars above gently swaying lanterns while smiling Nagas in gorgeous costumes serve delicious eco-friendly dishes and, perhaps, something a little more sophisticated than locally brewed rice beer.

Will the trick work? Possibly. The system of dishing out grants to fund Naga policies that suit Delhi is helping to weaken the traditional social bonds of the Naga tribes. Those who toe the Delhi line, by default or by design, are becoming a kind of Naga middle class. Traditionally, Naga tribes have been not just classless but often democratic, too. Women have been empowered for as long as anyone can remember and some of the great Naga heroes have been heroines. Today, that structure is under threat. While there has been a middle class of educated, besuited, churchgoing Nagas in Kohima and Dimapur for some years, elsewhere the hill tribes have maintained their grip on the traditional ways of life. If you get to Khonoma, such thoughts deserve to cross your mind. While you might see and enjoy an exotic and special place, beautifully located and eco-friendly to boot, the polite Nagas showing you around might just see things differently. And as Tajenjuba, a retired Ao headhunter, said to me over a paper mug of rice beer in Khonoma, 'They're telling us to be ecological. What were we before the Indians came to tell us this? Did we have steam engines? Did we have cars?'

Not far away is, perhaps, the most exquisite part of Nagaland foreigners can reach without being turned back by the Indian military or bumping into Naga militia, who can be equally zealous when it comes to the question of documents; understandably, they have every reason to be suspicious of outsiders. This truly unspoilt landscape is the Dzuku valley. Less than twenty miles south of Kohima, this is a safe place to trek. Here anyone can be a Wilfred Thesiger or Eric Newby for a day or two. Imagine some Alpine valley as green as Ireland at its best surrounded by rolling hills, punctuated by rivers that freeze, fairy tale-style, in winter, laced with lilies and rhododendrons in summer. There are forty species of orchid here. Wild pigs. Leopards. Black bears. And those rarest of pheasants, the tragopan. A part of this valley is, though, in some ways contentious. For the ecologically minded flying in from developed countries, including mainland India, the creation of the Khonoma Nature Conservation and Tragopan Sanctuary in the Dzuku valley can only have been a good thing. Fought for from the early 1980s by Tsilie Sakhrie, a village elder, the sanctuary was established in 1998. Under threat of fines, from Rs300 to Rs3,000 (about £4 to £40), hunting in the area is forbidden.

Traditionally, Nagas are keen hunters, and while the foundation of the sanctuary might have gone against their grain, it has brought economic benefits, especially for the emerging

Naga middle class in terms of central government grants, through the Department of Tourism and a slowly increasing influx during the dry season of tourists who can commune with virgin nature here and send home seductive images of a picture-book landscape via their mobile phones. The children of Khonoma may have benefited, too. Quite a number of them have won places in universities in Calcutta, Delhi and Bombay.

Education has certainly taken some Nagas a long way from their revered villages. One of their wisest champions, now working in the United States, is Dr Paul Pimomo, Professor of English and Co-Director, Africana and Black Studies, at Central Washington University in Washington State. Dr Pimomo is also a founder of the thoughtful nagablog.com that keeps his homeland and the growing Naga diaspora up to speed about ideas aimed at helping Nagaland to develop intelligently. In March 2009 Dr Pimomo returned to Khonoma after twenty-five years away to give a public speech on the future of Nagaland. These were his opening lines:

Being a Naga in the world sometimes feels like an ant among elephants in the forest. You feel tiny, vulnerable, almost non-existent. You can be crushed underfoot by all sorts of animals, not because they hate you but because they don't know you exist.

So as Nagas, we learn to do two things to survive: first, like ants, we have to come together and build a large mound or anthill so that even elephants take notice of it and don't walk all over us. Second, like some ants, we have to adapt, evolve, and grow wings with which to take flight and soar even above the elephants. I'm talking about imagination, vision, and acquired world-class professional skills. Wings. And if there are enough of us who can fly around the anthill at the approach of other animals, we can ward off threats and protect our city and our spot in the forest. Every creature in the forest knows ants can bite and sting. Ants know that too, but that doesn't carry us far. Every ant knows that it cannot survive alone; it must be part of a large anthill. This is true especially for small groups of people like the Nagas.

Pimomo believes that Nagas have been too busy fighting among themselves to have yet formed a viable modern society. He worries that money pumped in from mainland India is only helping to widen the poverty gap between those who choose to remain in the old villages and those who flock to the towns hoping for jobs, money and modern creature comforts.

Until recently, the village was the Naga universe; the rest could only be imagined. The village was the centre of Naga life to a degree that constituted our very identity as human beings. Even today, economic circumstances have forced many of us to leave our villages, but the village has not left us. The yearning for community quintessentialised in the Naga village is deep-seated in the Naga being. There is a reason for this, of course. Our forebears did not have a literate educational system in the form of colleges and universities. But they had an effective oral and practical system of education within the village community. Those of us who are familiar with Easterine Iralu's historical novel titled A [Naga] Village Remembered know that it is based on Khonoma village, but we recognise our own villages in it.

Easterine Iralu's novel, published in 2003, is the first to be written in English by a Naga author. In trying to get the story of the Nagas heard, she upset both Indian and Naga politicians. She is currently in political exile with her husband in Norway. Her non-violent protests in Nagaland have brought accusations of terrorism from a suspicious Delhi and of treason from radical separatists. 'I sometimes imagine', she told an audience at the Gothenburg Book Fair in 2006, 'that my people are those people

67

living on the edges of the earth, crying out to be let in but dismissed by those inside as just howling wind. These are the stories I am struggling to tell, the invisible stories, of a nation denied birth, and the long struggle that is killing itself from within.'

Dr Pimomo's point, meanwhile, is that Naga identity, born in a village system with many virtues, needs to remain strong even as Nagas take advantage of education, and not simply of state handouts. Nagas need to put away their warring rivalries and to nurture the land that is so much a part of their identity.

One successful attempt to preserve both the land and Naga identity is in the Dzuku valley, where a government plan to build a mighty dam that would have channelled water to Kohima and Dimapur at the expense of wildlife in the area and villages around it has been warded off. This 1990s campaign won the support of one of India's greatest writers, Vikram Seth, in his poem 'The Elephant and the Tragopan' (1991), in which he imagines the animals fighting against witless technological 'progress':

> Reduce your runoff and your waste
> Rather than with unholy waste
> Destroying beauty which, once gone,
> The world will never look upon.

There are other and equal beauties to be found at Dzulekie, twenty-five miles west of Kohima, where rare ray-finned fish as well as familiar rainbow trout swim in the streams, and in the ascent of Japfu, less than ten miles south of Kohima and the second-highest peak in Nagaland. The views across the Dzuku valley are eye-searing. The great rolling hills beyond the University of Washington must remind Dr Pimomo of his home country and of the struggle of its essentially village-minded people.

Perhaps, though, to a young tribesman or woman from Khonoma in search of a university education, the madness of central London or Manhattan would seem equally exotic.

4

Headhunting and Basket Weaving

How many Naga tribes are there? Nagas themselves seem unsure, estimates varying between thirty and seventy-seven. The reason for this is twofold. First, the distinction between Naga tribes and sub-tribes is often blurred; second, many tribes who are not ethnically Naga, including several Kuki tribes from the Kohima district, call themselves Nagas when it suits them to be seen as allies of the most powerful and politically active of the indigenous peoples of the Indian north-east. It is important to understand that the ambitions of Nagas, and of Naga wannabes, are partly wrapped up in their individual tribal loyalties. For an outsider, these can be hard to fathom.

'The expression Naga', wrote John Henry Hutton, a Nagaland deputy commissioner and Naga specialist, in his introduction to J. P. Mills's study of the Lhota Nagas published in 1922, 'is useful as an arbitrary term to denote the tribes living in certain parts of the Assam hills, which may be roughly defined as bounded by the Hokong valley in the north-east, the plain of the Brahmaputra Valley to the north-west, of Cachar in the south-west and of the Chindwin to the east ... the south of the Manipur valley roughly marks the point of contact between the Naga tribes and the very much more closely interrelated group of Kuki tribes, Thao, Lushei, Chin etc.' This is the area Naga independence groups call Nagalim, Greater Nagaland.

Anthropological studies of the Nagas are, as yet, far from definitive. Naga tribes are, as Hutton and Mills rightly observed, spread across what today are the borders of Nagaland itself and into the fringes of Manipur, Assam, Arunachal Pradesh and northern Burma. There are probably between three and a half and four million Nagas, although no one is quite sure as records in Burma have long been poor, and because official Indian censuses are still a bit confused on the issue of who exactly is a Naga and who isn't. And, of course, the fact that the Indian government has made Nagaland a no-go area for so many decades means that few experts have travelled through the state or through Nagalim. Home-grown Naga expertise is still in rare supply, although growing as an ever increasing number either further their education abroad or abandon this troubled part of the world altogether and seek refuge in Europe, the United States and elsewhere.

What we do know is that there are sixteen tribes living strictly within the borders of the state of Nagaland. They are, although spellings vary, the Angami, Ao, Chakhezami, Chang, Chiru, Khiamniungan, Konyak, Lhota, Mokware, Phom, Rengma, Sangtam, Sema, Tikhir, Yimchungru and Zeilang. Of the other Naga tribes, the Zemis are from Assam and the Wancho, Ranpang and Nocte tribes from Arunachal Pradesh. Manipur is home to the Anal (an honorary tribe), Kabui, Lamkang, Mao, Marram, Poumai and Tangkhul. The Burmese tribes are the Mekuri, Pangmi, Para and Somra. The Hemi are spread between Burma and Arunachal Pradesh. The Khiamniungan and Konyak straddle the border between Burma and Nagaland, and the Zeliangrong can be found in Nagaland and Manipur along with the Kuki, a second tribe of 'honorary' Nagas.

None is ethnically Indian. Sharing a common, if uncertain, ancestry, some scholars believe that the tribes arrived in waves over several centuries from about the time of Christ to settle in the far-eastern foothills of the Himalayas. The Hague-based Unrepresented Nations and Peoples Organisation (UNPO), on the other hand, says that the Nagas came to their hills from Mongolia in the tenth century. No one is quite sure. There is a reference made by the Greek historian Ptolemy in the second century to a 'Nangalogae' or naked people in this general area, but no one seems to know quite who these people were and where exactly they lived. When Christoph von Fürer-Haimendorf titled his *The Naked Nagas*, this was probably the German classicist in him at work, referring back to Ptolemy, rather than some definitive naming of the hill tribes themselves, or even their state of (un)dress.

Most of the early research on the history of the tribes was carried out by enthusiastic British soldiers and civil servants from the mid-nineteenth century. Some of their first works were destroyed during early insurrections. We know this because the loss was reported by Major General Sir James Johnstone, one-time political agent in Manipur, who wrote in 1896, 'Where the Angami [Nagas] came from must be uncertain till the language of our Eastern Frontier has been scientifically analysed. The late Mr. Damant [G. H. Damant, appointed political officer of the Naga Hills district in 1879], a man of great talent and pioneer of research, had a valuable paper regarding them in hand, but it perished in the insurrection of 1879. The probability is, that they came originally from the South-Eastern corner of Tibet.'

There were, of course, many other languages and theories as to the origins of the Nagas yet to be analysed. It is, though, to such men as Major General Johnstone that we owe the beginnings of studies into Naga ethnography and culture. Johnstone would only ever claim to be an amateur, but such military men tended to be fit and confident; they thought little of marching up and down the Naga Hills to meet fierce-looking hill tribes in villages where no white man, indeed no outsider, had ventured before. Of Johnstone himself, it is significant, perhaps, that among the most prized artefacts he donated to the Pitt-Rivers Museum, Oxford, were a Manipuri polo saddle and stirrups; a man of robust, if stylish, action to the last.

Naga legends and folk tales, however, make no evident reference to Tibet, although when Johnstone himself had contacted Nagas at Samagudting in 1874, a man claiming to be at least a hundred years old told the British officer that the Nagas had come from the 'north-east' – north-east of the Naga Hills, that is – and that his people were the seventh generation living there. Was he referring to Tibet, or could he have meant China?

Years later, in *The Angami Nagas* (1921), J. H. Hutton observed that 'all sorts of origins have been connected with the Head-hunters of Malay and the races of the Southern Seas on the one hand, and traced back to China on the other hand'. He also noted that the distinctive, and to the first-time visitor utterly unexpected, terrace rice cultivation system of the Angami resembled that of the Bontoc and Igorot tribes of the Philippines.

William C. Smith, a missionary, who was to publish tribal studies and folk songs of the Nagas in the 1920s, suggested that they had moved south down the Brahmaputra valley and then on into Burma, the Malay Peninsula, Borneo and the Philippines. Dr M. Horam, a Naga scholar, has synthesised these theories in *Nagas: Old Ways and New Trends*; he says that 'there can be little doubt that at one time the Nagas must have wandered about before they found this their permanent abode; from their myths and legend one gathers that there is dim relationship with the natives of Borneo in that the two have a common traditional way of headhunting; with the Indonesians, as both use the loin loom for weaving cloth. The embroidery on the Naga clothes resembled the kind done on Indonesian clothes.'

The headhunting practices of the Nagas have indeed been connected to those of, among others, the Igorot tribes of the Philippines. These practices gradually died out with the arrival of European powers and the resultant spread of Christianity. The last time a headhunting mission in Nagaland was officially recorded was in 1958, although in remote villages there are plenty of heads on display on shelves lining the walls of village long houses. Significantly, the great ritual celebration of gathered heads for which the Iban tribe of Sarawak, Malaysia, were once famous was called Gawal Kenyalang, or the Hornbill Festival. This is the same name given to the major annual cultural gathering, now state sponsored, in Nagaland. Today, the Hornbill Festival is quite innocent, although the bird, sought for its large, bright and distinctive feathers, might once have been associated by the Nagas, as it was for the Ibans, with Singalang Burung, or his equivalent, the bird-god of war and, in pre-Christian times, the most important of all the animist gods.

There is no evidence to suggest that Nagas have ever been cannibals. Why, then have they so often been portrayed as such? One possibility is that the Nagas share many characteristics, both physical and cultural, with hill tribes in Indonesia who were cannibals until recent times. The Bataks of Sumatra, for example, isolated for many centuries, used to behead and eat both enemies and lawbreakers (head and hands being displayed either as trophies or as a warning to would-be miscreants).

Headhunting aside, many Indonesian tribes have several cultural connections with the Nagas. The seafaring Bugis, for example, who inhabit many islands in the archipelago, build timber and bamboo houses with pairs of crossed roof finials symbolising cattle horns. Crossed mithun horns are very much a characteristic of timber-and-bamboo Naga longhouses.

There are clearly many links between the Nagas and the tribes who, historically, made their way by land and sea to the southern oceans from somewhere in the east-central Asian land mass. Gathering the evidence of British, Indian and Naga sleuths and scholars, it seems most likely that the ancestors of the Nagas emigrated south from a source in the Asiatic mainland, very possibly in China's Yunnan province. Yunnan borders Burma. It is also where the earliest known human beings lived in China and remains a place of extraordinary human diversity. Of China's fifty-six officially registered indigenous minorities, twenty-five live in Yunnan, where they form 38 per cent of the population. It has always been one of the world's junction boxes, with peoples criss-crossing its extensive borders on treks to other parts of Asia and Oceania.

Significantly, from the 1960s, it was to Yunnan that Naga guerrillas trekked to be trained, armed and, to a certain degree, politically indoctrinated. The Maoist element in Naga insurgent thinking may be due as much to subconscious cultural links with the Chinese as to a commitment to the Great Helmsman's revolutionary theory.

From Yunnan, the people who became the Nagas might well have made their way down through Burma, through what today is the rather seedy Chinese border town of Ruili, rife with prostitution, arms and drug-trafficking, through the great river valleys and jungles and so to the sea at Moulmein, now Mawlamyaing, on the west coast of Burma. Moulmein will be known to British readers as the hostile town featured in George Orwell's disturbing, anti-imperialist short story 'Shooting an Elephant' (1936). More enjoyably, a reference to the city launches Rudyard Kipling's rollicking rhyme 'Mandalay', published in his popular *Barrack Room Ballads* of 1892:

> By the old Moulmein Pagoda, lookin' lazy at the sea,
> There's a Burma girl a-settin', and I know she thinks o'
>   me;
> For the wind is in the palm-trees, and the temple-bells they
>   say,
> 'Come you back, you British soldier; come you back to
>   Mandalay.'

For some reason, some of the ancestral Nagas, unmoved by the calls of girls 'a-settin' by an old pagoda by the sea, moved north-west again and into the security of what the British came to know as the Naga Hills. Other Nagas, meanwhile, continued south and on to Malaysia, Indonesia, Sumatra, Taiwan and the Philippines. Some, on the trek back north, settled in the Chindwin and other river valleys in what became Burma.

All this seems to make sense. I have often wondered why Nagas make such rich use of cowries and conch shells in their traditional costumes when they live so far from the sea. They may well have adopted this tradition from those distant times when their ancestors did so. The Naga scholar R. R. Shimray, author of *Origin and Culture of Nagas* (1985), believed that the forebears of today's Nagas might well have lived in a coastal region:

> The hypothesis that the Nagas must have come from the sea-coast, or at least seen some Islands or the seas, is strengthened by the life-style of the Nagas and the ornaments being used till today in many Naga villages. The Naga, being left undisturbed for such a long time, have retained the culture of the most ancient times till today. Their fondness of Cowries shells for beautifying the dress, and use of Conch shells as ornaments (precious ornaments for them) and the facts that the Nagas have many customs and way of life very similar to that of those living in the remote parts of Borneo, Sarawak, Indonesia, Malaysia etc. indicates that their ancient abode was near the sea, if not in some islands.

Among those customs was headhunting, while the traditional thatched homes of the Nagas are very similar to those found in Borneo and Indonesia.

Those seashells do indeed tell us something special about the roots of the Nagas; their way of life has always pointed, and even travelled in distant memory, away from the hot plains of India and towards the peninsulas and archipelagos fingering out into the south seas and the Pacific Ocean. I remember the excitement I felt at my own bit of archaeological sleuthing when I filled my hands with tiny, ancient seashells while scooping desert sand away from the remains of the Sumerian ziggurat at Eridu in southern Iraq. Eridu was, arguably, the world's first city, and its ziggurat, although rebuilt as many as sixteen times in the ancient era, one of the world's very first designed buildings. When I visited in the ember days of Saddam Hussein's regime, it was just possible to reach Eridu, with a military escort and along a pot-holed track lined with the detritus of the first Gulf War. We got to Eridu at about midday. The sun blazed. The temperature was exactly 50 °C. And all around was the silence of a scorching desert stretching as far as screwed-up eyes could see.

Having got to Eridu by happy accident, and not yet having read the evidence tucked away in the Iraqi Museum in Baghdad and in the vast echoing vaults of the British Museum in Bloomsbury, I had not understood why such an important place – the first great venture into urban planning and monumental architecture – was hidden in such a deathly hot and dry place. The seashells were the obvious clue. My discovery would seem very naive and simplistic to a professional archaeologist, yet for me, at least, it was a magical moment to put two and two, or sand and seashells, together and to realise that thousands of years ago Eridu must have stood by the sea. This had to make sense. Why otherwise would all those thousands of tiny seashells, washed up and bleached by the tides of the desert, be there?

Now, standing on top of the shallow remains of a once-proud Sumerian temple, I could see, in my mind's eye, ships emerging from the shimmering desert horizon. I could imagine Eridu as the centre of seaborne trade and commerce. Looking at Nagas and their costumes – those seashells, the feathers, the similarity between their looks and details of their way of life, from farming methods to the design, materials and construction of their homes – I could see the reasonableness of the case for them having once lived by the sea.

This also made sense because Bronze Age travellers journeyed extensively along trade routes shaped by the wind and with the tide. Perhaps at last I had discovered the answer to a question that had always puzzled me as a child, turning the pages of old encyclopedias and picture books: why 'primitive' peoples living as far apart as the mountain villages of Bolivia, the buffalo plains of Wyoming and the deep jungles of Burma looked as if they might be cousins separated by a few days' trek rather than thousands of miles of ocean.

I remember one day walking into the Naga village of Lahe, in Burma, and catching sight of a festive gathering of tribesmen in magnificent feathered headdresses; they could easily be Cherokee or Iroquois, I thought. On reflection, this was not such a potty notion. The Nagas may have lived in the secret fastness of their landlocked blue hills for many centuries, and yet they remain part of a vast diaspora that has spread south and east and west from somewhere in China or Mongolia, and possibly right around the Pacific. The one direction they didn't take, so very significantly for their future, was west to the great plains of India. I feel slightly bad for thinking that Nagaland and India go together like the Sioux and General Custer.

There are, in any case, Naga folk songs, handed down over very many generations, and not always written down even today, that tell of ancient journeys of the people from the sea to the hills. What we know for certain, and from the earliest written documents available, is that the Nagas were long known to have been fierce warriors. Certainly, the Nagas were renowned fighters when, in the early thirteenth century, the Ahom kings of Thailand managed to conquer Assam, but not the neighbouring Naga Hills. The Nagas clearly liked to keep themselves to themselves; their raids down onto the Ahom-held plains were largely for livestock and booty, never for land or political gain, and certainly not to spread their religious views or way of life. Ninety per cent or more of Naga history, however, has never been written down – no Naga even knew how to write until the late nineteenth century – the ancient history of the tribes remains the stuff of myth and legend.

By the time of the Mughal invasion of Assam in the early seventeenth century, led by Mir Jumla, a Persian-born diamond merchant turned governor of Bengal, and chronicled by Shahabuddin Talish, the word Naga itself appears to have stuck and was associated with fierceness as much as with nakedness. Mir Jumla conquered Assam with an army of 12,000 cavalry, 30,000 infantry and a fleet of 323 ships sailing up the Brahmaputra, manned in part by English, Dutch and Portuguese sailors, although even this great military caravan slewed to a halt as the monsoon rains fell and the Naga Hills loomed ahead. Mir Jumla refrained from sending his spent army into the heights of the mist-enshrouded hills to do battle with tribal warriors who knew each sodden nook and cranny of an exhausting landscape that spelt mysterious death to the soldiers of conventional armies. The Naga Hills were never to be a part of Mughal India, for all that great empire's distinction in arms and soldiery.

As for language, although they share common roots, each Naga tribe has its own language or dialects, largely incomprehensible to members of other tribes, let alone to foreigners. Today, Naga speaks unto Naga in what I have heard called both Nagalese and Nagamese, a pidgin mix of Naga languages with a bit of Assamese and Nepalese stirred into the verbal mix. Sometimes they communicate in English, or in a fusion of Nagamese and English. Nagaland is the only one of India's twenty-eight states where English is still the official language, which, as much as anything else, marks it out as different from anywhere else in the federal republic and puts noses out of joint elsewhere in India.

The few available tourist guides and histories of Nagaland insist on saying that Nagas are a naturally democratic people with no social hierarchy. This, though, is not exactly true. Certainly, the Angami have always appeared to have lived democratically, without formal leaders; yet, in sharp contrast, Konyak society, for example, remains fundamentally autocratic. The Aos, meanwhile, have long practised a form of parliamentary democracy, voting for their leaders.

Women have the same rights as men in a number of tribes. On the other hand, there are few women officers in the various Naga rebel armies, and in some of the most intensely tribal areas, notably in the east, across the Burmese border, Naga women seem to do the tiger's share of day-to-day work, and barely seem equal. For the most part strong and wiry, Nagas, men and women, tend to be long lived, despite poverty and the wars of independence that have been simmering or boiling for much of the past sixty years; the average life span of men and women is currently 73.4 years, much the same as it is in most developed countries and in stark contrast to mainland India. Anyone, I suppose, who has to walk up and down the Naga Hills day-to-day would very quickly be fit or dead.

Well educated in comparison to people living in poor and remote countries elsewhere in the rest of the world, partly by mission schools and because many new state schools have been built since the 1980s as part of India's attempt to pacify the Nagas through economic development, the Naga literacy rate, recorded as 67.11 per cent in 2002, is a little above the Indian national average. I have no idea how accurate this figure is. In remote villages, many people remain barely literate, although, and perhaps because of this, story telling remains an enthralling communal activity.

Quite clearly, Nagas are not the primitive peoples living in huts in distant jungles that all too many citizens of distant Delhi, Bombay and Calcutta still believe them to be. Although an increasing number of young Nagas are in tertiary education in major Indian cities today, the popular, folkloric image of the 'naked Nagas' has yet to vanish. The truth, though, is that there are several Nagalands within Nagalim. There are, for example, the Nagas living in the former 'administered areas' of the British colonial system. Based for the most part in Dimapur, Kohima, Mokokchung and the lowlands, these are the most exposed to India and the Western world. Other tribes living in the higher hills in the old 'unadministered areas' are much more likely to be cut off from the advance of the modern world, while those living in Burma, the eastern Nagas, continue to survive, and, at their best, thrive, in a world that has changed remarkably little over the past God only knows how many centuries.

Nagas might well describe their life in distant times as being something like that of the citizens of Greek city-states, although it takes a stretch of the imagination to liken a shaggy, fortified Naga hill village to the architectural sophistication of an ancient Greek hill town adorned with marble. The idea, however, is both charming and apt. Hidden up in their hilltop eyries and unmolested for many centuries, Nagas led a life that was, at heart, and for the most part, 'democratic'; they also happened to fight one another with gusto. Naga villages tended to be highly independent of one another, self-sufficient, too. The slightest degree of trespass or interference of any kind could readily lead to war and a fresh bout of headhunting. The idea of a common Naga cause or a Naga nation is very recent indeed, while chasm-like divides in the Naga independence movement in recent decades only reflect the deeply tribal nature of the Nagas. It should also be remembered that the word 'Naga', although used by outsiders for several centuries beforehand, was accepted by all Naga tribes only during the past century.

What brought Nagas together even before their experience of global conflict and politics in two world wars was their willing and mass conversion to Christianity from the late nineteenth century. In a 1997 *Journal of World History* article the historian Richard Eaton wrote that the Nagas' was 'the most massive movement to Christianity in all of Asia, second only to that of the Philippinesi'. The part that Christian missionaries have played in the Naga independence movement is a fascinating if rarely deliberate one. In translating the Bible into several key Naga languages such as Ao, Angami and Sema and printing these in Roman script, missionaries encouraged young Nagas from different tribes to learn these core languages; and, ultimately, they learned English, too.

The process of creating a written Naga language began with the American Baptist mission of Edward Winter Clark, founded in the Ao village of Molungkimong in 1872. The Aos insisted they once owned a written language, but the scripts, marked on a leather parchment, had been eaten by a dog at the time of the tribe's migration to the Naga Hills centuries ago. So, the dog ate their homework – a story that must have been familiar to a teacher like Clark – and yet, by 1880, Clark and his wife Mary, having learned to speak the tribal language, hand-printed their first Ao alphabet and grammar. Three years later they printed a translation of St Matthew's Gospel. St John – some achievement – followed in 1906. An Ao dictionary was published in 1911, while the first complete Ao edition of the New Testament was completed, with the help of Ao tribesmen Idijungba, Subonglemab, Kilep and Allem, in 1929.

After Clark's death the Baptist missionaries R. B. Longwell and C. W. Smith teamed up with Mr Mayangnokcha, the first Naga headmaster of the mission school, to continue the work. With major contributions by tribesmen, notably Nokdenlemba and Bendangwati, who gave whatever spare time they had to this truly Herculean task, a single edition of the entire Holy Bible was finally published in November 1964; three thousand copies were sold within an hour of the book going on sale.

Not that this is what the Clarks would ever have intended, and yet being able to read the Bible, to write in a Roman script and to speak in English were all ways in which Nagas defied India after the British left in 1947. This is why Baptist missionaries working in Nagaland are often looked on as deeply suspect, as rebels in disguise, by the mainly Hindu politicians in mainland India. The spread of Christianity, common languages, education and writing has gone hand-on-Bible with guns, war and the demand for independence. It can seem that wherever you walk in Nagaland, Jesus walks with you. In India, Naga missionaries are busy today spreading their message in Arunachal Pradesh, Assam, Manipur, Orissa, Uttar Pradesh and West Bengal. I have come across Nagas in Burundi, Cambodia, Hong Kong, Japan, South Africa, Thailand and the United States, where a few Nagas attempt, rather heroically, to preach the word of Jesus in the white Bible belt.

The importance of the translation of the Bible cannot be overestimated. Naga literature, teaching and story telling was, from the 1890s onwards, increasingly affected by the 'Good Book'. Biblical metaphors and idioms became a way of communicating among newly educated Naga officials and, eventually, among Naga independence armies.

This combination of a new-found nationhood and an enthusiastically embraced and shared religion revolutionised tribal society in the Naga Hills within a remarkably short period. When Christoph von Fürer-Haimendorf returned to visit the Konyak Nagas in the 1970s for the first time since before the Second World War, he noted how 'only those who have experienced traditional Naga society can appreciate the magnitude of the transformation'. The Konyak villages he had trekked through were often isolated to the extent that Konyaks in surrounding villages were considered to be enemies and, thus, legitimate targets for headhunting raids.

It was the Christian missionaries who made the most impact on traditional Naga culture. But, while nurturing literacy and education, the missionaries also did much to undermine age-old traditions and ways of life as well as spiritual beliefs. Converts were instructed not to take part in traditional song and dance, not to drink rice beer and not to play the drums. They were not to sleep in morungs, the traditional common dormitories for young, unmarried men. They were to dress in Western-style clothes. Some of the more zealous missionaries went so far as to destroy morungs and much-revered tribal artefacts in the belief that the only sure way of instilling a Christian belief was to break down the Nagas' communal way of life. British administrators with a romantic view of the tribes looked with increasing suspicion on the work of the largely American missionaries. They wanted the Nagas to stay more or less exactly as they were, but this was never going to happen once the British themselves introduced the rudiments of a market economy into the administered areas of the Naga Hills and began to spread a quietly insidious Western influence among the tribes they were closest to.

J. H. Hutton was one of the fiercest critics of the work of the missions. In *The Angami Nagas* he wrote:

It is barely forty years since Captain Butler [John Butler, *Travels and Adventures in the Province of Assam* (1855)], wrote, but many customs of the Angamis at war which he records are almost or entirely forgotten by the sons of those from whom he learnt them. With the Aos and Lhotas matters have gone even further. Old beliefs and customs are dying, the old traditions are being forgotten, the number of Christians or quasi-Christians is steadily increasing, and the spirit of change is invading and pervading every aspect of village life . . . their [anthropologists'] opportunity, however, is not entirely gone, for there are still across the frontier happy tribes, which have not yet touched pitch and become civilised like their administered [cousins] . . . which know not the seed of conversion and the sword of dissention which missionaries bring, nor have yet been made to eat of that forbidden fruit which drove our first parents into fig-leaves and banishment. The diseases which follow, like jackals, in the wake of invasion have not yet touched them, and they go clothed with modesty rather than with 'dhutis'. No paternal Government forbids them the taking of heads or their fittest to survive, and no profane hand is raised against their customs of primaeval antiquity.

Curiously, this paean in praise of headhunting reads rather like a chapter from the Old Testament. What Hutton presumably could not see at the time was the fact that, although Christianity has indeed either watered down or eradicated many traditional Naga beliefs and practices, the missionaries did arm Nagas with the education and literacy that have enabled them to fight their own battles in the modern world.

Because Nagas were so very diverse and divided, whether Christian or animist, and because so many villages were, and remain, hidden away in heavy vegetation on remote and largely inaccessible hilltops, the British had been keen to map the Naga Hills in as much detail as possible before Indian independence. The Anthropological Survey of India was founded in December 1945 in a rather rushed pre-independence attempt to identify, locate and describe all the indigenous peoples of the subcontinent. The idea was rooted in both practicality and romance. At the time, no one knew exactly how many tribespeople there were in India, while for many British colonial officers and for anthropologists like von Fürer-Haimendorf there was an urgent need to protect the tribes from an all-powerful future Indian state. In particular, a lobby comprising the likes of von Fürer-Haimendorf, J. P. Mills, J. H. Hutton and other concerned local officers, including B. S. Guha, who had run the anthropological unit within the Zoological Survey of India since 1927, were pressing hard for the creation of a crown colony in the northeast that would have served as a protectorate for the very tribes, Nagas prominent among them, fighting various wars of independence across the region. In the end, the British gave India its independence in what proved to be a swift and decisive, if nasty, brutish and bloody rush, and any thoughts of creating a protectorate in the north-east were quickly dispelled, leaving the Nagas to find their own way in the new political settlement.

Indian governments were eventually to become keen on the Anthropological Survey of India and its successors, not for any romantic reason but, academic interest aside, because it could be used as a census of sorts, a way of mapping the subcontinent's five thousand or so different peoples and, to an extent, keeping them in their place. This, though, was always going to be difficult in Nagaland for the simple reason that Nagas do not keep still. There has always been a 'leakage' of highland Nagas to the lowlands, and vice-versa in times of floods, crop failures and famine. Much to Delhi's dismay, the Nagas are not, nor ever have been, an easy people to govern.

When the British first marched into the Naga Hills they found the political workings of Naga society baffling. When, in 1845, Captain Butler went on a lengthy mapping and diplomatic expedition through the region, he was told by Naga chiefs and elders that they had no control of their people except in time of war, and, while they happily agreed to British protection, this was only because they hoped that the British soldiers would help them attack people in neighbouring villages who might well be from the same tribe. Six years later, after two expeditions to the Angami Naga country in Manipur, Lieutenant Vincent reported to the governor general of North-East Frontier Agency that 'in every Angami village, there were two parties, one attached to the interests of Manipur and the other to the British, but each only working for an alliance to get aid in crushing the opposite faction'. Nor, of course, could the British read the complex sign languages used by Nagas to plot wars, or alliances, behind the backs of the intruders.

The big question of whether or not there is such a thing as a Naga nation has been used both to justify the existence of the modern state of Nagaland, created in 1963 in an attempt by Delhi to pacify the natives, and to deny and undermine it. The official, or Indian national, view is that Nagaland state serves to hold the Naga people together for their mutual benefit as well as for the good of India as a whole. The unofficial view is that the state is an artificial construct, as well as a tool of oppression, that fails to include all Nagas within it. In 2000, under the direction of S. C. Jamir, the state's chief minister, the Nagaland State Congress Party published a pamphlet, 'Bedrock of Naga Society', which set out once and for all, as far as the party was concerned, to explain what being a Naga meant and why, of course, the state of Nagaland had been and continues to be a necessary construct.

Had the Nagas, asked the authors of the pamphlet, ever been an independent nation? 'The stark and inescapable truth', they wrote, 'is that neither did we have a definite and unified political structure and nor did we exist as a nation. We were actually a group of heterogeneous, primitive and diverse tribes living in far-flung villages that had very little in common and negligible contact with each other. The main contact between villages was through the savage practice of headhunting. Mutual suspicion and distrust was rife. Internecine war was the order of the day. There was no trust or interaction between different tribes. In these circumstances, the question of a unified Naga nation did not arise.'

Inevitably, this 'Bedrock' document generated heated controversy among the independence groups we will meet close-up in later chapters of this book. Its official justification was to convince Nagas that the Indian state they live in is a good thing, and not least because it has given this group of 'heterogeneous' peoples 'worth and significance in the eyes of the world'. This statement is, it must be said, patently absurd. If anyone outside the borders of Nagaland knows anything about the state, or its peoples, then this is because of the activities of the various independence groups who have fought so hard, and messily, over half a century to free themselves from India.

Naturally for those lowland Nagas who have happily gone along with Indian rule, the usual rewards, in terms of salaries and a comfortable way of more or less modern life, have been high. For the majority of Nagas, however, their state is an Indian yoke, and the sooner it goes and an independent Nagalim is created, the better for everyone. Even then, Nagas living in Manipur are divided in their loyalty to the cause of Nagalim. If such a country ever came into existence, the boundaries of Manipur would be diminished. All Manipuris, whether Nagas, less than 15 per cent of the population, or Meitheis forming nearly 60 per cent, believe that they were cheated in 1949 when their kingdom, independent for centuries, and only a British protectorate of sorts during the Raj, was signed away to India behind their back and by their very own king. As a consequence, Manipur, although a beautiful land surrounded by mountains, has never been a happy state. Its people want their independence back. They are even further from Delhi and mainland India than Nagaland. So, here, the Naga cause is blurred, at best.

India's desire to keep Nagaland, Manipur and the other five north-eastern states in its orbit and control is really driven by national security. Without the 'Seven Sisters' acting as a buffer zone between Bengal and China, India would feel exposed or, indeed, naked.

*

The word 'naked', derived from Sanskrit, Assamese and Hindustani as well as from Ptolemy, has long been applied to the hill tribes living at the far end of Assam. As William Robinson wrote in *A Descriptive Account of Assam* (1841), 'The origin of the word Naga is unknown; but it has been supposed to have been derived from the Sanskrit word, Nanga, and applied in derision [by Hindus] to the people, from the paucity of their clothings, but there seems little foundation for the etymological derivation, as the term has never known to be applied to either the Khasias or the Garos with whom they were better acquainted with a greater degree of nudity than the Naga tribes with whom we [the British] are acquainted.'

There are other theories struggling to find an origin for the 'naked' epithet, but what matters most is that the word has always been an imposition made by outsiders. Traditionally, Nagas called themselves either by the name of their individual tribes, or simply 'man', a word they used to express both a commonality and the idea that they lived in a society free of hierarchies; everyone, including women and children, were simply, and unequivocally, 'man'. But, the 'naked' tag has long been used by mainland Indians to suggest that the Nagas were somehow inferior, and this attitude remains rife today.

Casual and institutionalised racism among mainland Indians

is underlined by out-of-date books giving the impression that Nagas are still living in the early twentieth century. One schoolbook I leafed through that was still doing the rounds in Calcutta in the 1990s lists the essential characteristics of the Nagas and their culture thus:

Headhunting
Common dormitory for unmarried men
Dwelling house built on posts
Disposal of dead on raised platform
Betel chewing
Trial marriage system
Aversion of milk
Tattooing by pricking
Absence of political organisation
Double-cylinder vertical forge
Loom for weaving cloth
Large rectangular wooden shield
Residence in his region
Crude agriculture

So, if you ever happen to be in north-east India and stumble across a common dormitory raised on posts and full of probably naked unmarried men chewing betel nut, operating double-cylinder vertical forges and refusing offers of milk, then you will know for sure that here be Nagas. Except in some far-flung villages, notably those in Burma, traditions have often broken down or vanished. The morungs, or common dormitories, where young men lived together from puberty till marriage, have mostly disappeared; a combination of Christian mission teaching and an acceptance of a 'modern' way of life means that the family unit has become more important in recent decades, although the village remains the heart of Naga life.

The further you climb into the hills away from the Dimapur Junction and Kohima, the more likely you are to find traditional villages in all their hilltop glory. The best of these are still fronted by avenues of menhirs erected as part of a quiet cult of ancestor worship, while behind wooden barricades, huts crowned with great shaggily thatched, deep-eaved roofs might well still be adorned with horns and antlers. Those morungs that survive are still filled with hunting trophies, while the young men who sleep in them are unlikely to commit themselves to ideal, missionary Christian marriages. Traditionally, Nagas have been sexually uninhibited, 'marrying' many times, 'just for one night', as they like to say, and getting wed officially only on an experimental basis until they find their true partners; once found, however, Naga marriages tend to be long lived and loyal. The divorce rate today is high largely because the missionary way of life is not a perfect match to traditional Naga ways that are far more fluid and pragmatic than ascetic Christian missionary ideals.

Coming from Victorian Britain, with its uncomfortable marriage of tightly corseted public virtues privately underpinned by guilty lust and a largely unrequited desire for exotica, the discovery of the Nagas was indeed thrilling for young men trekking out into these fierce hills. Those high cheekbones, almond eyes, bronze skins and flashing smiles. Those sensational costumes. Nagas themselves judge the beauty of a person, or potential partner, by the shape of their calves, for them the most erotic part of the body. The naked or barely concealed breasts of women on accidental or innocent display in the most old-fashioned villages in Burma are not objects of slavish attention from men as they would be in the Western world.

To see today's Nagas in their intricate tribal finery on a feast day, of which there are very many indeed, however, is still very much a visual thrill. Imagine how such people would have appeared to Victorians trying their damnedest to maintain a stiff upper lip. And imagine Scottish soldiers coming across warriors in tartan kilts. Each tribe has its own designs and colours; they are all quite beguiling. Significantly, an official Indian government guide to Nagaland describes its people as being 'of sub-medium height, the facial index is very low, the nasal index corresponds to a medium nose, the hair is generally straight, the skin is brownish yellow'. Or, it might have said, primitive, sallow and ugly, which is far from the truth.

After initial bloody clashes between their first encounter with the Nagas in 1832 and 1879, by which time they had established their military superiority, the British settled down reasonably well with the hill tribes. The one big problem both sides faced was the question of headhunting. To the British, the practice was abhorrent, but to the Nagas it was more than a way of life. A captured head was a source of good luck and fertility; the more heads on display in a village, the more prosperous that village would be. And for a youth, he could only prove himself to be a fully fledged warrior, a real man, when he had taken his first head. Then he would have had his body tattooed and his chance to wow the girls. To justify headhunting on the grounds of 'cultural differences' (an excuse used today by vicious men in societies who enjoy beating and stoning people to death, lopping off hands, the genital mutilation of young women and other forms of unspeakable behaviour, often in the name of religion and poor old God) is, however, to be unaware of the fact that Nagas also chopped off heads for the sheer fun of it.

One story that does the rounds in Naga villages tells of a chief eating little at lunchtime and claiming to feel unwell. When asked what was troubling him, the chief said, 'I feel bad because my warriors haven't hunted enough of our enemy's heads.' So his young warriors rushed down to an enemy village and hunted the heads of some women and children. These were served to the chief for supper, by which time he had regained his usual hearty appetite. Nagas like telling stories like this. When Ursula Graham Bower, of whom much more later, took her Naga guard with her on a shopping trip to Calcutta in the 1930s, she found him happily scaring polite Hindu travellers to death with tall tales of his insatiable cannibal appetite. It was certainly a good way, she told me, of his getting a compartment on the crowded Assam mail train to himself when he wanted to lie down and sleep.

The British did convince the Nagas, by and large, to give up headhunting – the source of many inter-village and tribal wars – but I have yet to be convinced that the practice stopped, as official documents both British and Indian like to say, well before the Second World War. Old customs die hard. Official Indian government reports, for example, state with wonderful assurance that just 0.3 per cent of Nagas still practise traditional religious beliefs, and that these are mainly concentrated in Peren and the eastern districts of the modern state. Perhaps. And, yet, any remotely sharp-eyed visitor travelling through England today would quickly be aware that this is not a particularly Christian country, despite the official statistics; if anything, England is an aggressive, largely pagan or simply irreligious country, yet its people are good at singing enchanting carols at Christmas, after a few drinks down the pub, and calling on God in times of trouble. Statistics give little idea of what people believe in their bones. The fact that Nagas have, even as animists, always believed in a Supreme Being, made it that bit easier for Christian missions to do their work when they first came this way in the 1880s.

Festivals held throughout Nagaland have clearly changed little over the centuries, despite the extraordinary rise of Christian baptism and worship. This makes good sense, though, to members of most religions, for the principal festivals are concerned with sowing or preparing the land and with harvests. The rites and rituals involved are reproduced in recognisable forms around the world: ablution, sacrifice – cock, pig, bull – watering the land, communal singing and, of course, feasting are commonplace in many countries and all have their modern, if sanitised, equivalents in Europe and the United States. Whether the food on offer is beef, frog, yam, sticky rice or tapioca, and whether it is washed down with rice wine or rice beer, depends on which tribe is celebrating what event, but these Naga festivals are recognisable to anyone who comes from or has ever lived in an agricultural community.

If you come across such a festival, you will be made welcome. Nagas tend to be a hospitable people, but then these agricultural feasts have a habit of bringing out a generous spirit in people across the world. Only recently, one Sunday, I was driving through rural Provence and, having stupidly just missed lunch, stopped near a crowd outside the church in a stone village near Uzès, hoping to find something to eat at this time in the afternoon. This was the day of the village bull run. Join us, they said, as I was wheeled to an improbably long trestle table creaking under the weight of magnificent food and local wine. The party was followed by the bull run, a gloriously ancient event, all connected, of course, to old fertility rites. What, I couldn't help thinking, was the difference between this event and those held in Naga villages? Not much, really. Beneath the stately veneer of many religious events are age-old rituals concerned with making the land fruitful, respect for ancestors and physical and spiritual rebirth.

The big difference between a feast held by the Ao or Sema Nagas and Provençal farmers is largely one of dress. Where my French hosts were clothed drably, Nagas dress in all their exotic finery on festival days. Hand-woven and dyed shawls and kilts, striped, patterned or plain of many different colours, are embellished with beads, cowrie shells, precious materials and goat's hair. There are feathers galore, and headdresses more exotic than anything found in the bright pages of a Tintin story, fashioned from even brighter red beans. Hats, some like the busbies of British guardsmen, are enlivened with bear or dog fur, the tusk of wild boars and bright, hand-wrought jewellery. Necklaces hang heavy with shells, bronze bells, tiger teeth, brass heads and beads the size of golf balls. Ears might be pierced with horns and bamboo hats pinned with the tusks of wild boars. Upper and lower arms are banded around with wooden rings. Faces might be tattooed or painted with paste.

An exhibition of traditional Naga dress, headgear and even modern textiles would surely be a hugely popular sensation in any major world museum or art gallery; Nagawear could set any number of new trends in fashion. Sadly, although Naga women remain, to a happy degree, highly skilled and imaginative weavers, crafts in Nagaland are gradually becoming servants of the slowly growing tourist market in Dimapur – look at the wood carving on display at the Diezephe Craft Village – and Kohima. And, increasingly, when they can afford it, villagers throughout Nagaland are buying aluminium pots and pans instead of making their own pottery bowls and cooking dishes. I suppose this is inevitable, even though for anyone with the slightest romantic inclination or visual sensitivity, the global rush to American leisure clothes (made anywhere except in the USA) and supermarket-style goods is a demeaning phenomenon and one that strips away individual, tribal and other local identities. Rather comically, festivals for tourists subsidised by the state have insisted on tribesmen wearing shorts and running shoes, rather than loincloths and bare feet, just in case visiting VIPs from mainland India or US missionaries, I assume, are offended by truly traditional costumes.

The songs you hear at festivals today can be a curious mix of the traditional and the very modern, too, the latter in the guise of American Baptist hymns, none of which I seem to know from my own Catholic upbringing. Some of the Naga sporting entertainments still very much alive during festivals as well as other times of the year are happily unaffected by puritan concerns; Naga wrestling, kick-boxing, pole-climbing, and tugs-of-war remain enormously energetic and hugely popular communal entertainments, as, less happily, does cock-fighting. One thing the artistically inclined might notice, though, is that not everything in these festivals is quite what it should be. Look at some of those headdresses. Are those real feathers? No. Because Nagas have hunted wild animals with abandon, much-prized hornbill feathers are becoming increasingly rare and an increasing number of the 'feathers' on display are made of painted paper. There are a few wildlife sanctuaries in Nagaland, yet what survives of traditional Naga culture is as much threatened by a lack of concern for the natural environment as it is by Western, Indian and other foreign influences.

Will traditional Naga culture survive? Not as it was, no, and yet there are healthy signs that a young, computer-literate generation is beginning, through music, writing, fashion, craft and other means to connect traditional Naga beliefs, values, rituals and aesthetics to a modern and increasingly globalised world. Again, it is not difficult to see how Naga fabrics and costumes could be a major influence on the world's fashion industry or how Naga bamboo and cane craftsmanship might become far more than the inspiration for a few tourist trinkets in the bazaars of Kohima. In fact, Naga bamboo designs for everyday life, from hats and baskets to dishes, containers, fishing tackle, flutes, trumpets and violins, are both delightful and useful. Even a child usually glued to a computer might enjoy learning to play a bamboo mouth organ, a delightfully simple instrument that nevertheless encourages the player to explore its range. Such beautifully made objects would sell easily in smart design-led shops around the world. Especially, perhaps as they are wrapped around with enjoyable legends and folk tales. I like the Ao Naga story of the discovery of basket making: Once upon a time, there lived a magician called Chankichanglanga who used to perform many miracles as well as entertainments; when he was about to die, he told his fellow Ao people that if they were to open his grave after six days then they would find something that they had never seen or thought of before. And so they did. What was in the grave? The designs for all the basketwork the Aos would ever make; and some of these are quite miraculous.

Even though Naga culture will twist and turn itself one way or another into the modern world, the Nagas themselves will, I imagine, retain their deep loyalty to their tribes. Christianity, capitalism and consumerism have all, unintentionally or not, helped in levering the Nagas away from their old form of communal life. But listen to the voice of Kaka Iralu, speaking on the subject of the Indo-Naga conflict at the Indian Council of Social Sciences-sponsored National Seminar on Resolving Ethnic Conflicts in North-East India held at Guwahati in November 2002:

> I am from Khonoma village of the Angami tribe. My political status and identity as a Naga starts from that village level . . . every Naga village is a sovereign democratic republic with its own sets of laws governing the village. Now, within the village, I belong to the Iralu clan. The Iralu clan belongs in turn to the Meyasetsu clan. The Meyasetsu clan in turn belongs to the still wider and larger clan group called the Merhuma Khel. The Merhuma Khel is in turn one of three major Khels that make up Khonoma village. The Khonoma village in turn belongs to the Angami tribe and the Angami tribe belongs in turn to the Naga nation. My sense of political identity, therefore, starts from the Iralu level to the Meyasetsu to the Merhuma to the Khonoma to the Angami and ultimately to the Naga national level.
>
> At every level of my political identity, I have hundreds of clansmen, khelmen, village men, tribesmen and fellow Nagas who have the obligation to protect me as a Naga. I, in turn, owe the same obligation and allegiance to all these levels of my political identity. This is how the Nagas, though they are a very small nation, have defied the mighty British Empire for over a century and India for over half a century. In actual political reality, no Naga stands alone. Hence, if any foreigner harms a Naga, they will find themselves pursued by hundreds of the victim's clansmen crying for their blood!
>
> Land ownership of an individual also spreads across all these various levels of clan, Khel, village and tribal lands. Every Naga, therefore, is a man with many clansmen and

many lands. As far as I am concerned these ethnic and national identities are precious to me. They, in fact, define my political existence as a man with a country to call his own. As such, I can never surrender this birthright to India or any other nation on earth.

5

Everything Stops for Tea

The British have long been a nation of tea drinkers. Tea came from several parts of the British Empire during Queen Victoria's reign, and notably from Assam, where the tea bush is a native plant. Unknown to the British, its leaves had been chewed and sometimes brewed by Bodo tribespeople in Assam, and by Nagas, for centuries. In 1832, Britain lost its monopoly on the Chinese tea trade. This was a serious blow. Until then tea had been exported exclusively from China. No one knew that a different strain of tea bush was growing by the banks of the Brahmaputra and up along the fringes of the Naga Hills.

What happened next is astonishing. Examples of the leaves of the Assam tea bush, first discovered by Major Robert Bruce in 1823, were taken by his brother, Charles, a pioneer tea planter, to the Botanical Garden in Calcutta for analysis in the early 1830s. This was an important moment. Tests proved that this was tea all right. Now Britain could fight its way into the hugely lucrative international tea market without China. Indian and Chinese strains were cross-fertilised, for taste and durability, and then planted across Assam. Here is the source of the strong black leaves many of us know as English breakfast tea.

From the moment it was first brewed and tasted in London, at India House in 1839, Assam tea was a roaring success. That year, after fifteen years of warfare against the Burmese who had recently annexed Assam, and skirmishes with local tribes, the British had completed their takeover of the province. Now, thousands of acres of jungle were cut down to make way for a new generation of Indian tea plantations. Nature fought back. Planters were killed by contaminated water, insects and tigers. Cheap labour was imported from central India. About one in ten immigrants died on the long journey to Assam, where more fell ill and died working horribly long hours in foul conditions. The tea trade, though, was an instant and hugely profitable commercial brew. Its success meant that Assam's borders needed protecting against potential invaders as well as from marauding tribes coming down from the hills. Over countless cuppas, the scene had been set for the British to meet, and fight, the Nagas.

At this time, the British were also looking for a reliable route from Assam to Imphal, the capital of Manipur, a satellite kingdom bordering Burma. This was to be a useful passage for British troops as they made their way into Burma, a kingdom that was finally wholly absorbed by the Empire in 1885. The eight hundred soldiers exploring the route up through the Naga Hills in 1832 were mostly Manipuris, led by Captain Jenkins and Lieutenant Pemberton. Almost immediately they were attacked, and harried all the way to the British fort at Dimapur. Reprisals took the form of punitive raids from Assam. Between 1839 and 1846 six major British expeditions attempted to subdue the Nagas. For the next thirty-five years the British and Nagas fought one another, stones and arrows flying in one direction, bullets and artillery shells in the other.

For a short while, in the 1850s, the British, perhaps tired of so much fighting for no gain, left the Nagas alone, but repeated raids from the hills on Assam and its tea plantations sent the troops up and down and up again. In one year alone Naga warriors are said to have killed 232 British subjects in Assam. The biggest fight, involving some five thousand British soldiers, was at Khonoma in 1879, a battle that dragged on until March 1880 when the Nagas, if not wholly defeated, were at least subdued.

Between 1866 and 1881 the Naga Hills were formally declared a British district, although 'excluded' or 'unadministered' zones, those that were to remain ungoverned, amounted to some two-thirds of the area. Between 1881 and 1939 Nagas continued to fight the British at Chinlong, Pangsha and elsewhere. British and foreign citizens were allowed to enter the Naga Hills with permits. These were rarely granted to those wishing, for whatever reason to push on into excluded areas. British motives for isolating the Naga Hills were complex. There was certainly a growing belief among young officers and administrators that, as long as the interests of the Empire were served, the Nagas should be left to their own devices, and even protected for their own good. Equally, the British had realised early on just how important the Naga Hills were from a strategic, as well as tea- and rice-growing, point of view.

Why, though, did the British divide the Naga Hills so readily into governed and ungoverned areas? Because the part of Nagaland that mattered to them was its south-east corridor, from the railhead at Dimapur along the road to Kohima and down through Manipur to Imphal, and so, eventually to Burma and all imperials points south. If this area could be tamed, the British would have a highly effective buffer zone between Burma and India and a protected overland trade route from Bengal to Malaysia. But the divide in Nagaland was also due to the fact that the higher and the further from Kohima and Dimapur tribes lived, the more likely they were to fight the British. Deeply suspicious of land-grabs by soldiery, they were determined to keep their homes in the hills free from foreign domination; and, as the British noted (C. U. Aitchison's *Treatises, Engagements and Sanads*, 14 volumes, 1909–33), 'the Nagas are the only undefeated people who refused to sign treaties ceding their territory to us'.

There was also the fact that tidy-minded imperial officers tended to find the Naga way of life either improbable or downright impossible. Chiefs of individual tribes could not be relied on to establish treaties because, as they themselves argued, their people might not go along with them. Nagas have always been fiercely independent peoples, running many of their tribes in a loosely self-governing fashion. In 1845 Captain Butler was sent on a mission to conciliate rebellious tribes while mapping the areas he journeyed through. The chiefs he met paid him handsome tributes of ivory, cloth and spears while telling him they could not guarantee that their tribes might not go to war and even asking him to employ his soldiers to attack rival tribes. As British officers quickly discovered, Nagas often felt they had to attack a rival tribe because of the need to cut off heads to release the spirits that would help nurture bountiful crops.

The Nagas and British muddled along together from the 1880s. Something, though, began to change. Slowly at first, and then with gathering speed, the Nagas began to develop a sense of nationhood. There were several reasons for this. First, British administration brought members of rival tribes together, particularly in the new administered villages and hill-stations including Kohima, Mokokchung, Wokha and Zunheboto. Second, the English language allowed them to speak to one another more readily than they had ever been able to before. What were described as tribal 'dialects' often proved to be individual languages. Members of different tribes resorted to sign language when unable to make sense of what others were trying to say.

The English language, taught largely by mission schools, helped to bring tribes together. From then on it was possible for Nagas to discover the outside world and to understand why the British had occupied their country. Today, literacy in Nagaland is above the Indian national average, while speaking English, as many mainland Indians have discovered to their economic advantage, has drawn them with increasing success into the world of modern global electronic communications.

The spread of Christian teaching through the Naga Hills taught the tribes brotherly love; in converting local spirits into Christian saints and prophets under the umbrella of a single

God, missionaries had found a powerful way of uniting Naga culture. Nagas have long believed in a single almighty spirit. And they have believed in a Heaven of sorts: the soul of any Naga who has lived a good life will be turned into a star.

When Nagaland was incorporated against its will into India when the British left, conversions to Christianity increased dramatically, especially when Delhi tried to ban Christian missionaries from entering. The Christian faith of Nagas is, in part, a wilful and determined challenge to India's predominantly Hindu culture; it has brought Nagaland's sixteen tribes together in a way that would have been inconceivable to British soldiers and civil servants serving here a century ago. It was also to give Nagas a recognisable moral authority when dealing with the British and, much later on, on the international stage; it was always going to be difficult for Westerners and the peoples of 'civilised' countries to deal on an equal footing with a nation of headhunters divided among themselves.

A further reason for the rise of Naga nationhood was the Nagas' experience of the First World War. Something like two thousand Nagas (some authorities suggest four and even five thousand) from different tribes served with the Allied Labour Corps in France from 1916. Their common experience of the horrors of modern warfare brought these men closely together. A copy of the *Illustrated War News* from 1917 listed and described the 'tens of thousands of black men, brown men, and yellow men, Asiatics and Africans, Mongolians, Negroes, Indians, and Egyptians, working under British officers and British military discipline at the wharves, railway sidings, roads, and transport centres of Northern France'.

The journal drew particular attention to:

Indian companies who know nothing of priests or padres. These are the Nagas, who are 'animists', with no belief in anything in particular except ghosts. They are wild-looking little fellows, with shocks of long black hair, and big knives in their girdles, with which, it is said, in their native hills they may do a little headhunting when the humour takes them. Also they have no castes, and no prejudices about diet, and will, if allowed, eat anything in the nature of animal food, from bully beef to dead ammunition mules. Here in France they are quite good-tempered and jolly, and their quaint ways and broad grins have endeared them to the inhabitants.

Those who made it back home to the Naga Hills became allies and even close friends. The British, it has to be said, were quietly delighted. They helped establish a Naga Club in 1918 for the returning heroes of France, hoping that this would go some way to putting an end to internecine war while making it easier for the British to run the country. What actually happened was that the members of the Naga Club learned to articulate national rather than purely tribal demands. The British were impressed and from the late 1920s began to discuss their future in a way that, while not exactly treating Nagas as equals, at least took their demands seriously.

German troops who occasionally came up against Naga warriors in the trenches during the First World War were shocked to have to fight 'savages'. They thought this demeaning, and complained to their High Command. What worried them most, though, was the fact that Nagas saw war in the trenches, no matter how alien, as an opportunity for headhunting on an epic scale. In the event they agreed to bring back the spiked helmets of their victims rather than their severed heads.

My grandfather spent some time commanding Indian troops in France and looking after, so far as he was able to, Naga tribesmen. He was fond of them and of the Naga Hills, where he liked to ride and record what he saw of nature and of village life. In any case, here is a brief extract from the diary of John Henry Hutton, then a district officer, dated 18 July, 1918: 'To Chuntia. One of the coolies returned from France and asked if there are any more wars he could get to, as he badly wanted to "cut" a man; a rare and laudable ambition in an Ao. I promised him his belly-full of campaigning in the cold weather.'

Although the Nagas kept up a fight with the British right up until the latter left for good in 1947, they did come to some understanding with the white imperialists. They even formed loyalties and genuine friendships. This had been largely impossible in the days of early encounters between Naga warriors and British soldiers. At this stage, between the 1830s and 1880s, the British saw the Nagas as, to put it bluntly, a bloody nuisance; they interrupted the day-to-day business of Empire, conquest and trade, and the fact that each tribe had different customs, laws, languages and habits made governing them all but impossible for those with inflexible minds.

*

As the British gained a more or less comfortable toehold in the Naga Hills, they began to face up to the Nagas honestly. In any case, to maintain some sort of peaceful coexistence with the warring tribes, it was necessary to try to understand them. It was this that led to a slow trickle of explorers and anthropologists to the Naga Hills, and, eventually, to a breed of distinguished colonial officers who bridged the gap between academic and man of action. The need to administer the area effectively encouraged what was to become a detailed study of the Naga tribes. Initially, this was undertaken by a number of highly intelligent, and equally curious, British soldiers.

The first serious studies of the Naga tribes were made by Colonel R. G. Woodthorpe, who, as a young lieutenant, carried out detailed surveys in the Naga Hills in 1871–2. In the following decade Woodthorpe gave lectures on the subject in India and England, illustrated with his own excellent sketches and watercolours. Other officers kept detailed records of their tours through the Naga Hills, several filling sketchbooks with fine drawings of what they saw. As the British began to understand the Nagas better, so civil servants tended to take over the role of administrator and anthropologist.

The best known of these among the Nagas in the early part of the twentieth century was John Henry Hutton, who gained a doctorate when he finally returned from India and was Professor of Social Anthropology at the University of Cambridge from 1937 to 1950. Between 1909 and 1935, Hutton served with the Indian Civil Service almost entirely in the Naga Hills. As a young district officer he, like so many of his generation, had to learn how to collect taxes, administer justice and to strike a balance between the demands of Empire and local ways of life.

Encouraged by Henry Balfour, director of the Pitt-Rivers Museum in Oxford from 1890, many of whose students went on to become colonial officers, Hutton collected examples of tribal crafts, from daos and tools to textiles and jewellery, and had them carefully and dutifully shipped to England. He took hundreds of photographs of his travels through the hills and many of the 1,200 or so villages that straddle them. He made wax-cylinder recordings between 1915 and 1919 that today are the stuff of magic – as, of course, they would have been for Nagas listening to them in the early twentieth century. It is a haunting experience to hear a lament sung all those years ago by a young Angami warrior spurned by a beautiful girl named Lozofewu, and to hear the song of Sema tribespeople working in the fields. Some of the recordings are introduced, in a clipped and efficient manner, by Hutton himself.

Hutton matters so much to my story because he sought out the Nagas, found out about them in exhausting detail and brought them out of the deep jungle of history and, if not exactly into the limelight, then to the attention of considerate imperialists and even to the mandarins in Delhi and Whitehall.

From 1922, Hutton wrote at least three studies of individual Naga tribes, published by Macmillan on behalf of the Government of Assam. Hutton was exactly the kind of British colonial officer Christoph von Fürer-Haimendorf was so keen to defend when I met him in 1982. Hutton's tour diaries and letters reveal the man, and the spirit of many others like him who were as far from the stereotype of the starchy and careless imperial Blimp as it was possible to get. Contemporary black-and-white photographs might show very obvious-looking young British officers, but as Nagas themselves are well aware, appearances can be truly deceptive. We fool ourselves if we think that just because a keen young man staring out from an old photograph in khaki and a sola topee looks like a parody of a bumptious British officer of a nearly a century ago, he must have been aloof and narrow minded. Turning the pages of Hutton's diaries, a rather different type of man emerges.

On 17 June 1922 Hutton was at Dimapur, organising improvements to the well and local drains. After breakfast he had to adjudicate in a case in which local Christians were accused by 'Garo ancients' of cutting down their 'puja erections', or festival decorations:

> They could not say who had done it on this occasion, but they demonstrated that on previous occasions it was the Christians and I have not the least doubt that it was the Christians again this time . . . if these religious quarrels go on there will be nothing for it but to separate the Christians from the ancients entirely and forbid their going to each other's villages at all. I wonder why it is that it is so often the least pleasant of the community who turn Christians first. I suppose they stand in greater need of salvation. With the exception of one or two of the older men – ex-sepoys – the Garo Christians of Darogapathar struck me as a most unsatisfactory selection compared to the ancients.

Not, perhaps, what you might expect an upright, Church of England educated English officer to think.

The industrious Hutton was followed by the equally busy J. P. Mills, who spent the years between 1916 and 1938 in the Naga Hills, returning to become a Reader in Anthropology at the School of Oriental and African Studies. This was the same Mills who escorted von Fürer-Haimendorf on his epic tour of the Naga Hills of 1936–7. Like Hutton, Mills sent Balfour at the Pitt-Rivers Museum a supply of wonderful artefacts bought from Naga villagers. Here is a March 1927 diary entry by Mills that captures the fine balance such men were to able to maintain between anthropology and practical affairs:

> It is the custom here to set up monoliths by the side of the path in the name of dead men, with a line of small stones at the side representing the various affairs of the heart in which the hero has succeeded in overcoming the scruples of the girl concerned. The best score I saw was 27, near Hegokulwa. The connection between such stones and fertility is obvious. Another fertility rite which I noticed today is that of digging a round pond by the side of the path in the name of a dead man. Laisong [another village] have recently dug one and lined the top with stone. One is reminded of the way-side ponds outside some Ao villages.

The following January, Mills finds himself dealing with marital affairs one morning in the village of Paija and coping with land disputes while having one eye on something special to send Balfour at the Pitt-Rivers:

> 25th Jan. Halted. Today there turned up, breathing fire, the wife of the Christian whom we listened to yesterday. She threw fresh light on the character of that smug gentleman. According to her he was turned out of the mission for adultery in various villages. She forgave him, but he has turned her out and taken to himself another (and younger) wife. She demands compensation and the right to tear the new wife's clothes, pull off her beads and scratch her face – all in public.
>
> We went to Losker and back (5 miles). It is the only village in which I have seen nice old things. I acquired an outstanding

and unique piece of old metal work, bought from a Bete village 40 years ago. Not being ancestral the owners were quite ready to sell. It is here that the Kacharis from the North and the Rhangkols from the South meet. There is consequently rather a difficult land case.

Quite how remote, and potentially threatening, much of the Naga Hills could be to the British nearly sixty years after the Battle of Khonoma can be felt in this diary extract when Mills was leading von Fürer-Haimendorf through unexplored parts of his own district:

22nd November 1936

Major Williams, Mr. Smith, Dr. von Furer-Haimendorf and I visited Yimbang with 50 rifles and came back via Waoshu. This meant a walk of 12 to 14 miles, with countless stiff climbs and steep descents over shoulders. Yimbang has never been visited before. It is a mixture of Yimsungr and Kalyo-Kengyu with a few households of Changs. Our reception was not exactly enthusiastic, but a tune on the pipes quieted nerves all round . . . On the head tree were five heads taken from Saochu in the raid in which Yimbang joined Pangsha. As the raid was a gross act of treachery against a village with which Yimbang were at peace, and as it was a slave raid I had the heads removed from the tree and taken outside the village. They will not be hung up again. The heads of men had been scalped to provide hair for trimming dao-holders, but those of the women were not scalped, as Saochu women cut their hair short.

When we got back we heard that Noklak (East of sq.60) had sent a war party to move parallel with us on the range to the East and watch our movements, and that as we walked out of Yimpang three Noklak men walked in: the three said that Noklak had sent a party to help Yimpang in case we attacked it. Noklak men can visit small Yimpang with impunity, but Yimpang are afraid to visit powerful Noklak. I got them however to promise to send an old lambu tomorrow. Lambus are supposed to be sacrosanct, but several have been killed round here lately and the old men may refuse to go. In that case I shall approach cautiously and try to get in touch. Noklak and Chingmei are at war, and Noklak have so far refused to clear their portion of the path of panjis and traps, and Chingmei are sending out a party tomorrow to see how far they can make the road safe for us.

In December, Mills's party pushed on into further unexplored villages and dealt with local slave-traders.

3rd Dec.

To Panso. A pleasant and easy march of 5 miles ended in a spacious camp all ready prepared for us. We first went up to Yukao, which has never been visited before, but is most friendly. It is a colony of Panso. They have in their houses huge, padded crash-helmets which they wear for village quarrels. In these quarrels the use of edged weapons is forbidden, but you can hit your opponent as hard as you like on the head with a club. Hence the helmets. Panso, though very inefficient in bringing anything we wanted, gave us a great welcome as the conquerors of Pangsha. The story is worth recording as an example of the heights of insolence (and bravery) to which Pangsha had attained. Panso is very big and is reckoned a stout opponent in war. Yet Pangsha sent a large war party to them about the time of the raid on Kejuk. The intruders stood outside the village fence and challenged Panso to come out and fight. Panso accepted the challenge and lost 12 heads before they knew where they were. Pangsha waved the heads at them and said, 'We did this just to show

109

you the kind of men we are. We shall not trouble you again. Do not pursue us or we shall retaliate.'

They then went quietly away.

Letters between Mills and Hutton reveal the extent to which these colonial officers were determined to get to know the territories they nominally governed in minute detail, whether tribal rites or the plumage of local birds:

3/11/1918

Dear Hutton,

I'm afraid I made a mistake about a bird. The crested eagle you asked about (Sema 'alu'?) is quite certainly 1209 LOPHOTRIORCHIS KIENERI Rufous-bellied Hawk-eagle and not spizaetus nepalensis. I only found out my mistake this morning.

Splendid news about Turkey [the surrender of Turkey at the end of the First World War]. I have given the wherewithal to rejoice all round.

J. P. Mills

Other letters between the two men are concerned with language and tribal customs, with myths and legends. Throughout their diaries and letters, Hutton and Mills exemplify a type of colonial officer very much forgotten today in the populist quest to reject everything the British ever tried to do in Asia. What comes over strongly is a keen sense of justice, as well as a love for landscape, a fascination and care for everything and everyone they met that challenged what they knew and how they had been taught to see the world as Victorian schoolboys and students. They were also, quite clearly, very brave, and sometimes a little foolhardy. Here is Mills writing to his wife Pamela at home in Assam:

Camp Chingmei

November 22nd, 1936

Twelve to fourteen miles up and down these hills is not conducive to good letter writing. We went to Yimpang, one of the slave-raiding villages, with fifty rifles. To say we got a hearty welcome would be an exaggeration. The people were pretty frightened for no white man has ever been there before. It is over 7,000 ft. up, and the first thing we did was to look at the view. It was rather thrilling, looking down on to unsurveyed country, and we were busy for some time taking bearings and putting on the map villages which were mere names before. The range which marks the boundary with Burma was quite close and I was told a Column with 50 horses, i.e. mules, visited Himbu, a village just the other side of it, last year.

The sight of Sepoys with rifles and fixed bayonets must have been rather shaking to Yimpang's nerves, but we had a piper with us and after one of your National Airs the people began to look more cheerful.

Hanging from the Head Tree were five heads of the wretched Saochu people they killed in the spring. As the raid was for slaves and was a gross act of treachery I was determined to confiscate them, but I bided my time till we were safely outside the very strong fortifications. A double fence with a ditch in the middle simply bristling with poisoned bamboo spikes. Then I demanded those heads, and waited outside with my 50 rifles till they were produced. We got them and the Yimpang Head Tree is bare: and the Pitt-Rivers Museum will get some fine specimens if I can ever manage to send them.

Events like this one do mark a divide between our generation and that of the colonial administrators. Whatever his respect for Naga culture and fondness for individual Nagas, Mills demonstrates that he has the power to use these people for his own ends. He is the master; they are the servants.

*

Despite pioneering and detailed work by Hutton and Mills, the official Anthropological Survey of India was not set up by the British until as late as December 1945. By this time the colonial authorities had long established geological, botanical and zoological surveys of all India, to map the resources of the country as well as for the purpose of good governance. Even then it only came about through intense lobbying by, of course, Hutton, Mills and von Fürer-Haimendorf, among other colonial officers and anthropologists concerned with the long-term future of aboriginal tribes. Initially the pleas they made for the Anthropological Survey were turned down by New Delhi and the India Office in Whitehall. It was felt that Britain could ill afford such niceties, given the parlous state of Europe and the impending threat of war with Germany.

It is interesting to see the British anthropologists' position from an Indian point of view. According to the distinguished historian Kumar Suresh Singh, 'Their special interest in the tribes derived from a romantic tradition that presented the tribes in pleasant contrast to castes [elsewhere in India], the "unravished" hills and plateau where they lived which reminded the colonial rulers of their homeland, and from their appreciation of the strategic location of the tribes and the enormous resources that their lands contained.'

And, yet, as Singh himself has to admit, it was adminstrator-academics such as R. B. Seymour Sewell, director of the Zoological Survey from 1924 to 1932, who campaigned hard for an Anthropological Survey because of the importance this could have to an independent India. Seymour Sewell, like Hutton and Mills, was determined to ensure that however India was governed in the future its aboriginal tribes would be looked on as special rather than merely primitive, and in need of some form of protection. The Anthropological Survey was established soon

Above: The beauty of the Naga Hills captured in this 2005 view, close to the traditional gated village of Shamnyu on the Burmese border. Note the terraced fields and thatched timber houses.

Below: Longsha, a Konyak elder and celebrated head-hunter in his younger days, sporting a tusked straw and bear-fur hat crowned with a monkey skull, his ears decorated with horns. Mon village, 2002.

Above: Mauwung, Konyak Ang (chief) of Longkhai village, photographed by Christoph von Fürer-Haimendorf. On the right, he performs a ritual war dance, holding his short sword or dao.

Below: Survey of India map of 1932 showing the 'unsurveyed' area in white, around Tuensang village and the Burmese border. District officers, soldiers, missionaries and guides filled in these maps as they trekked ever further into remote corners of the Naga Hills.

Above left: J. P. Mills, deputy commissioner of the Naga Hills district, sits with a Naga boy rescued from slavery, Chingmei, 1937.

Above right: Christoph von Fürer-Haimendorf strikes a matching pose with a young Konyak woman at Longkhai, 1937.

Below: The Ang of Sheangha Chingnyu (second from right) and Ang of Chui (centre left) share a bamboo tube of local rice beer with von Fürer-Haimendorf (front left), 1937.

Above left: Young Phom musicians at the Ouliengbu spring festival, Wakching, 1937; the single-stringed instrument is still played today as an accompaniment to Naga folk songs.

Above right: Phom dancers pose for Verrier Elwin, the British missionary and anthropologist, Longleng, 1954.

Below: Princess Ngapnun of Longhkai has her hair braided by her mother before the princess's appearance at the local spring festival in 1937. They are adorned in superb handcrafted jewellery.

Above left: Young woman of the Yimchungru tribe from the Kiphire district; the tribe's name means 'the ones who have reached their place of choice'.

Above right: Phom elder – and former head-hunter – with his prized collection of skulls, Yongnyah, 2002.

Below: Konyak woman displaying a magnificent necklace made from split and engraved conch shells over strands of coloured glass beads. Yonghong, 2005.

Above: Portrait of the Konyak Ang of Lemwang, Mon District, 2003.

Below: Vividly decorated gable end of a morung, a communal village house, at Tuensang.

Above: Young Phom women dance at the Monyo (fertility) festival, at Pongu Village, 2002. This is one of the many festivals held in Nagaland that are as yet unseen by tourists.

Below: Local people from Kohima dressed in modern western clothes sporting slogans mix with those from hill villages dressed, more or less, in traditional costumes, at the Hornbill Festival.

Above: What will his future be? An Ao boy in a t-shirt and shorts poses in front of an Indian Mahindra 'Jeep' with a realistic model of the kind of assault rifle used by Naga independence armies. Ungma village, Mokukchung.

Below: New technology meets the Naga world: a Konyak man uses a shapely leaf and sweet-smelling 'alpine' flowers for earrings, and decorates his bear fur hat with a CD. Yonghong, 2005.

after this campaign led by experts on the ground. Its first director, appointed in 1946, was a Hindu, Biraja Sankar Guha, who had run the anthropological unit very effectively within the Zoological Survey since 1927. Since then, the Anthropological Survey has blossomed. Today it is an ambitious study of all the peoples of India, and, to date, it has identified no fewer than 4,694 different 'communities', a polite modern word for what were once known as tribes. People living on the plains of India would be aghast, I think, to imagine themselves as members of tribes. Tribes live in hills, and especially the north-east. Communities live on the great plains in teeming cities.

The wholly well-meant idea of protecting the Nagas, however, was to backfire soon after Indian independence. In August 1946 Jawaharlal Nehru wrote to the fledgling Naga National Council, founded the year before, emphasising that 'it is obvious that the Naga territory in Eastern Assam is too small to stand by itself politically and economically. It lies between the two countries, India and China, and a part of it consists of rather backward people who require considerable help.' This was patronising stuff. It also made it quite clear that India's uncertain relationship with China at the time, and for many years to come, would determine the fate of what, nearly twenty years later, was to become the Indian state of Nagaland.

This, of course, is exactly the fate that the Nagas were trying to avoid when, after the First World War, they began to see themselves as a nation rather than as a land of rival tribes with little or no idea of national boundaries and why these appeared to matter so much as the twentieth century drove on. When, in 1928, the India Statutory Commission, chaired by Sir John Simon, arrived in India to map out a new political future for India, members of the Naga Club made two very clear pleas to its seven members, all of them British MPs. The first was to keep the Nagas outside the reformed and semi-autonomous government proposed by Westminster and New Delhi. If this was impossible for any reason, then the Nagas asked to be left 'as they were before the British arrived'. They feared what might happen to them if they were to become a fixed part of the Indian political map. They delivered a memorandum to the Commission pointing out that 'before the British Government conquered our country in 1879–80 we were living in a state of intermittent warfare with Assamese of the Assam valley to the North and West of our country and the Manipuris to the South. They never conquered us, nor were we ever subjected to their rule.'

Indian nationalists did not see things the same way. They were little interested in the fate of aboriginal tribes in the northeast. To them, the Simon Commission was an outrage. Appointed by the Tory prime minister Stanley Baldwin in December 1927, its members were all white, and there was no Indian representation. It did, though, include the Labour MP Clement Attlee, who as prime minister in 1947 would force through Indian and Pakistani independence. The Commission arrived in Bombay in February 1928 to face mass protests. These ended in a bloody riot in Lahore later in the year. The findings of the Commission, published in seventeen volumes in 1930, recommended representative regional government in India established by the Government of India Act of 1935. Despite the rage felt by many Indians, whether Hindu, Sikh or Muslim, many of the new statutes laid down by the 1935 Act were to be written into the Indian Constitution of 1947.

For now, at least, the Nagas, could breathe a sigh of relief. The government agreed to the Naga Hills, or much of them, remaining an 'excluded area' outside the terms of the Act. By now Naga leaders knew that the solution was a temporary one. On 14 August 1947, a day before India became independent, the Naga National Council declared Naga independence. It was a brave move. A month earlier, a nine-strong Naga delegation had met Mahatma Gandhi in New Delhi. Its members told Gandhi of their decision. 'Nagas have every right to be independent,' he replied during their meeting at Bhangi Colony, New Delhi, on 19 July. 'We did not want to live under the domination of the

British and they are now leaving us. I want you to feel that India is yours. I feel that the Naga Hills are mine just as much as they are yours, but if you say "it is not mine", then the matter must stop here. I believe in the brotherhood of man, but I do not believe in force or forced unions. If you do not wish to join the Union of India, nobody will force you to do that.'

But I am rather jumping the gun in going straight from the conclusions of the Simon Commission to Nagaland's premature declaration of independence, because they are separated by one monumental event that changed the world for ever: the Second World War. And it was, perhaps, what happened during this global cataclysm, which I shall examine in the next chapter, that sealed Nagaland's fate so far as the new masters in Delhi were concerned.

*

Pre-independence, although Nagas were increasingly suspicious of mainland India, many also wanted the British to go. When in 1941 Sir Robert Reid, a former deputy commissioner for the Naga Hills and governor of Assam, recommended a new crown colony carved from the Naga Hills, the North-East Frontier Agency and upper Burma and directly administered from Whitchall, the Nagas opposed the idea. They were beginning to make their own plans.

Opposition to the British had been continuous, if sporadic. Tribes had been as likely to support the British if they thought their soldiers would attack a rival tribe as they were to attack British patrols anyway. There were no all-embracing rules. Life in the Naga Hills had an unpredictable momentum of its own. And at no time more so than when, in 1932, the most unlikely rebellion broke out, initially among Nagas in Manipur before spreading into the Naga Hills. It happened like this.

In the early 1920s Haripau Jadonang, a young Naga of the Rongmei tribe, born in Kambiron, Manipur, and a one-time British soldier in Mesopotamia, started a campaign to drive the British out of Naga territories. Jadonang became something of a mystic, championing a new religion, the Haraka cult, marrying elements of Hinduism and Christianity to traditional Naga beliefs. His first disciples were drawn largely from the Kabui and Kacha tribes, and in 1929 Jadonang declared himself 'Messiah King of the Kabui Kacha Kingdom'.

Gradually the movement became more specifically political as Jadonang and his followers began a campaign of civil disobedience including a refusal to pay taxes. Clearly this irked British administrators in Manipur who, it seems, were on the look-out for one good reason to arrest Jadonang. This came in 1931 when four itinerant Meitheis traders were killed in Kambiron for insulting the religious beliefs of Jadonang. Nagas had long been sensitive to criticism by the Meitheis, who were, as far as anyone can be sure, the very first people to encounter the tribes who had settled somewhere from the East in the Naga Hills. Nagas paid tribute to the Meitheis of Manipur, sometimes in the form of ivory or slaves. Many Nagas were recruited into Manipuri armies. To the Meitheis, Nagas were regional underdogs.

Whoever murdered the Meitheis traders, Jadonang was accused of the crime. After what was perceived by Nagas to be an unfair show trial he was hanged in Imphal, the capital of Manipur, on 29 August 1931. He was twenty-six years old. And that was the beginning of one of the great, and almost wholly forgotten, Naga rebellions. This was led by Gaidinliu, who for the best part of a year fought a guerrilla war, from Manipur up into the Naga Hills, against the British in retaliation for what many Nagas considered to be the judicial murder of Jadonang. Amazingly, Gaidinliu, from Nungkao village in the Tamenglong district of western Manipur, was just sixteen years old, born on 26 January 1915. Even more amazingly, Gaidinliu was a girl. Variously described as the third daughter in a family of eight children, or the fifth child of a family of six girls and a boy – the history of Nagaland has yet to be set in stone – Gaidinliu was Jadonang's cousin. Although she had no schooling, she was highly articulate and, as Nagas will tell you today, a natural-born leader. She led her army with considerable success before finally being captured on 17 October 1932 in Poilwa village by a British troop led by a Captain MacDonald. He must have been astonished to meet this fierce girl-warrior face to face, especially when, so Nagas say, she bit him in the hand and had to be handcuffed. The district commissioner at Kohima who handed the prisoner over to the authorities in Manipur was J. P. Mills. Sadly, I have been unable to find Mills's letters and tour diaries of the time; it would interesting to know what this thoughtful colonial officer made of what must have seemed an unusual situation even in this unusual country. In the event, Gaidinliu was sentenced to life imprisonment. She was held in several prisons including Aijawl, Gauhati, Tura and Shillong. She was released, by order of India's first prime minister, Nehru, on 14 October 1947, but refused permission to return to her native village in Manipur until 1952.

Gaidinliu is indicative of the fact that many Naga women have long been equal, and sometimes superior, to their men. This may partly explain the failure of fundamentalist Islamic missions in Nagaland today. While these have been supported by Pakistan as one means of undermining Indian authority in the north-east, few Naga women are prepared to be subordinate to men. Nor, traditionally, have Nagas believed that the Supreme Being is inevitably male. Their instinctive beliefs pre-date the male-dominated religions that emerged in the Bronze Age when earth goddesses were ousted by sky gods, and usually very angry ones at that, keen on smiting their enemies and generally spreading hatred, death and destruction. Membership of the pantheon of gods tends to vary from tribe to tribe, however, each with a different emphasis on male and female deities.

There is a twist to Gaidinliu's tale. Free again, and back home among the Nagas of Manipur, she proved to be a fierce and influential critic of the Baptist Christian Naga National Council rebels fighting the Assam Rifles and other elements of the Indian

Army from the early 1950s. This was because of her religious beliefs. She was opposed to the loudly professed Christian sentiments of Naga insurgents, and took up arms against them in 1960. Her guerrilla army, up to four hundred strong and known as 'Kampai', was badly mauled at Mandu (or Bandu) village during a lengthy fight in 1963. Gaidinliu vanished into a cave at Magulong for three long years, only reappearing following an agreement with the Indian government.

Her fight against both the Nagas and Christians, and her support of elements of Hinduism, made Gaidinliu a great favourite in mainland India. In truth, this raising of Gaidinliu to national hero status was rooted in pure political opportunism. When she had been fighting the British, she had been hailed by Jawaharlal Nehru. There was no mention of her religious beliefs then. Nehru had visited Gaidinliu in prison in 1937, promising to do everything he could to secure her release. Then, as reported by the *Hindustan Times*, he subsequently declared her 'Rani [Queen] Gaidinliu of the Nagas', comparing the young guerrilla fighter to Joan of Arc and Rani Laxmi Bai of Jhansi.

Rani Laxmi Bai, or Lakshmibai, was another young woman who had fought the English, as well as soldiers drawn from across the United Kingdom and India, at Jhansi, Gwalior and Kalpi during what is commonly known in Britain as the Indian Mutiny of 1857, and in India as the First War of Independence.

The young rani had been pro-British, and not least perhaps because the British had outlawed *suti*, the custom by which a Hindu widow was obliged to throw herself on the funeral pyre of her husband. She had a vested interest: the old Raja of Jhansi, Gangadhar Rao, some forty years older than his teenage wife, had died in 1853. Some say that Lakshmibai was forced at gunpoint by her rebellious soldiers to make a stand against the British, others that she took arms against them only after the deaths of seventy-odd British men, women and children caught up in the events of 1857 in Jhansi. Naturally, the British sought justice, or revenge.

Whatever the truth, the British, under the command of Major General Hugh Rose (later Field Marshal Rose, 1st Baron of Strathnairn and Jhansi) besieged Jhansi in days of terrific heat. Lakshmibai escaped at first to Gwalior and then to Kalpi, keeping up attacks on her late husband's allies, her enemy. Dressed as a man, she was run through with a sabre, though some say shot, in a final cavalry battle with Rose's much-depleted detachment on 17 June 1858. Her soldiers cremated her.

Of her bravery and qualities of leadership, Lakshmibai's enemies were in no doubt. Major General Rose said that, 'although a lady, she was the bravest and best military leader of the rebels'. Rani Lakshmibai remains an inspiration to Indian freedom fighters today. The irony is, of course, that today's freedom fighters are on the warpath against India itself.

When the Nagas began to fight the Indians, suddenly the Hindu element of Gaidinliu's belief came to the fore. She was, as Nehru wanted his countrymen to believe, like Rani Lakshmibai, an all-Indian hero. In 1972, when fighting in Nagaland was fierce, Delhi honoured her with a tamtaptra, a bronze plaque, celebrating her role as an Indian freedom fighter. Nine years later she was made Padma Bhushan, India's third highest civilian honour. In 1996 I bought a one-rupee stamp in the magnificent domed General Post Office (1864–72; by Walter Granville) in Calcutta's Dalhousie Square, emblazoned with a portrait of the veteran rebel dressed in traditional Naga costume and a pair of fashionable sunglasses. Sadly, I never got to meet this formidable woman.

*

The British undoubtedly changed the Nagas, or at least the Naga way of life in a large part of the Hills as well as Manipur to the south under colonial administration, providing roads and a railhead. They introduced Nagas to modern weaponry, literacy, written history and a sense of nationhood. But perhaps Christianity has been responsible for the greatest changes of all.

No one seems quite sure when Christian missionaries first set foot in the Naga Hills, although the Revd Miles Bronson, an American Baptist, and his family were here in 1839 when he set up a school supported politically by British officialdom and financially by British officers in Namsang village. This was a natural extension of the American missionaries' work in Assam that had begun in 1835, encouraged by British tea planters.

This first attempt at preaching the Christian message to the Nagas ended in failure as Bronson and his family fell ill from fever. His sister Rhoda died on 8 December 1840 and the mission closed. The Bronson family moved back to Assam, where the first Naga to convert, Hubi of the Nocte tribe, was baptised in Sibsagar on 12 September 1846. Before Christmas that year, Hubi contracted cholera and died. The second Naga Christian, Longjanglepzuk, an Ao Naga from Merankong village, was baptised in autumn 1851. He returned to his tribe to find a wife. Whether or not he did is unclear. What is certain is that Longjanglepzuk was killed in a traditional headhunting raid in 1853.

The great wave of evangelical American Christians who spread across the Atlantic through Britain to the 'heathen' world beyond at the time encouraged a second generation of Baptists to try their luck in the Naga Hills. The most determined and successful of these were Dr Edward Winter Clark and his wife Mary. The Clarks arrived at the Baptist Mission in Assam from Boston in March 1869. 'It is certainly painful for us in Sibsagar', wrote Clark, 'to be unable to lift our eyes without seeing these hills and thinking of the men who have no knowledge of Christ.'

Clark began to make contact with Nagas through a mission undertaken by Godhula and Lucy Brown, two young Assamese Christians, in early 1872. Some months earlier, Godhula had been escorted up to the Naga village of Molungkimong by a friendly hill man, Supongmeren, who was baptised in October 1871. At first, Supongmeren's fellow villagers had taken Godhula for a 'company' spy. All white men, or Indians in their employ, were referred to as 'company men' by the Nagas. (They had first heard of the East India Company in 1826 at the time the British had driven the Burmese from Assam. From then on, they assumed that all white men belonged to the East India Company tribe, which, in a sense, indeed they did.) Godhula was shut into a makeshift hut on his first night in the village, set about with guards. And yet, we learn from Clark's diaries, he sang hymns all night, and so beautifully that the Nagas were soon wanting to join in. This is probably a true story. The Nagas really do love singing, and especially together, and this really is one good reason that the Christian missions were to be so very successful in the north-eastern hills. The singing in Nagaland's churches today is as harmonious and as heartfelt as that found in any Gospel church in the Deep South of the United States or in the shanty towns of sub-Saharan Africa.

Soon enough, Godhula and Supongmeren came back down from the hills to Sibsagar in the company of nine young men wishing to be baptised. When they discovered that Clark was the leader of the Christian tribe, they invited him up into the Naga Hills. The British authorities warned him against it, and yet in December 1872 Dr Clark disappeared into the hills escorted by sixty young warriors from Molungkimong. Of course, there was an Englishman somewhere up there ahead of him; not a rival missionary, but Colonel Buckingham, a tea planter, who was able to offer tea, and something stronger if required, to the hill-bound expedition if not to the fiercely teetotal Dr Clark. In the days before Christmas, Clark not only kept his head, but founded the first Christian church in Nagaland. He returned to Sibsagar after an absence of twelve days in company with fifteen baptised warriors.

Clark returned to his new church soon afterwards, and lived and preached among the Nagas until he retired in 1911. He was joined by his wife in 1878. Between them, they taught Nagas to read and write, and printed Naga books in Roman script. They did all this before the Battle of Khonoma, and so were living with the possibility that any day they might lose their heads to tribes beyond the new Christian pale. The mission work was slow and not without problems and misunderstandings. Converts were initially ostracised by fellow villagers, and even after the turn of the century just a small clutch of the thousand or so villages in the Naga Hills could be said to be Christian. In 1905, though, Clark wrote: 'Thirty years ago I took up residence in these Naga Hills in a village where some work had been done by a native evangelist [Godhula Brown]. Save at this place, over all these ranges of hills hung the black pall of heathen, barbaric darkness. Now from some twenty of the fifty villages [of the area around Molungkimong, presumably] crowning the mountain crests floats the glorious banner of Christ, held by the Naga disciples. The softening twilight of Christianity is here. Soon the broad daylight with its transforming powers will reveal a Christianized people.'

Whatever you make of their evangelising mission, the Clarks had sparked a revolution, the Pentecostal fires of which would spread to almost every crest and dell of the Naga Hills. Theirs was a truly extraordinary achievement. It was also to be a spiritual wedge driven between the north-east and mainland India. Ever since, the message of Christianity has been a rallying call for the Nagas in their fight for independence.

It is fascinating to see something of the ways in which colonialists and missionaries were seen by the Nagas themselves. A document issued by the Naga National Socialist Council, before it split in two in 1988, had this to say:

The good side of the civilisation they brought was immense and Nagas owed them as much. The south-west areas were brought under effective control. Administration was excellent. They stopped headhunting which was common among the Nagas. It was this savage practice which created hostilities and feuds among themselves. Before long Nagas were brought much to their senses. Schools were opened and they had the chance of learning the three 'R's for the first time. But the propagation of Christianity by the American missionaries along with the imparting of education by opening mission schools gave the greatest contribution to the rising of the Naga society. It was through them that the heathen Nagas learned of the existence of the Absolute reality and the better way of living. Nagas could comprehend the meaning life has and they wouldn't anymore part with it. They now felt blessed though endless hurdles remained. Nagas would be forever grateful to them.

Although many Hindu fundamentalists see the advocacy of Christianity in Nagaland as a political weapon aimed at undermining Indian authority in Nagaland and the north-east and Hindu values elsewhere, Christianity has long been rooted in India. St Thomas, one of Christ's apostles, and possibly his brother, is said to have landed at Kodungallur on the Malabar coast in AD 52. There is no reason to doubt the story. Some of the first Indian Christians were first-century Malabari Jews who are said to have settled in India during the reign of King Solomon. Today, there are twenty-four million Christians in India, the majority Catholic, but with a very strong Baptist presence in Nagaland thanks to Dr and Mrs Clark and their energetic successors. Between them, British forces and American Christianity effectively put an end to raids by Naga warriors on the tea plantations of Assam, the very places that first caused the British to meet the Nagas, and fight them.

In September 1939, when Britain declared war on Germany, the Naga Hills were on their way to becoming one of the most important areas of a globally militarised world. Here, not only would both the fate of the British Empire and the future of India turn, but loyalties would be placed and misplaced in the fight for Indian independence. The Naga Hills were to be crucially important to world politics in the mid-1940s, but even then very few people indeed would have been able to put a name to this part of India, much less to locate it. And although one of the most important battles of the Second World War was fought here in 1944, the Naga Hills were to remain as unknown and as mysterious as they had ever been.

6

Thermopylae Revisited

The Battle of the Tennis Court hardly has the resonance of Waterloo, the Somme or Stalingrad. Yet this was the fiercest episode of one of the most important battles of the Second World War, Kohima, which came to be known as the Stalingrad of the East.

The tennis court in question is the one marked out in the centre of the military cemetery on the terraces of Kohima's Garrison Hill. At the time of the prettily named battle, it belonged to the deputy commissioner of Nagaland, the highly competent and much-liked Charles Pawsey. From 4 April to 22 June 1944 British troops, including the Assam Rifles and the Assam Regiment of the Indian Army, fought the invading Japanese to a standstill here. Between these dates, all that stood between the Japanese and Delhi was this most distant rectangle of what might be mistaken for a patch of Betjemanesque Surrey, were it not for the fact that Kohima is set 4,700ft up in the Naga Hills. The two armies fought hand-to-hand in savage, kill-or-be-killed bayonet charges. Hand grenades were volleyed and machine-gun fire served over an increasingly ragged net and a small apron of black pitch.

The RAF, flying from Calcutta, was able to supply British and Indian troops, while the Japanese, far from their main bases in Burma, Malaya and Singapore, gradually ran out of food and ammunition. Twin-engined Dakotas, for the most part, flew an astonishing 19,000 tons of supplies to the Kohima battlegrounds. They ferried 12,000 soldiers in, and 13,000 casualties out. They rescued 43,000 non-combatants in the area. The Japanese had no such supply line; moreover, unlike the Nagas, the Japanese found it hard to survive on a last-ditch diet of rats and grubs. Their withdrawal on 22 June 1944 marked the turning point in the war in South-East Asia. This was Japan's first significant defeat in what Tokyo called the Greater East Asian War. Following the reversal, the British, with Indian and American support, would push slowly and painfully deeper into Burma, and so gradually into Malaya and then across to the Pacific islands towards Japan itself.

The Battle of the Tennis Court was the intense and bloody epicentre of the wider Battle of Kohima fought over the same period. The importance of this all but forgotten battle that cost the lives of 5,764 Japanese soldiers and 4,604 British, Indian and African troops, can hardly be overestimated. Kohima, as Lord Louis Mountbatten, the Allied Supreme Commander in South-East Asia from 1943 to 1946, said, was 'the Battle of Burma . . . the British-Indian Thermopylae'. He was right. The Japanese had intended to fight their way through the Naga Hills and to destroy the British armies gathering in and around Kohima and Imphal as they prepared for a push into Burma. If successful – as, of course, they assumed they would be – the Japanese armies would push on almost unopposed into Assam and so to Calcutta. The Raj would be toppled. On the way to Kohima, the Japanese also aimed to cut the British–American supply line to southern China, and thus severely weaken the Chinese military effort led by Chiang Kai-shek against Japan. At the same time, they would shut off the supply of fuel from India that enabled the 14th US Air Force commanded by Major General Claire Lee Chennault and his legendary 'Flying Tigers' to maintain their highly effective bomber and fighter raids against Japanese-occupied China. This was quite some plan.

The pinch-point, though, for the invading Japanese was the narrow pass at Kohima. Once they had forced their way through this, then nothing, or so most generals of the Japanese High

Command believed, would keep them from the plains of India. Many Japanese generals also believed, not without justification, that they had the broad support of the Indian people behind them. Fighting alongside Japanese soldiers in the summer of 1944 was the Indian National Army (INA), under the political leadership of the Bengali hero Subhas Chandra Bose, a man whose hatred of the British was so great that he and his followers were blinded to the realities of Japanese ambition.

To many Indians the Japanese were soul brothers, albeit of a very unusual kind. In 1905 the Japanese had inflicted a severe defeat on imperial Russia, the first in modern times by a Far-Eastern army over a western neighbour. Indians keen to witness the death throes of the Raj hailed the Japanese as liberators of Asia. Tokyo played up this false assumption to the best of its ability. The imperial Japanese government had, however, no intention of liberating India from British rule. The 'Children of the Sun', as the Japanese saw themselves, believed, much like many contemporary Germans, that they were a chosen race, far superior to Malays, Thais, Burmese and certainly to what they saw as the dog-eating savages living like monkeys in the trees of the Naga Hills. What the Battle of Kohima was to prove, however, was just how very important the Naga Hills, and the Nagaland of the future, were to be in geopolitical terms. For the rest of the war and beyond, the Nagas, however despised by the Japanese, would be at the centre, a strangely silent and unknown centre as far as most of the rest of the world was concerned, of international ambition. The battle brought home to Delhi the strategic significance of the area and put an end to any debate concerning regional autonomy: Nagaland was far too important to be entrusted to the Nagas alone.

Many Nagas remained as neutral as it was possible for them to be during the savage, close-combat fighting that took place in their hills during the Second World War. Some fought alongside British and Indian Army troops, while a minority sided with the Japanese and the INA. What they all came to realise was that they were caught in the middle of political and military forces wholly beyond their control.

At the beginning of the Japanese march on India, things had been less clear. To break into India proper, Japanese forces would have to force their way through the 'thermopylae' ('hot gates') of Kohima. The comparison Mountbatten made between the legendary battle fought in central Greece in the early autumn of 480 BC between the Greeks and the Persians remains appropriate and justified, even though the ultimate outcomes of Thermopylae and Kohima were to be very different indeed.

At Thermopylae, a small force of some three hundred Spartans and seven hundred Thespians led by King Leonidas held back the vast Persian army, led by Xerxes I, attempting to break through a narrow and mountainous passage into the main body of Greece. Disorganised at the time, the country's defences would have been no match for the Persian military juggernaut if it had been able to take the pass easily. Until they were betrayed, and a secret goat track leading up behind their positions was revealed by a fellow Greek, Leonidas's small band held the Persians at bay for three days. There were just two survivors. One, ashamed to be alive, committed suicide; the other brought news of what the Spartans had achieved, a tale of heroism that stirred the Greeks into united action against a seemingly unstoppable enemy.

The Battle of Thermopylae gave the Greeks the jolt, and the critical time, they needed to organise retaliation against Xerxes. Within months they had crushed the Persian navy at the Battle of Salamis, and soon afterwards, the Spartans led the Greeks to a defining victory on land against their army at Plataea. The Persians – or the barbaric Asian horde, as the Greeks would have seen Xerxes' army – had been pushed back into their world of tyrannical darkness across the sea.

Greece prospered after Thermopylae. With the country more or less united, Athens entered its legendary Golden Age. It celebrated its victory over the Persians by constructing, among other monuments, one of the greatest buildings of all time, the Parthenon, a temple that was, through complex mutations over the centuries, to inspire the architecture of neoclassicism and Empire, in India as elsewhere, in the late eighteenth and early nineteenth centuries.

Kohima stopped the enemy but, unlike ancient Greece, the country it saved was far from united by the battle. As the British and Indians drove the Japanese from Burma, Indian soldiers loyal to the Raj fought their countrymen in the INA. But even those loyal to the British, Hindus, Sikhs and Muslims, would soon be fighting one another after August 1947, when the British left a country split in three – India and the two Pakistans, East and West – not to mention the numerous internally contested districts, princely states and kingdoms of the north-east. The Battle of Kohima was a heroic victory for the British, British Indians and Nagas at the time, yet it also pointed the way to a fragmentation of the subcontinent that has never been repaired.

At Thermopylae the Greeks erected a burial mound incised with an epigram by the lyric poet Simonides of Ceos. In *The Hot Gates* (1965), William Golding translates it as:

Stranger, tell the Spartans that we behaved
as they would wish us to, and are buried here.

The monument erected alongside the tennis court at Kohima reads:

When you go home tomorrow, tell them of us and say
For your tomorrow, we gave our today

These words are by John Maxwell Edmonds, an English classicist directly inspired by Simonides. What sort of tomorrow those who fell at Kohima were fighting for was, however, difficult to say even then. In a little more than three years, the British were gone, not just from Kohima and the Naga Hills, but from the whole of the subcontinent. As for the Nagas, Kohima was a proud moment of sorts, but they were soon to be subject to a new form of imperialism, neither British nor Japanese, but Indian. Kohima was a turning point for Naga political ambition. If the First World War had nurtured a sense of nationhood among Naga tribes, the Second World War gave them some real understanding of global politics. In less than a decade, they would be fighting a more or less united war for liberation against India, with erratic support from Pakistan and China, and they would be actively seeking international support for their cause.

Wars of liberation against British rule came to haunt, and finally to kill, Lord Mountbatten. Sailing out from the small harbour close to his Irish home at Mullaghmore, County Sligo, on 27 August 1979 aboard his fishing boat *Shadow V*, the last Viceroy of India and his crew were blown to smithereens by explosives planted in the hull by members of the Irish Republican Army. How the INA would have cheered. Its leaders had, in part, been influenced by the organisation and campaigns of the IRA.

*

The British declared war on Japan in December 1941. This was in response to the unprovoked Japanese attack on the US fleet at Pearl Harbor on 7 December. Britain promised to support the Americans in their fight against the Japanese if the Americans backed their struggle in Europe against Hitler and Mussolini. Not that President Roosevelt had much choice in the matter. On 11 December Hitler declared war on the United States. Other nations rushed in to line up on one side or the other. China declared war on Japan, along with Costa Rica and Cuba. To add to this absurdist mayhem, Bulgaria declared war on Great Britain and the United States on 13 December. This was a few days after Hungary had done the same. Britain, meanwhile, declared war on Finland, a country it had supported the previous year. Truly, this was a confusing as well as global conflict. The Nagas, meanwhile, were to be swallowed up by events far beyond their control as the war moved, as if inexorably, towards their remote hills.

Initially, the Japanese appeared to reproduce the successes German armed forces had enjoyed in the early 'blitzkrieg' stages of the Second World War in western and northern Europe. During the course of 1941 Thailand, Hong Kong, Guam and Wake Island fell like a stack of dominoes to the Japanese as they set out on their warpath. The next year the Japanese successfully invaded Burma, the Dutch East Indies, New Guinea and the Solomon Islands. They seized the key South-East Asian cities of Manila, Kuala Lumpur and Singapore. Bali, Timor, Java and the Philippines were lost to seemingly unstoppable imperial Japanese might. Rangoon followed, and then Emperor Hirohito's armies scythed north through Burma towards Manipur and the Naga Hills.

India had not necessarily been the logical target for Japanese aggression. The original plan as the Imperial Army moved north up through Burma was to attack the British dug in at Imphal, capital of Manipur, before they had time to strike back, at the same time cutting off the Allied supply route from Dimapur to both Imphal and China further north. There had been no real need to bother with Kohima. Dimapur was the key target. Here, trains were bringing increasingly heavy loads of war materiel to supply both the British in Burma and the Americans and Chinese further north.

Before the war, the metre-gauge railway through eastern Assam, built to serve tea plantations, carried no more than 600 tons of goods a day in each direction. By late 1943 this had been increased, with the help of the military, to 2,800 tons a day. From early 1944 the American army muscled in, and by the time the Japanese were heading for Kohima on the backs of elephants and mules as well as on foot and by bicycle, powerful new US-built locomotives were hauling 7,000 tons and more of supplies each day to Dimapur, including the light tanks that would appear so very dramatically in the last bloody, mud-soaked days of the

Battle of Kohima. The city was hardly an easy target, then, yet an obsessiveness on the part of the Japanese High Command demanded the capture of the capital of the Naga Hills, even though to do so would delay their crucial march on Dimapur.

The plan to drive on to India, although questioned by leading Japanese staff officers in Tokyo, was championed by Lt General Renya Mutaguchi, who convinced the Japanese prime minister General Hideki Tojo of the rightness of his ambitious plan. The commander on the ground, Lt General Kotoku Sato, expressed serious doubt about the adventure, code-named operation U-Go. Nor did Sato trust Mutaguchi; the two generals were old rivals from military academy days.

With their headquarters in Imphal, the British were still in a fairly strong position. If, however, Sato could cut their supplies by blocking the only road from Dimapur, and its railhead connecting the Naga Hills to the rest of India, the British might well be starved out of their positions. In the event, and as Sato had predicted, the Japanese overstretched themselves. And, despite what the INA claimed, local people, especially aboriginal tribes, did not come running in large numbers to support the Japanese.

The British, meanwhile, were increasingly well supplied as the weeks wore on and as the Japanese clawed their way towards Kohima on one flank and Imphal on the other. Their inspired and much-liked commander Lt General William Slim (later Field Marshal Viscount Slim, Chief of the Imperial General Staff, 1948–52, and Governor General of Australia, 1953–60), forged what was to become an extremely effective multi-ethnic force comprising British, Indian, Gurkha and East and West African troops. This was the newly formed, million-strong, 14th Army, later to be known as the 'Forgotten Army'. Slim ensured that the 14th was supplied from the rear at all times and wherever it moved by the RAF and USAAF. At the height of the Battle of Kohima, as troops under the dogged Colonel Hugh Richards fought the Japanese virtually eyeball-to-eyeball over the deputy commissioner's tennis court, aircraft were ferrying in artillery, ammunition, food and fresh troops as near to the hill town as they possibly could. Even then, it was extremely hard work to supply Kohima. Water was pumped into the inner tubes of lorry tyres and dropped to the dehydrating troops from C-47 Dakotas flying just above tree height, in clear range of enemy guns. During the height of the battle, fought in temperatures of around 100 °F and into the monsoon, the water ration for the defenders of Kohima actually rose from one to three vital pints a day.

The Japanese fought tenaciously at Kohima, but quite simply ran out of everything. At the beginning of the battle, though, an Allied victory was far from assured. A motley garrison of some 3,500 soldiers (some accounts give a figure of as low as 1,200 and, of these, just 500 are said to have been crack troops) faced between 12,000 and 15,000 seasoned Japanese soldiers from the 31st Division. When relief finally arrived with Lt General Montagu Stopford, his British, Indian, African and Gurkha soldiers fresh to the battle found the little hill town in ruins and the surviving defenders thin, unshaven and just about in one piece. The monsoon had broken, so Kohima was running in mud. And the mud was running with rats. The dead, Japanese and British alike, were piled up one on top of another. Corpses were bloated and stank. The place swarmed with flies. The chimney stack of Charles Pawsey's bungalow rose above the carnage like some abstract monument. Stopford, a Great War veteran, said that Kohima – all mud, hastily dug trenches and shell holes – looked like the aftermath of a First World War battle. The intensity of the fighting had been comparable to anything he and his senior fellow officers had experienced between 1914 and 1918. Lt Horner, signals officer of the 2nd Royal Norfolks 4th Infantry Brigade, wrote in his diary that 'the physical hammering one takes is difficult to understand. The heat, humidity, altitude and the slope of almost every foot of ground combine to knock the hell out of the stoutest constitution. You gasp for air which doesn't seem to come, you drag your legs upwards till they seem reduced to the strength of matchsticks, you wipe the sweat out of your eyes . . . so you stop, horrified to be prodded by the man behind you or cursed by an officer in front.'

Writing in 1950, Major Michael Lowry of B Company, The Queen's Royal Regiment, recalled an attempt to assault Japanese lines on 10 May 1944:

[T]he terrain was not easy, there being many shell-holes, horizontal tree stumps and the odd trench to negotiate. As we were going down the slope we caught the full blast of about three light machine guns and rifle fire, and, of course, grenades as we tried to negotiate the obstacles. This, I am afraid, resulted in many more men dropping . . . after this there followed a sniping duel, and then things happened the like of which I have never seen before. It was the nearest approach to a snowball fight that could be imagined. The air became thick with grenades, theirs and ours, and we were all scurrying about trying to avoid them as they burst. This duel appeared to go on non-stop for an unreckonable time . . . for the rest of the day we dug like beavers – everything we could find, plates, mugs, bayonets and entrenching tools – not so much digging as is normally done, but by making a hole and burrowing and tunnelling ourselves forward below ground. By the evening we were completely dug in . . .

Even in the relative safety of a position at the rear of the battle zone life could be hazardous. Soldiers had to avoid stepping on poisonous snakes; tarantulas and other spiders hid in latrines, waiting to bite; leopards carried off animal mascots. Quite simply, there was no escape from danger of one sort or another, and no question of rest. One private, at the height of the siege, had asked Colonel Richards, 'When we die, sir, is that the end, or do we go on?'

Eventually, the Allies prevailed, but it had been a close-run thing. And as the Duke of Wellington said after Waterloo,

'Nothing except a battle lost can be half as melancholy as a battle won.'

The Japanese defeat at Kohima was matched by their huge losses at Imphal during the same bloody weeks. Here again, the 'Children of the Sun' had been over confident. They believed that British and Indian troops were inferior to their own. Perhaps that had been true in the Far East in the early stages of the Second World War, but not now. And, again, they believed the fiery oratory of Subhas Chandra Bose, who insisted that the Burmese, Indians and even the savages in the hills, would turn against their British oppressors as the heroic Japanese armies marched gloriously on Delhi.

In the event, the Japanese lost an officially recorded 54,879 men in the combined battles of Kohima and Imphal, with more than 7,000 killed around the famous tennis court alone; the Allied side suffered some 4,000 dead, missing and wounded in Kohima, and about 17,500 altogether in this intense campaign. Nearly as many Japanese soldiers died through disease, starvation, snake-bites, attacks by other wild animals and sheer exhaustion as were killed by bullets, bayonets and bombs. The conditions they operated in, especially at Kohima, had been vile. Rather than face capture, ordinary soldiers clustered in small gangs over hand grenades and blew themselves up. Officers disembowelled themselves. Other Japanese soldiers had their heads cut off by Nagas as they tried to escape from the hills. When General Sato, commander of the Japanese 31st Division, ordered the first of his units to withdraw, he wrote, 'We fought for two months with the utmost courage and have reached the limit of human fortitude. Shedding bitter tears, I now leave Kohima.'

*

My father, who loved the Naga Hills, and held their tribes in high regard, witnessed at least some of this while serving with the RAF. His letters home were always cheery, concealing the brutality of the fighting. To an extent RAF officers were remote from the worst of the fighting, although my father, for whom talk of combat was almost wholly anathema, did recall the time he was writing home to my mother near Imphal when a Japanese infantry officer strode into his tent, sword drawn. Too taken aback to do anything, my father could only watch as the man fell, gunned down by RAF Regiment guards. The sword came home with him in 1946, although it was always kept well hidden from his children.

Flying, though, had been far from a doddle. Although equipped with three squadrons of superb new tropical-issue Spitfires, together with four squadrons of Hurricanes and a detachment of night-flying Beaufighters, and supported by USAAF long-range Lightning and Mustang fighters, Allied airmen were never masters of the skies. By this time, the Japanese air force was little or no match for the Allies, but Nature did not allow British and American pilots to have things all their own way. Flying Officer, later Wing Commander, H. D. 'Hank' Costain of 615 (County of Surrey) Squadron was caught in a sudden tropical storm on 10 August 1944 between Kohima and Imphal. His Mk. VIII Supermarine Spitfire was no match for the monsoon. 'Within seconds, I was completely out of control and with the artificial horizon toppled, I had not the faintest idea which way was "up". Outside it was so dark that I could not even see my wings, and the pounding of the hailstones on the fuselage drowned out even the noise of the engine.'

Costain and his aircraft were drawn up a 10,000ft current of angry air before being sent spinning down into an equally vicious downdraught. He bailed out at 1,000ft and came to land, fracturing a leg, in the relative comfort of a rain-beaten paddy field. Three of his fellow pilots were killed flying through the monsoon, including his commanding officer. Other survivors found themselves being hurled by a force far, far greater than the 1,475hp Merlin engines of their Spitfires into clear blue skies high above the storm before flying safely to base at RAF Baigachi, Calcutta. 'When it is angry,' Costain wrote, 'the sky is a foe without mercy.' Or, as King Lear might have warned him, 'As flies to wanton boys are we to the gods, they kill us for their sport.'

Even heavy bombers and Dakota transport planes could be hurled from the skies in tropical storms. Some were lifted so high that their crews succumbed to hypoxia and crashed into the jungle below. If they survived such trauma, and were very lucky, Allied aircrews might be rescued from their aircraft by Naga warriors and carried to safety. Capture by the Japanese meant almost certain death, either by a lunge and twist of a bayonet, or by ritual decapitation with an officer's sword. One of my father's colleagues went missing; his body was later found in a jungle clearing, chopped to pieces.

Nagas had, of course, suffered in the fighting, too. The Japanese had occupied the Naga village at Kohima. Humiliation, rape, torture, beatings and executions were par for the course. The Nagas, though, fought back, mostly with the British, and, as they did, they gathered an arsenal of weapons and ammunition that would surprise rare visitors to Nagaland, including me, forty years on. Before Nagaland I had never seen, much less picked up, an Arisaka Type-99 rifle, made in Nagoya and complete with a sixteen-petalled chrysanthemum etched into its butt. This was the standard-issue Japanese service rifle between 1941 and 1945. Here, too, I was handed a Nambu Type-14 pistol, an 8mm weapon carried by officers along with their swords. And there are quite a few swords to be seen, especially examples of the razor-sharp Type-94 Shin Gunto (New Army Sword) mass-produced in Japan between 1934 and the end of the Second World War.

Many Nagas supported the British by acting as guides, porters or lookouts. Until they came this way, the Japanese had prided themselves on their ability in jungle warfare. On the march north through Burma to Imphal and Kohima, they had travelled as much by mule and elephant as they had by bicycle and lorry. They had no intention of getting bogged down in the mud.

Local, rice-based meals were, more or less, familiar and readily digestible. What they had failed to take into account was the fact that the jungles become ever more dense, the hills steeper and closer together, the sheer number of dangerous animals ever greater as northern Burma folds and refolds itself into the Naga Hills. The Nagas knew this densely planted part of the world like the backs of their war shields and, like the Japanese, they were long used to the idea of taking no hostages in battle. Only heads. Japanese soldiers came to fear the jungle while British and Indian troops were learning, if slowly and painfully, to come to terms with it. Some British soldiers, notably the Chindits – a guerrilla force named after a mythical Burmese lion, formed and led by the Bible-bashing Christian Zionist Major General Orde Wingate – crawled through the very heart of the Burmese jungle to undermine Japanese positions, and confidence, although at a terrible cost. The deeply eccentric, Indian-born Wingate died when the USAAF B-25 bomber he was being flown in crashed into the Naga Hills.

Wingate is one of the many reasons I had long wanted to come this way. His famous guerrilla exploits in northern Burma fuelled my boyhood imagination, yet all I ever saw of Wingate and his jungle world were tantalising moments of grainy black and white film occasionally shown on television and snaps in fading books. What was that jungle really like? Where exactly was the River Chindwin, which Wingate's men had crossed in search of the enemy? In upper Burma, of course, a part of the world never easy to get to and today virtually inaccessible to foreigners under Burma's authoritarian military regime. I was told of a possible route over the hills and into 'eastern Nagaland', or upper Burma. I decided to follow in Wingate's footsteps.

I had no illusions that the going would be easy. This is a land of dense jungle, leeches, disease, snatching plants, poisonous snakes, oozing mud and unfeasibly large, biting insects. As a homage to Wingate, though, the hardships had to be worth it. At least Nagas I met on my trek to the banks of the Chindwin found

Wingate interesting, too. Like them he was a deeply committed Christian, and although the name of his guerrilla army had Burmese roots, he took it from the Naga word *chindit* rather than the Burmese *chinthe*.

Some years earlier I had visited Wingate's birthplace, the small garrison town of Nainital founded by the British in 1841 in the foothills of the Himalayas in what is now the state of Uttarakhand, the source or the Ganges and home to some of the most sacred Hindu shrines. Brought up in such a remote land in a family governed by his mother's zealous Plymouth Brethren brand of Christianity, Wingate was always going to be a little different from regular British army officers. He was constantly, it seems, in search if not of Shangri-La, then perhaps of the Holy City itself, the New Jerusalem. During a successful spell of service from 1928 to 1933 with the Sudan Defence Forces, tracking down and ambushing slave traders and ivory poachers, this Arab-speaking officer set out on an expedition to find the mythical city of Zerzura.

In Arabic legend, Zerzura exists somewhere deep in the infinite folds of desert somewhere west of the Nile, possibly in Egypt, perhaps in Libya. The fifteenth-century *Kitab al-Kdnuz* (*Book of Hidden Pearls*) tells of the gleaming white city in the desert. On its gate is carved a bird. The beak can be turned, admitting lucky visitors to Zerzura and its untold treasures.

A number of British officers were swept up in the craze to find Zerzura in the 1920s and 30s. The English-educated Hungarian Count László de Almásy, however, claimed that his discovery of the third and final group of wadis (oases) in the Gilk Kebir marked the end of the search, because the 'city' of myth would, in all likelihood, have been an oasis, or a complex of them. Like the New Jerusalem, Shangri-La or any other mythical city, Zerzura remains undiscovered because its streets cannot be walked in this life. Not that these ventures are always a waste of time. Ralph Bagnold, a Royal Engineers officer, veteran of the trenches in the Great War and a pioneer of desert exploration, who had made every effort to locate Zerzura at the same time as Almásy, used his experiences to found and command the British army's daring and successful Long Range Desert Group during the Second World War. The great explorer Wilfred Thesiger was a member of the group. He had previously served under Wingate in both the Sudan Defence Force and Wingate's Gideon Force, a guerrilla army formed in Abyssinia to harass the Italians who had brutally invaded that country in 1936. In 1941, meanwhile, Bagnold found time to publish *The Physics of Blown Sand and Desert Dunes*, a book that NASA has used to help plan landings on Mars. He was made a member of the Royal Society in 1944. As for Almásy, he went on to serve with Rommel's Afrika Korps, although he was said to have passed on German secrets to his old 'Zerzura' friends in the Long Range Desert Group, and, much later, became the subject of Michael Ondaatje's novel *The English Patient*.

Wingate, meanwhile, after service in Abyssinia and Palestine, where, a fervent Zionist, he led the Special Night Squads that taught the nascent Jewish army, including future Israeli leaders such as Moshe Dayan, much about guerrilla warfare, was asked by his old desert commander General Wavell to form a guerrilla army in India. The purpose of the 3,000-strong 77th Indian Infantry Brigade, the 'Chindit' force, was to undermine Japanese positions and confidence in Burma.

Badly affected by bouts of malaria and increasingly eccentric – Lord Moran, Winston Churchill's personal physician, noted in his diary, '[Wingate] seemed to me hardly sane . . . in medical jargon, a borderline case' – Wingate did penetrate deep into Burma. The Chindits covered between a thousand and fifteen hundred miles on foot, by mule and without motorised land transport. His latest mission, however, was not wholly successful. The terrain was simply too exhausting even for such well-trained and exceptionally brave soldiers as his. After initial successes in early 1943, the Chindits were forced to escape Burma as Japanese troops closed in on them. Wingate, however, did establish a new form of close, cooperative strikes by fast-moving troops on the ground covering difficult terrain and supported from the air with supplies dropped by the air force. The tactic would later be used in many theatres of war around the world. In Wingate's case, air support was provided by a clutch of Dakota and Hudson aircraft flown from Agartala in eastern Bengal by RAF 31 Squadron. Fighter cover for these dangerous long-range operations was limited.

A second Chindit mission employing gliders and parachutes began in March 1944, just in time to divert at least some of Japan's extensive forces away from their objectives of Imphal and Kohima. It was during this operation, on the return flight following a visit to three Chindit bases deep in Burma, that Wingate was killed. The jungle he had wrestled with so fitfully had claimed his life. As, of course had Nagaland. I have yet to find the spot where he went to meet his fierce, if loving, God.

Other, far less intense, soldiers were involved in the Burmese and Naga Hills campaigns. Major General Douglas Gracey, commander of the 20th Indian Division, looked on the jungle as nothing more tricky than ill-managed woodland in an otherwise well-kempt country estate. Gracey walked out each morning, stick in hand and accompanied by his Labrador, for a spot of shooting before training his men in the art of jungle warfare as if they were out for a trek in the New Forest. The general had little but contempt for the notion that the Japanese were superior jungle fighters to the British, Indian or African troops under his command. (It was Gracey who, in October 1945, controversially rearmed the Japanese prisoners-of-war he had rounded up in Saigon the previous month when the Viet Nimh threatened to attack the French-Vietnamese city. Better the Japanese than communism. The unflappable Gracey went on to become commander-in-chief of the independent Pakistan Army from 1948 until 1951.)

Something like 200,000 Nagas served the British cause one way or another during the war, mainly in non-combatant roles.

The armed Nagas who rallied around the extraordinary Ursula Graham Bower are a remarkable exception. Such was the fame of this young English woman that she was the cover girl of the 1 January 1945 issue of *Time* magazine. An eye-grabbing article headlined 'Ursula and the Naked Nagas' told of 'half-naked tribesmen from northeastern India', directed by 'pert, pretty Ursula Graham-Bower [*sic*], 30, an archaeology student who looks like a cinema actress'. The Nagas, according to *Time*, were 'lithe-limbed warriors' who 'lead a somewhat humdrum existence punctuated by occasional raids to cut off their neighbours' heads, which they carry about in wicker baskets'. They used drugs to catch fish, an American readership learned, and 'begged Miss Graham Bower to name their babies. She named most of them Victoria Elizabeth.' Which was, perhaps, a little unfair on the boys. Now, the 'Roedean-educated debutante, rally driver, traveller and anthropologist' was fighting the Japanese and helping Allied soldiers with the help of what *Time* clearly saw as her naive, if warlike, adopted jungle children. *Time* also went to see Ursula's mother in Leigh Hall, Cricklade, Wilts, who commented that her daughter was 'an extraordinary girl; she never would sit still'.

Ursula Graham Bower was certainly an extraordinary young woman. She was also an extraordinary older woman, who poured tea for me at her house in the New Forest after I had come back from my first trip to Nagaland. She was a formidable lady, very grand, wonderfully informed, highly articulate and with a sparkling sense of humour. It was not too difficult to imagine her as she had been forty years earlier, a Bren-gun-toting guerrilla leader serving both British and Naga interests with an official rank of captain. One of the very few British women combatants during the Second World War, Graham Bower was dubbed 'The Jungle Queen' by American servicemen, and 'The Naga Queen' by their British counterparts. As for the Nagas, they too saw her as a queen, or in the case of the Zemi tribe she lived with during much of her time in the Naga Hills, a goddess. Many Nagas regarded her as a kind of 'reincarnation' of Gaidinliu, at the time languishing in jail, who had promised on her arrest that she would come back to fight for her people in an unrecognisable form. That she should have chosen the guise of a very proper, and very white, Home Counties 'gel' did not seem to strike them as odd.

Graham Bower had first ventured into the Naga Hills in 1937. Born into an old military family, she had hoped to go to Oxford from Roedean, but her parents were none too keen on the idea of university-educated girls. Palming her off with an Aston-Martin sports car and a promise of world travel, they were not particularly surprised when she sailed off to India before journeying on into the Naga Hills. Graham Bower might not have thought this at first, but she, too, was looking for a wild place to call her own. In her best-selling book *Naga Path* (1950) she noted:

> In the administered areas [of Assam and the Naga Hills] Mission and Plains influence have altered the tribes much. Caps, boots and trousers replace the former simplicities, and a desire for sinecures and soft jobs seduces men from the old, hard way of the soil. There are, though, blessed oases in the drab desert where beads and feathers, red-dyed goats'-hair and rich-hued plaids still gladden the eye; where the ancient candours and ancient moralities survive uncorrupted, where chipped enamel and cheap glass have not ousted the hand-carved product; where men go armed with spear and dao instead of notebook and fountain-pen; where the dog-eat-dog existence of modern economics has not swamped the primitive decencies, and where life is simple and pagan and brief and happy.

Two sights made her want to stay in the Naga Hills even after one brief trip. As she was driven up from Dimapur to Kohima:

[A] group of hillmen scattered before us and stood on the roadside, staring. They were not the slim-built Assamese of the low ground. The sight of them was a shock. Here were the Philippines and Indonesia. Bead necklaces drooped on their bare, brown chests, black kilts with three lines of cowries wrapped their hips, plaids edged with vivid colours hung on their coppery shoulders. Tall, solid, muscular, Mongolian they stood, a little startled, as we shot by.

This was Graham Bower's first glimpse of the Nagas.

And then there were the views. Over breakfast in Kohima she looked out beyond the town to:

[A] progression of ranges which faded out into the haze of the east and the unmapped country. Bridle-roads led there, winding down spurs and curving round contours till they were lost in the intricate folds. On every ridge there was a shaggy village, its thatched roofs smoke-stained and weathered. One behind the other the hills stretched away as far as the eye could see, in an ocean of peaks, a wilderness of steep fields and untouched forest, of clefts and gulfs and razor-backs which merged into a grey infinity. That landscape drew me as I had never known anything to do before, with a power transcending the body, a force not of this world at all.

This lovely prose recalls Coleridge's exultantly romantic and dream-like poem, Kubla Khan:

In Xanadu did Kubla Khan
A stately pleasure dome decree:
Where Alph, the sacred river, ran
Through chasms measureless to man
Down to a sunless sea.
So twice five miles of fertile ground
With walls and towers were girdled round:

And there were gardens bright with sinuous rills,
Where blossomed many an incense-bearing tree;
And here were forests ancient as the hills,
Enfolding sunny spots of greenery.

In this highly charged dream, and its exotic places and people, there is a hint that somehow, no matter how impossible this might seem, we might just find this Shangri-La . . .

And, yet, as Graham Bower returned, and returned again, to the Naga Hills, not without a little help from that old Naga hand Professor J. H. Hutton at Cambridge, she learned that such beauty, wildness and exotica came at a price. She entered Naga villages where children died of diarrhoea and men from syphilis. Hailstones the size of golf balls could destroy traditional homes in storms. She was taken for a queen, and a goddess, by the Zemi Nagas, and being a practical, although romantic, sort found this more of a threat and a nuisance than an honour. And, as she had read Rudyard Kipling's spine-tingling and chastening tale 'The Man Who Would be King' as a girl, she knew in her bones that for a mortal to be taken for a deity in such climes was not such a clever thing. In Kipling's tale, those two British soldiers of fortune, Daniel Dravot and Peachy Carnehan, together with 'Billy Fish', a friendly sepoy, make their dangerous way into the unknown mountain country known as Kafiristan. Here, mistaken as descendants of Alexander the Great who passed this way thousands of years before, they are worshipped as gods, and Dravot is crowned king of the tribes he has united. It all goes horribly wrong when Dravot is bitten in the hand by the native beauty he plans to take as his wife. Revealed as a mere mortal, Dravot is sent plunging into an impossibly steep ravine from a rope bridge cut by the maddened locals, Carnehan is crucified before being sent free to tell his awful tale, and Billy Fish has his throat slit from ear to ear. As for the last living Naga deity, Gaidinliu, she was currently serving a long stretch behind British Indian bars.

The wildness of the Nagas was, however, deeply attractive to Graham Bower. Here, as she said of the hill tribes, 'war was the natural state; to them, the Pax Britannica, was but an interlude'. With the coming of the Second World War and the threat of invasion by the Japanese, Graham Bower's extraordinary standing with the Nagas meant that she was able to get them to work for 'Watch and Ward', a local defence and intelligence-gathering organisation she set up with the encouragement of General Slim. 'Watch and Ward' was a local offshoot of V Force, the British military underground unit working in Burma and the north-east. Graham Bower's V Force contact was Colonel Rawdon Wright, who, by chance, was acquainted with her parents back in Wiltshire. Rawdon Wright had been badly wounded in the First World War; his gammy leg, with its open wound, made it difficult for him to walk, though he had still managed to serve between the wars with the Assam Rifles. A friend of J. P. Mills, he knew the area and many of its peoples well. Quite simply, he loved the Naga Hills. Bad leg and all, Rawdon Wright set out on a trek up and down the hills in August 1942 with Graham Bower soon after she had talked her way back to Assam from England, to see if the Zemi Nagas could be persuaded to join 'Watch and Ward'.

Understanding that he was a valiant soldier who had fought in the war against Germany three decades earlier, the Zemis offered to carry the limping colonel in a litter. Rawdon Wright would have none of it. This very much impressed the Nagas, who told Graham Bower that this was not a man, but a tiger! Rawdon Wright had been worth his weight in ivory, or heads. After his visit, the Zemi Nagas pledged themselves to 'Watch and Ward'. Sadly, just three months later the Colonel's injured leg was amputated. That last trek had been too much even for this gallant and uncomplaining Indian Army officer. He died just before Christmas.

Commissioned as a captain, Graham Bower performed quiet miracles with her 'Watch and Ward'. Many RAF pilots owed their lives to her as they were stolen away into the jungle, and into safe hands, after crashing. Matter-of-fact to the last, Graham Bower had decided exactly what to do if she was ever in danger of falling into Japanese hands. She would shoot herself, and her faithful servant Namkai would chop off her head and present it to the Japanese as proof that she was dead to avoid the enemy torturing local people in an attempt to discover her whereabouts.

The 'Naga Queen' was certainly well versed in the use of guns. 'My father was a keen shot,' she told Major General Julian Thompson, author of *Behind Enemy Lines*, a book published in 1998 for the Imperial War Museum. 'I learned to use a rifle when I was twelve. I started on a .22, and while he was in the Navy he gave my brother and me training on the standard service rifle, the Lee Enfield .303. I could use a shotgun and an automatic pistol.' Naturally she was aghast when the first 'rifles' given by the Indian Army to her 'Watch and Ward' Nagas were antique breech-loading affairs that were dangerous to handle, slow to fire and pretty much useless in the face of contemporary Japanese infantry firepower. Many were later re-equipped with shotguns.

In the event, Graham Bower was able to help the British and Allied armed forces without losing her head, despite the price put on it by the Japanese, but she did lose it in a happily different way when she fell for Lt Colonel 'Tim' Nicholson Betts, a fellow V Force officer. The colonel was a former Assam tea planter who had later grown coffee in southern India and then gone on to join the Indian Army. When he learned of Ursula Graham Bower, he decided that he had to seek her out and marry her. Which is what he did. 'As we both seemed to be mad along the same lines,' wrote Ursula, 'it appeared a very suitable match.' It was. When the war ended, and V Force had been disbanded, Nicholson Betts was appointed first political officer to the stretch of India between Nepal and Tibet. No maps. Fierce tribes. Freezing cold. Ursula went with him, and that, for some while, was the end of her direct contact with the Nagas.

Graham Bower had been well aware of her propaganda value during the war. She believed that her own role had been exaggerated out of all proportion and that she had been made into the object of some sort of real-life Rider Haggard romance. But although she won the loyalty of many Nagas, Graham Bower was often regarded by British officers as anything but 'She-who-must-be-obeyed'. In fact, many of them were rather dismissive of her extraordinary efforts. But 'Uncle' Bill Slim was not among them, of course, and in this theatre of war it was his support that counted for most.

The Nicholson Bettses went on to grow coffee in Kenya and to work with the Masai tribes. The violent Mau Mau uprising, the armed struggle for Kenyan independence during the 1950s, encouraged them to leave, especially after a friend of their young daughter, Trina, was killed. They next moved to the island of Mull, off the west coast of Scotland, where they farmed, studied wildlife and brought up their two daughters. It was here in the early sixties that the Nicholson Bettses were visited by four neatly suited Nagas who had come to explain what had happened since the British had left shortly after the end of the war with Japan, and to ask their former 'goddess' for help. Although a Naga government in exile was established in London, and despite the best efforts of the *Observer*'s Gavin Young, then reporting live from Nagaland, there was little Ursula Nicholson Betts could do. She had persuaded Nagas to fight with the British in 1942, but what could she do now that Nagaland was a part of India?

After her husband died of a stroke while out riding in 1973, Ursula moved to a house in the New Forest to be near her aged mother. Ursula died in 1988. At the funeral two of the pall-bearers were Naga warriors. Another pair were British veterans of the 'forgotten' Burma War.

*

The Naga contribution to the Allied cause was warmly celebrated by General Slim in his 1956 memoir *Defeat into Victory*:

The Nagas whose loyalty, even in the most depressing times of the invasion had never faltered. Despite floggings, torture, execution and the burning of villages, they refused to aid the Japanese in any way or betray our troops. Their active help was beyond value or praise. Under devoted leadership of the very highest quality they guided our columns, collected information, ambushed enemy patrols, carried our supplies and brought in the wounded under the heaviest of hostile fire. No soldier of the 14th Army will ever forget that, nor will he ever think of them except with admiration and affection.

Which is fine, except for the fact that many Nagas were neutral during the war, while some were distinctly pro-Japanese. The latter were a minority, yet a significant one. At the time they confused loyalty to the Japanese with an allegiance to the INA that, they believed, would rid them of the British and guarantee their future independence.

As Graham Bower had discovered by living with the Nagas, there was no set rule determining whether they would be loyal to the British, the Japanese or simply themselves. What mattered more to them than the regard of the British or the Japanese was the way they felt about one another. Age-old rivalries between tribes were just as likely to determine their attitudes towards the war and its protagonists as any promises by representatives of occupying and other imperial powers. Nevertheless, although one of the reasons the British had decided to 'protect' the Nagas was to keep them well away from dangerous lines of Indian nationalist thought, the tribes did tend to side with the colonials. The experience of Japanese brutality aside, tribesmen with an increasing sense of Indian national politics had no intention of blurring their identity with that of an independent India. If that is what supporting the Japanese meant, then it was better to stick with the British.

In any case, the Japanese were not exactly besotted with the Nagas. They thought them primitive, and thus simple. This patronising racist judgement was useful to the British; because the Japanese believed the Nagas to be fundamentally stupid, Naga spies working on behalf of the British were able to wander freely into Japanese camps, as long as they kept up the pretence of being dim-witted apes.

Slim delighted in telling Graham Bower the story of two Naga tribesmen employed as batmen to Japanese officers in Manipur. When the pair decided to steal a vital map concerning future Japanese operations in the area and to hand this over to the British, they also took some valueless bits and bobs along with them, guessing, rightly, that the Japanese would assume that theirs had been a routine and purely opportunistic robbery. In all likelihood the dumb Nagas would eat the map, or use it to help make a fire; the joke, however, was on the Japanese. The map was duly handed over to the British.

Nagas who sided with the Japanese, including Angami Zapu Phizo, the first leader of a united Naga independence movement shortly after the Second World War, might have thought that they had a better chance of independence when the fighting stopped if the British were pushed out of India. Perhaps, though, they had overlooked a key problem. The main allies of the Japanese in the push against the British during the Second World War were soldiers of the Indian National Army led by Subhas Chandra Bose. Bose believed that only an armed struggle would lead to Indian independence and that the Japanese were, somehow, Asian brothers in arms. So keen, in fact, was Bose to fight the British out of the subcontinent that he sided not only with Japan but also with Nazi Germany, and not merely by default because both were Axis powers. Bose, as we will see, courted the Nazis directly.

From the Naga point of view, did this matter? Surely whoever guaranteed their future independence was in the right? What did they know of Nazism or concentration camps, or the annihilation of the Jews? But the folly of supporting the Japanese, Bose and the INA was that none of these was much interested in the Nagas or in their independence. As time proved, Indian nationalists not only believed that the Naga Hills were a necessary part of an independent India, but guaranteed this by force. In supporting Bose, pro-Japanese Nagas made both a tactical and a strategic error. Even Gandhi, opposed to violence, preferred the idea of a future Nagaland within India, while Bose was wholly scornful of Gandhi's peace-loving ways.

The story of Subhas Chandra Bose remains controversial even today. A Hindu nationalist and Bengali hero, he is forever associated with the Japanese attempt to invade India through Manipur and the Naga Hills. Yet very few Indian histories have much to say about Bose and the Nagas. He probably didn't think much about them himself; they just happened to be the people who lived in what appeared, in 1943–4, to be the Achilles heel of British India. How odd, then, that it was Bose who unintentionally did so much to draw the Naga Hills and their 'naked' headhunting tribes into the world of global affairs and international political ambition. For from 1941, when Bose courted first Hitler and then the Japanese High Command, the Nagas lost their political innocence. From now on, the Naga Hills, and the future Nagaland, would play a key, if largely forgotten and often secret, role on the world stage.

With the story of Bose, we find the Nagas connected unwittingly to the ambitions of Hirohito, General Tojo and Adolf Hitler. We discover Indian soldiers fighting Indian soldiers in the battles of Imphal and Kohima. And we witness Indian soldiers forming a Waffen SS regiment with the aim of fighting the British in India. In encouraging the Japanese to attempt an invasion of India through Manipur and the Naga Hills, Bose sealed the fate of Nagas for decades after his own mysterious death in 1945. After Bose, the Nagas would never be free.

Born the ninth of fourteen children into an affluent family in Cuttack, Orissa, in 1897, Bose was educated at the Scottish Church College, Calcutta, and Fitzwilliam College, Cambridge. Although privileged, he was violently anti-British from a young age. After a brief spell with the Indian Civil Service he joined the Indian National Congress Party. He quickly made himself a nuisance to the imperial authorities and was first imprisoned after encouraging the boycott of a visit by the Prince of Wales to India in 1921. In 1930 he was elected Mayor of Calcutta. He served two terms as president of the Indian National Congress in 1938 and 1939, but after a clash with Gandhi was ousted by a vote of no confidence.

Bose then set up his own All India Forward Bloc, and initiated a campaign of civil disobedience when, in September 1939, Lord Linlithgow, the Viceroy, declared war on Germany on India's behalf without consulting Congress. Imprisoned for the eleventh time, he was sprung by supporters from house arrest with his nephew, Sisir Kumar Bose, in January 1941 and made his way, rather colourfully, to Afghanistan in various disguises – now as a deaf and dumb tribesman, now as a Pathan insurance salesman, although accounts of his escapade vary – and thus into the welcoming arms of German agents. In the guise of an Italian aristocrat, Count Orlando Mazzotta, Bose was whisked off to Moscow. And then, courtesy of a real-life German aristocrat, Friedrich-Werner Graf von der Schulenburg, German ambassador to Moscow (hanged 10 November 1944 after the 20 July 1944 attempt on Hitler's life), Bose was flown to Berlin.

Here he renewed the acquaintances he had made in the mid-1930s with such racist ideologues as Alfred Rosenberg, the Nazi 'philosopher' who gave intellectual underpinning to the regime's policies of anti-Semitism, Lebensraum and white Aryan supremacy; Thor only knows what Rosenberg would have made of the 'naked Nagas', although, of course, as a fellow Aryan – Indians are Aryans just as Nazi Germans were – Bose himself was not an *Untermensch*. At the same time, Bose made himself useful to Dr Joseph Goebbels, Hitler's minister for propaganda, and finally got to meet Hitler himself. An entertaining, if politically lop-sided film, *Bose: The Forgotten Hero* (2005), directed by Shyam Benegal, includes a bizarre, even funny sequence in which Bose lectures Hitler on military tactics.

As for the Nazis' ideas on race, Bose could only display both a certain confusion and contrapuntal arrogance. On 25 March 1936, during his first visit to the Reich, he wrote to Dr Franz Thierfelder of the Deutsche Akademie:

Today, I regret I have to return to India with the conviction that the new nationalism of Germany is not only narrow and selfish but arrogant. The recent speech of Herr Hitler in Munich gives the essence of Nazi philosophy . . . the new racial philosophy which has a very weak scientific foundation stands for the glorification of the white races in general and the German race in particular. Herr Hitler has talked of the destiny of the white races to rule over the rest of the world. But, the historical fact is that up until now, the Asiatics have dominated Europe more than the Europeans have dominated Asia. One only has to consider the repeated invasions of Europe by Mongols, the Turks, the Arabs (Moors), the Huns and other Asiatic races to understand the strength of my argument . . .

Hitler, who brushed aside such arguments, was only vaguely interested in the idea of pushing Britain out of India at some time in the future, while Bose's arrival in Germany was poorly timed in terms of the Führer's immediate ambition. In June 1941 Hitler unleashed Operation Barbarossa, the invasion of the Soviet Union. From now on, and even if it had mattered for a moment in Hitler's mind, India was little more than an exotic sideshow. Bose did, however, have some success in Germany. He founded a Free India Centre, established Free India Radio and formed the Indian Legion, a force of some 3,500, some of them Indian students studying in Germany, others Indian prisoners of war captured by the Germans in Libya. Bose visited POW camps and called for volunteers. These were to form the backbone of an army that would, or so the idea went, spearhead an attack on the North-West Frontier of India and so march on Delhi, where, presumably, flags sporting the ancient Hindu swastika would fly alongside those of the Third Reich.

Attached initially to the Wehrmacht, but later to the Waffen SS, the Indian Legion declared its allegiance to the Nazi regime in a ceremony first held in August 1942 at Königsbrück, where the soldiers were issued German field grey uniforms adorned with cloth badges bearing the legend 'Freies Indien' above a leaping tiger set against a backdrop of horizontal saffron, white and green stripes. Drilled by their German commander, Lt Colonel Kurt Krappe, each soldier barked, 'I swear by God this holy oath, that I will obey the leader of the German state and people, Adolf Hitler, as commander of the German Armed Forces, in the fight for freedom in India in which fight the leader is Subhas Chandra Bose, and that as a brave soldier, I am willing to lay down my life for this oath.'

Bose was awarded the title 'leader', which translates as Netaji in Hindi, and Führer in German. Hindu politicians and Bengali intellectuals continue to argue that Bose was opposed to Nazi Germany's active anti-Semitism among other crimes and excesses, and that he was a democrat and a socialist. Of a sort. The speeches he gave during the 1930s and 1940s were certainly those of a demagogue. Blood. Fatherland. Death. Glory. And he was not exactly averse to Nazi hospitality, enjoying a rent-free villa, a courtesy car and a generous personal grant of £800 a month. When he fell ill in 1942, he went to a good hospital in Vienna. Here he married his translator, Emilie Schenkl, who, that year, bore him a daughter, Anita, a professor of economics at Augsburg University today.

The last time Bose saw Anita, she was four weeks old. Anita, and Bose's sojourn in Nazi Germany, made news in 2005 when angry protests in India delayed the release of Shyam Benegal's film. How dare the director suggest that Bose had married. And even if he had, then surely he would have chosen a saintly Hindu

Indian virgin? Although a controversial figure, Bose remains an impeccable hero for many Indians. He was also fond of saying that he had no time for marriage; all his energies were taken up with his undying love for the Fatherland and all-consuming hatred for the British, and presumably for their third-rate Cambridge colleges, with their punts, clever young women, and strawberries and cream teas in summer, too. Hitler had also claimed that he had no time for marriage. All his energies were consumed by his love for the Fatherland.

Bose was discreetly dispatched from Germany to Japan where Hitler, quite rightly, believed that he could play a more useful role. Indian sources tend to say Bose went of his own accord, but this would have been impossible during the Second World War. For all his toadying up to Hitler, however, Bose remained a confused socialist, disturbed that Germany had invaded the Soviet Union, a country led by another of his heroes, the mass-murdering communist despot Joseph Stalin.

Leaving Germany for Japan meant abandoning both his new family and the Indian Legion. These soldiers, thoroughly trained by the German army, were to get nowhere near Delhi or the distant Naga Hills, although it seems that a hundred or so legionaries were parachuted into eastern Iran to infiltrate India through Baluchistan. I have yet to find out what happened to them. Leaderless, and demoralised, the rest of the Legion was left to fight sporadically against the British and French. After D-Day, the remnants retreated through France, gaining a reputation for sickening violence. As the former French Resistance fighter Henri Gendreau told the BBC in 2004, 'I do remember several cases of rape [in his home town of Ruffec]. A lady and her two daughters were raped and in another case they even shot dead a two-year-old girl.'

The Indian Legion eventually surrendered to US, French and British forces while trying to escape into Switzerland in May 1945. It was disbanded by the Allies, its members sent back to India. A smaller army of Indians loyal to Mussolini's fascist Italy

as well as to the cause of Indian independence, the Battaglione
Azad Hindoustan, formed by Iqbal Shedai, a Roman Indian
who had no intention of collaborating with Bose, had been
disbanded before it ever saw battle.

The Indian 'Führer', meanwhile, had been hidden aboard the
German submarine *U-180*, designed for long-range secret
missions, under the command of Captain Werner Musenberg.
On 28 April 1943, *U-180* rendezvoused four hundred miles
south-west of Madagascar with the Japanese submarine, *I-29*, a
big vessel with a crew of 101 and a range of 14,000 nautical
miles under the command of Captain Masao Teraoka. Bose was
duly exchanged for two tons of gold and Japanese naval officers
on their way to study the latest German U-boats. The Japanese
sub sailed on to Sabang, an islet off the coast of Sumatra, from
where Bose, posing as a Japanese VIP named Matsuda, was
flown in a series of hops, skips and jumps to Tokyo.

After addressing the Japanese parliament and a number of
very civil meetings with General Tojo, Bose left for Singapore on
27 June 1943, where, soon afterwards, he took over command of
the recently formed Indian National Army, or Azad Hind Fauj
(Free Indian Army). Tojo arrived to inspect the army and stood
alongside Bose as their new C-in-C gave one of his most famous
speeches:

> Throughout my public career, I have always felt that, though
> India is ripe for independence in every way, she has lacked one
> thing, namely, an army of liberation. George Washington of
> America could fight and win freedom, because he had his
> army. Garibaldi could liberate Italy because he had his armed
> volunteers behind him. It is your privilege and honour to be
> the first to come forward and organise India's national army
> . . . when France declared war on Germany in 1939 and the
> campaign began, there was but one cry which rose from the
> lips of German soldiers, 'To Paris! To Paris!' When the brave
> soldiers of Nippon set out on their march in December 1941,

there was but one cry which rose from their lips, 'To Singapore! To Singapore!' Comrades! My soldiers! Let your battle cry be, 'To Delhi! To Delhi!'

Bose then established a provisional independent government of India before setting out on a tour of Malaysia, Thailand and Burma to promote his cause and the INA. He raised something like 45,000 recruits, from among both Indian POWs interned by the Japanese and Indian civilians, together with large sums of money. On the night of 22–23 October Bose's government-in-waiting declared war on Great Britain, and, for good measure, the United States of America.

And then, lusting for blood, he marched with his army up through Burma and on towards the 'hot gates' of Kohima. In one curious way, the Nagas would have respected Bose. He saw women as equals, and even created a women's brigade in the INA. This was the 'Rani of Jhansi' regiment commanded by Lt Colonel Lakshmi Sahgal, a doctor and an active front-line fighter. As much a character as Captain Ursula Graham Bower, Colonel Sahgal went on to join the Communist Party of India (Marxist) in 1971 and was the rival candidate to A. P. J. Abdul Khan in the 2002 Indian presidential elections. Captured by the British, she was brought to Delhi where she received a hero's welcome. The British authorities promptly released her.

As for the march on the Naga Hills, it ended not just in defeat, but in the death of approximately half the INA. The retreat from Kohima and Imphal was a dismal episode, with famine, disease, exposure and dehydration taking their toll. Bose himself appeared to have learned the Japanese way of discussing defeat. 'Though the Japanese Army has given up the operation, we will continue it. We will not repent even if the revolutionary army to attain independence of our homeland is completely defeated. Increase in casualties, cessation of supplies, and famine are not reasons enough to stop marching. Even if the whole army becomes only spirit, we will not stop advancing towards our homeland.' In November 1944, when few Germans would have agreed with him, Bose announced that 'victory in this war [will] belong to Japan and Germany'.

Quite what happened to this fiery Indian independence fighter when the war ended, no one really knows. The official version is that he was trying to get to Moscow via Soviet-occupied Manchuria when the aircraft he was flying in crashed, and that he died either instantaneously or very soon afterwards. But conspiracy theories abound and official government investigations have led nowhere. Even today many Indians refuse to believe that Bose is dead, although he would be over 110 years old by now.

Bose remains a difficult figure for non-Indians to come to terms with. His falling in with the Nazis and imperial Japanese governments was based on the dubious premise that 'my enemy's enemy is my friend'. This seems horribly cynical. However bad the British had been in India, surely there were better ways of seeking independence than with two of the nastiest regimes in world history? Were the deaths of so many Europeans and fellow Asians, and the slaughter of six million Jews, the right sort of price to pay for Indian independence? Bose apparently thought so. His speeches were gory as well as blinkered, as if India were the only country in the world and Indians the only people that mattered. He said nothing that I have been able to find, though, about the nobility or otherwise of India's indigenous tribespeople, or about their right to independence from an India free of the British.

The last time I was in Calcutta I went to look at the statue of Bose that stands, arm raised in a German-style salute towards the road from which, during the Second World War, RAF Spitfires took off to defend India from the Japanese. To millions of Indians, though, Bose is a national hero. In Bengal, especially, he is beyond criticism. Calcutta's international airport, Dum Dum for many decades, has since been renamed Netaji Subhas

Chandra Bose International. There are daily flights to Berlin and Tokyo.

For many Indians, Bose's single-minded vendetta against the British was the key to Indian independence. Ranjan Borra, an American-Indian historian, journalist and founder of the Subhas Bose Society in Washington, once referred to a letter written by Chief Justice P. B. Chakrabarty of the Calcutta High Court in which this former acting governor of Bengal highlighted the importance from an Indian perspective, of Bose:

> Lord Attlee [formerly Clement Attlee, British prime minister, 1945–51], who had given us independence by withdrawing British rule from India, spent two days in the Governor's Palace at Calcutta during his tour of India. At that time I had a prolonged discussion with him regarding the real factors that had led the British to quit India. My direct question to him was that since Gandhi's 'Quit India' movement had tapered off quite some time ago and in 1947 no such new compelling situation had arisen that would necessitate a hasty departure, why did they have to leave? In his reply, Attlee cited several reasons, the principal among them being the erosion of loyalty to the British Crown among the Indian army and navy personnel as a result of the military activities of Netaji. Toward the end of our discussion, I asked Attlee what was the extent of Gandhi's influence upon the British decision to quit India? Hearing this question, Attlee's lips became twisted in a sarcastic smile as he slowly chewed out the word m-i-n-i-m-a-l.

Westminster passed the Indian Independence Bill on 4 July 1947. On 14 August, the Naga National Council, led by A. Z. Phizo, a wartime supporter of Bose, declared Naga independence. The message was relayed to both Delhi and the United Nations. The Nagas, though, were soon to discover that independence was very far off indeed. The events of the Second World War that had connected them to the political machinations of Tokyo and Berlin as well as those of London, Washington and Delhi had ensured both their importance in the Great Game of world politics and, perversely, their obscurity. For all the blood spilt at Kohima, the Naga Hills were about to vanish off the world map.

7

Christ Stopped at Chemong

'Our land is our heritage. To none shall it be surrendered. As whetstone, our opponents sharpen us.' This stirring inscription can be read on a simple monument set among pine trees above Kohima. It was raised in memory of Angami Zapu Phizo, the leader and, later, the conscience of the Naga independence movement. A mission-educated Angami Naga born at the turn of the century, A. Z. Phizo, who adopted the 'A' and 'Z' at mission school, worked as a teacher and as an insurance salesman before taking on the leadership of the fledgling Naga National Council in 1947. During the Second World War he worked for Japanese intelligence and fought with Bose's INA, believing that Tokyo would reward the Nagas with independence after the fall of the Raj. He was arrested and detained by the British in Burma, but released in 1946. He spent much of the second half of his long life not in the Naga Hills, but, from 1960, in London where he was to die thirty years later.

It was here that I first met this legendary politician and guerrilla leader in a nondescript meeting room in a block of offices in south-east London near the Elephant and Castle, though later I was invited to his home in suburban Bromley. He was in his early eighties then, small, fit and dapper, dressed, I recall, in a houndstooth-check suit, set off with a neatly knotted tie. His shoes were well polished. If he had tried to sell me an insurance policy, I wouldn't have been surprised. Not that I expected him to be dressed in a tartan kilt and sport a feathered head dress, spear and bow and arrow, but this national leader, so far from home, seemed an unlikely target for the frustration and wrath of Indian nationalist politicians. Over tea and biscuits, Phizo told me he had come to London in 1960, with a price on his head of 10,000 rupees, to spread the message of the Naga struggle.

'By this time, the Indian army had razed six hundred and forty-five of our villages,' he told me, 'and killed at least one hundred thousand of our people. Do you know when prime minister Morarji Desai flew from India to see me here in London, he flew into a rage and said he would exterminate all the Indian rebels?' Phizo handed me a copy of the speech he had made to the British press in London on 26 July 1960. It read:

> I have come to this country on behalf of the Nagas to tell the people of Britain, and through them the people of the whole world of the terrible tragedy that has overtaken our country . . . I should like to make a particular appeal to the people of India to understand what has been done in their names and to come forward to help bring these sufferings to an end.

The speech went on to cite rape, forced labour, concentration camps and sheer bloody murder. The yellowing press release, its pages held together with a rusty paperclip, was headed with the first address of the Naga National Council in exile: 81 Denison House, 296 Vauxhall Bridge Road, London SE1. The Naga Hills have never seemed so very far away.

In his quest for support in Britain, Phizo was only partly successful. David Astor, proprietor of the *Observer*, took an interest and dispatched Gavin Young, one of his finest foreign correspondents, to Nagaland. After a brief burst of interest, the story of the Nagas faded into a blur of minor wars of independence throughout the world, dropped behind the daily crossword, pets corner and nature-notes slots of newspapers, and then all but vanished from sight like the Naga Hills in the monsoon mist.

The story disappeared partly because Fleet Street tends to have a short attention span – the Naga struggle had been a promising little war for foreign news editors only until the next one blazed into action – and partly because Delhi had done its Machiavellian best to normalise the situation in the Naga Hills by creating the state of Nagaland on 1 December 1963. This event was barely noticed in the international press: a week earlier John F. Kennedy had been assassinated in Dallas; Nagaland could hardly be more than a hill of beans compared to this mountainous upheaval.

The creation of Nagaland was, on the face of it, a brilliant ploy by Delhi. Now, officially at least, this troublesome area was no longer some half-ungoverned land on the fringe of the recently independent republic, but part and parcel of it. Overnight, Naga freedom fighters became Indian dissidents, terrorists, even traitors. The Naga independence movement would from now on be referred to increasingly as an insurgency. A. Z. Phizo's daughter Adino, who, in her seventies, continues to run the Naga National Council from her modest Kensington flat in London, considers such descriptions not just unfair but disgracefully and deliberately misleading. 'How can Nagas be dissidents? Ours is not an insurgency. India invaded our country. We are not Indians. We do not belong to India.'

Of course, some Nagas have given in profitably to a more or less comfortable life within the Indian state system, but there are many more who despise the Nagaland tag. If Delhi had imagined that it could normalise the Naga district so easily, it was soon proved to be very wrong indeed. Almost immediately the fight for independence took blazing flight, and for the next thirty-four years Nagaland was engulfed by a vicious war. A peace agreement, of sorts, was signed in 1997 between the various warring parties but, even so, the fighting continues, largely between rival Naga factions, with the Indian Army standing by. The sad truth is that the Nagas have been at war with India, and among themselves, for the past sixty years. In July 2007 Delhi made an attempt to buy Nagaland out of its troubles. Atal Bihari Vajpayee, the Indian prime minister, paid a visit to the state, announcing new government investment of Rs1,050 crore (around £2.5m; 'crore' is the Indian measurement for 100,000), but as Adino Phizo says, 'Nagaland is not for sale.'

Although in Dimapur and Kohima you can buy Girls Aloud and angry rap CDs in shops selling plastic crucifixes and snowstorm-shakers depicting the Holy Family in the Christmas stable, and although mobile phones and laptops have long made their insistent presence felt, Nagaland retains much of its traditional culture. True, there are politicians in Kohima who will do anything to appease Delhi and so live a life of modest luxury, and yet the battle for the soul of Nagaland continues unabated. It saddens me that, over the years I have come to know Nagaland, the fight has turned inwards. Although tribal rivalry has always existed, today the stakes are very much higher than a dispute between one hilltop village and another. International forces, China and Pakistan chief among them, are constantly at work, pitting rival Naga factions against both each other and Delhi. The result today is an uncertain stalemate at best, a powder keg waiting to explode at worst.

It did not have to be like this. When A. Z. Phizo declared Naga independence on 14 August 1947, the Nagas might have been happily free of India, and India, independent the following day, unburdened of a conflict in which so many of its soldiers have died for a cause that few understand and fewer care about. A tailor on the Kamrup Express, on his way to make suits for politicians and placemen in Dimapur, told me over several generous tots of Bagpiper whisky how he had served with the Assam Rifles in the 1980s. He was posted to Dimapur two hundred miles north of his family home in Delhi. 'Until then,' he said, 'I really had no idea of exactly where Nagaland was. Even the Seven Sisters [the seven north-eastern states] were a bit of a mystery. I didn't know anyone who had been to Assam. Most Indian people have no idea about these places. All I knew was that the Nagas were insurgents, troublemakers, and that it was our duty to keep the peace in Nagaland. It was a most uncomfortable posting.'

'But,' added a government accountant from the ministry of agriculture, opting for my bottle of Jameson's while on his way to cope with the Byzantine intricacies of Naga finances, 'these people are a headache. Look! India is on the move. The Indian tiger is indeed roaring. We are part of the global economy, but here we are being held back, wasting crores [of rupees], and up to now many lives, when there are better things to do. And what, gentlemen' – a second tot – 'would become of an independent Nagaland? How would it prosper? With Chinese money?'

The argument passed a few hours as the Kamrup Express rumbled through Assam, a huge moon reflected in the carriage windows and in irrigated fields. Somewhere, on either side of the tracks, Assamese rebels might well have been planning the next move in their fight for independence. The spirit of the Naga rebellion has spread to other parts of the north-east.

'Today, though, and for all the bad things that have happened,' said the tailor, 'I am curious to go back.' To provide well-cut Western suits for Naga chiefs, I couldn't help thinking, who have accepted a decidedly wobbly Pax Indiana in return for crores from the coffers of Delhi.

*

A. Z. Phizo's Western suit appeared to be well cut, too, when I met him in London in 1983. How different he looked from his grandfather who fought the British at the siege of Khonoma, his home village, in 1879. That the man before me was a warrior, however, there was no doubt.

The Nagas' fight from 1947 has not been against India, especially, but for a cause. They simply want their freedom and cannot see why their fate should be decided by anyone else. At the time of Indian independence, it was unclear what would happen to the Nagas. Jawaharlal Nehru must have had his own ideas well before the Japanese were defeated in 1945, but no one appeared to want to play their cards before a date had been settled for the end of the Raj. This uncertainty is reflected in two plans championed by British Indian politicians in 1941 and 1946 aimed at protecting both the Nagas and long-term British interests in the region. The first was drawn up by Sir Robert Reid, governor of Assam, who proposed the creation of a Crown Colony, or protectorate, from parts of Assam, northern Burma and the Naga Hills. The second, the brainchild of Sir Reginald Coupland, an Oxford historian and British constitutional expert, was intriguing if rather awkward; the idea was for India and Burma, once independent, to share responsibility for the area 'in trust'. The Second World War did for the first idea; common sense for the second. India and Burma would have fought for control of the area.

The Nagas, meanwhile, had made it clear to the British that they wanted to be excluded from future plans for an Indian republic. In fact the Naga Club had told the Simon Commission of 1929 that they wanted to play no part in a revised British Indian constitution; as far as possible, they wanted to be left to their own devices. Until A. Z. Phizo came along, the Nagas were remarkably unwarlike in their demands. The Naga Club was really very polite. But Phizo had been galvanised by his experience during the Second World War. By 1945 he knew about modern weapons and he knew why the Naga Hills and north-east India as a whole had played such an important role in that global conflict. Perhaps he had fought on the wrong side with Bose's INA, although it might not have seemed like it at the time. In 1946 the cosy Naga Club was fused with the Naga Hills Tribal Council, an initiative of Charles Pawsey, the British deputy commissioner of the Naga Hills district over whose tennis court the most intense fighting of the Battle of Kohima had taken place, aimed at facilitating reconstruction work in the immediate aftermath of the Japanese retreat. The new body, announced at Wokha in April 1946, was the Naga National Council (NNC), made up of twenty-nine members representing the different tribes and sub-tribes and elected through a system of proportional representation. Here, for the first time, the words 'national' and 'Naga' were placed together. This was a significant moment. From now on it looked as if the Nagas would fight their corner as one.

For a moment, at least, it seemed that Naga independence was on the cards. In 1947 an agreement was reached between the NNC and the governor of Assam to the effect that the present arrangement of government, whereby the Naga districts would be governed from Assam independently from Delhi, would continue for the next ten years, 'at the end of which period the Naga National Council will be asked whether they require the agreement to be extended for a further period, or a new agreement regarding the future of the Naga people arrived at'. So, by 1957, the Nagas might be free. The Indian government, however, was dismissive of the 1947 agreement. As far as it was concerned the new Indian Union would include all the territories controlled by the British, and that meant the Naga district. As far as Delhi was concerned, that was that and there was to be no further argument.

Spurred on by Phizo, its most dynamic member, the NNC declared Naga independence the following year. In response, Jawaharlal Nehru, the new Indian prime minister, cracked down on Naga ambitions. 'I consider freedom very precious,' he announced, before immediately contradicting himself by adding, 'In the present context of affairs both in India and the world, it is impossible to consider even for a moment such an absurd demand for independence of the Nagas. It is doubtful whether the Nagas realise the consequences of what they are asking for. For their present demand would ruin them.'

This was deeply patronising, yet not enough for Nehru. In 1948 Phizo was arrested and charged with promoting a rebellion against India. Released from jail in 1950, and appointed president of the NNC, Phizo set about organising a plebiscite calling on Nagas to declare their desire for independence. He gave me a copy of the long and stirring document that accompanied the announcement made in Kohima in May 1951. It says so much of how the Nagas felt about themselves then, and how, I think, many of them still feel about themselves nearly sixty years on. It is an important document, too, in the sense that before this the Naga voice had only very rarely been heard. Nagas wrote nothing until Christian missionaries arrived in the 1870s; and even then, there are all too few written records from the Naga Hills. Phizo's voice comes across loud, clear, proud, and, importantly, very different from that of any Indian.

The document begins, in typical Naga fashion, 'Uncles, aunties, friends, brothers and sisters,' and continues:

Throughout Nagaland our people are ceremoniously observing this day, May 16th, as the day of our Plebiscite, which we are going to record by taking the thumb impression of our people.

Our country was an Independent country before the British conquered us with superior force of arms. Without making any special arrangement for our country the British abandoned us and we found ourselves under the mercy of the Indian people.

Our Naga people (the British subject Nagas) have demanded independence from the British on many previous occasions. Unfortunately, we never put it on record as our people are not accustomed to writing. The only written record submitted by our people to the British Government was submitted in the year 1929 January 10 when 'SIMON COMMISSION', under the chairmanship of Sir John Simon, came here in Kohima seeking our people's opinion about the 'New Reform' – as it was called. Our Naga people demand Independence and said, 'LEAVE US ALONE, AND WHEN YOU – the BRITISH – LEAVE US WE SHALL BE FREE AND INDEPENDENT AGAIN.'

Since [1947], we have tried to settle our political issue with India on various occasions. But we have not been successful. As a result we have gathered here together in order to try to convince India of our inherent right to be free and equal to any other nation as a distinct people. This time, and from now on, we shall put everything into writing.

We do not want to mix freedom, and our independence, with human blood. We do hope we shall not be compelled to live on a structure founded on human skulls and bones. We are determined to extricate ourself clear with understanding, by goodwill and through reason, so that we may continue to live in freedom and enjoy national independence.

We want our Indian brothers and sisters to know that we are not their enemy. We want the world to know that there is civilization in Nagaland. Academically backward though we may be, it is up to us to show to the world that we are not a people which has lost its raison d'etre. We are alive.

The Indians have no vested interest in our country and there is not a single Indian national who owns an acre of land in our Nagaland. Prior to 1947, that is, when the British were yet here, no Indian is allowed to enter Nagaland without a special permit and that good Regulation (which was in force before Naga territory was annexed) still happily prevails up to this day.

Phizo then moved on to Nagaland's economic attractions:

Nagaland is a surplus country in matters of food and in other daily necessities that makes life happier. We have a vast area of Oil deposit and we have been burning oil long before the British appeared in our country. The Indian government have already brought in other foreigners of Oil drillers and Geologists and they have shamelessly started exploiting our oil resources. Many of you have seen, and all of you know that drilling has been going on in Chumukedima, 37 miles from here. Drilling is being carried out against our strong protest. We hope it shall not turn out to be another Anglo-Iranian sort of affair. The position is very serious. We have foreseen the danger long before. There are coal deposits throughout Nagaland. The present coal mine is only a small fraction of what we have. For oil we just dig with hand and draw out, that is why we call it 'digged-water' (to tzü). We have mica, gas, lime, iron ores, nickel and many other essential materials for which India has an eye on our land.

Nagas, he says, are a happy people, and he compares their way of life to those of Indians:

We never hear suicide in Nagaland. Not only in youth alone but you are never a finished product even in your old age because there is an undiminished consciousness of the social link of youthful bloom in the perpetual companionate association with your fellow man day after day, month after month and with the change of seasons without end, singing even in your work regardless of how heavy the work may be. In all things, your community-groups stand by you, laugh and cry with you, so you are with them, throughout life. You enjoy your life's span till the last day comes to leave this earth. Was there any Naga who was ever abandoned on the day he died? Not that we know of even a single instance, it is unthinkable to our society.

It is a practice in India to kill their daughters because they cannot [find men to] marry them; that means, they have no tolerance, no consideration even toward womanhood who [are] the very fountain of their posterity. Their men are so selfish that they will not marry unless the wife to be brings wealth which they call 'dowry' for the price of marrying her, and, it is almost always the case the girl does not know the man who is to be her husband. A man old enough to be her grandfather is often represented to her as a handsome young boy. The selfishness reveals more tragically on the last day the man leaves this world. His wife is burned alive on his funeral pyre.

Extremes of poverty are unknown among classless, communal Nagas, says Phizo, while crime and attendant punishment are rare:

> There is no death sentence in Nagaland ... life to us represents prestige and honour. There is no pauper in Nagaland. There is no social 'out-cast' in our country. There are no professional beggars up to this very day. There is no families who are houseless anywhere throughout Nagaland. There are no landless persons among us. We have no unemployment problem. Economically, Nagaland is on a strong foundation.

Subservient to India, Nagaland, he prophesies, will soon become a dumping ground for that country's surplus population. Nagas love their children; Indians abandon them, or worse: 'Indian immigration to Nagaland by force will only create tension, a problem which did not exist in the last thousand years of human history . . . Nagaland need not imitate or adopt foreign institution like India in matters of political organisations.'

As for a distinctly Naga political programme, Phizo states the following ten principles or goals:

1. We want to feel that we are absolutely and unconditionally free as a nation. Nagas belong to a distinct people and live in a country entirely of their own. We want to remain outside the influence of any other nation, be it white or brown.
2. We want to develop our own culture unhampered in the way we like, without having to worry for a possible mixture of alien blood.
3. We want to direct our own education through the establishment of our own Universities.
4. We want to keep our own land in the possession of our own people for our own people.

5. We want to live our own lives. There should be no room for any possible interference, directly or indirectly, whether now or in days to come.

6. We want to keep in our possession as a heritage something which is exclusively of Nagaland; something which is bound to vanish and be lost to the Nagas if they were to live under an alien direction.

7. We want peace, real peace put into an abiding practice in the lives of men. We do not want war. And we do not want to see another war in our land. We do not want to make our country a defence line. We do not want to let our children live in battlefields.

8. We want to make our country a place of happiness, of security and rest. We hope and we cherish that we can make our country a meeting place of the East and an understanding centre of the world.

9. We believe that we shall become a better friend and that we can remain a better friend to India and the outside world if we are left to ourselves – unmolested and unexploited.

10. We believe that it is not only for Nagaland but for India and other surrounding countries as well that there is a better chance of creating and retaining peace and good will with a SOVEREIGN NAGALAND being in existence.

'Above everything else,' Phizo concludes, 'we want to be free as a distinct nation: and we shall be free.'

I have quoted Phizo at length, because here, for the very first time, is a distinctive Naga voice. And here is the first written explanation of just why Nagas continue to fight for their freedom. Indian politicians and commentators like to say that most Nagas wish to live in peace today and that it is just seven thousand or so 'insurgents', in league with the Chinese, Pakistanis, militant Muslims, the international drugs trade and so on who wish to prolong a futile war of independence. And, yet, whenever I have sat down with Nagas, whether in the hills, or elsewhere in recent years across the world, in London, Rotterdam and New York, these words of Phizo have echoed back in their sentiments. Ultimately, Phizo was to lose control of the Naga independence movement as it began to split into a hydra-headed disorganisation, yet he remains a truly national hero, an 'Uncle' for all Nagas.

The NNC's plebiscite went ahead. The result was a foregone conclusion: 99.98 per cent voted to call for an independent and sovereign state of Nagaland. The result was made known in 1952; it took NNC volunteers, among them many women and students, some while to trek to each and every village in the Naga Hills to read Phizo's declaration and to collect thumbprints.

Nehru dismissed the plebiscite out of hand. In retaliation, Phizo organised a boycott of the 1952 Indian general election. It was entirely successful: not a single Naga candidate put his or her name forward. A meeting was arranged between the Indian prime minister and the Naga leader in Chime in March 1953. It was, needless to say, fruitless. Ten thousand Nagas had turned up for the meeting. They were expecting a discussion, of sorts, and not a lecture by Nehru, who seemed bent on telling what he saw as recalcitrant tribespeople what to do. When he refused an interview with a Naga elder, his entire audience walked out in disgust at such an overt display of bad manners. Now members of the NNC began to talk of direct action, and a number of guerrilla raids were made on brand-new Indian Army security posts. It was, though, to be another three years before the NNC established an interim Naga Federal Government without Delhi's involvement, much less its approval, and formed an armed wing, the Naga Federal Army.

In September 1954 Phizo declared the establishment of a Sovereign Republic of Nagaland, refounded as the Naga Central Government in 1956 and the Federal Government of Nagaland three years later. At the same time he formalised rebel factions into a unified Naga army, known, initially, as the Naga Home Guards. The guards were equipped with obsolete weapons left over by the British, and to a lesser extent by the Japanese, after the Second World War. These were mostly Lee-Enfield .303 rifles, but they also included 9mm Sten guns, 2-inch mortars, a small number of heavy-duty Browning machine guns, grenades and pistols. The army's arsenal was slowly increased later on when, between 1967 and 1977, groups of Naga soldiers made the long trek to China, returning with modern sniper rifles, AK-47 'Kalashnikovs', M-20 pistols and hand-held rocket-launchers. Replacements for these have since, I gather, been manufactured in Nagaland itself. The army was also furnished with fascinating remnants of imperial British weaponry; where else in the world, outside a military museum, could you come across Nepalese Snider-Enfield and Martini-Henry rifles in working condition?

Phizo, meanwhile, had further incensed Delhi by making stronger links with the Pakistani government, which certainly paid for rebel arms. Delhi responded by declaring both the Federal Government and the Home Guards illegal and put a price of Rs10,000 on Phizo's head. In June 1960 the Naga leader was spirited to London through East Pakistan with the help of Revd Michael Scott, a Baptist missionary and famous champion of 'underdogs', whether in South Africa or India.

Indian Army action against the Nagas, meanwhile, had begun days after Nehru's visit to Kohima in 1953. Accusations of rape followed as the army moved in. On 29 May a force of up to 1,200 Indian soldiers raided Khonoma, Phizo's village, and destroyed 550 houses. On 24 August Delhi issued an order to abolish the traditional Naga court run by the Tribal Council. On 9 September it issued a further order stating that any Naga refusing to act as a coolie for Indians would be punished by a fine of Rs500 or a year in prison, or both. On 7 June 1954 the Assam Rifles raided the village of Chingmei, killing and wounding indiscriminately. Sixty men, women and children died in a particularly infamous army assault, from Noklak camp, on Yangpang village on the morning of 15 November.

According to the NSCN:

the killing lasted from five till seven, led by a political officer and his assistant. The political officer had been boasting previously that he would show the Nagas that Indians were better headhunters, and he carried out his boast with punctilious accuracy. All the victims were beheaded, some while alive, some after being shot and their heads were taken back to Noklak to be photographed. He rewarded his soldiers that night with a feast of looted pork from Yangpang. Among the stories told by survivors was one about Subonglemla, the cheerful young woman who was the village schoolmistress; she was dragged on the ground by her long beautiful hair, four feet long when loose. She begged for mercy and wept, but the killer scalped her while she was alive and then cut her head off. The political officer took the scalp. Afterwards he was heard to have said that he would plait her hair into a 'holy thread' and would keep it for luck. Subonglemla's husband and their two sons, one five years and the other seven months, were slaughtered too.

On 27 November what remained of Chingmei was bombed to pieces. In Chemong village, the same day, two young Nagas, Chenemong, aged twenty-three, and Shemshimong, thirty-five, were crucified in a ritual aimed at mocking their Christian beliefs; after several hours on their crosses, they were shot dead. Meanwhile, their fellow villager Yemkhotong, thirty-five, was pinned to the ground by Indian soldiers. They bored a hole through his thigh with a bayonet. A cord was tied through the hole and attached to a post. The tribesman was then taunted before being flayed alive, soaked with petrol from an army jerry can and set alight.

I single out these atrocities because, having visited these villages forty years on, the same stories were repeated in exactly the same detail by any number of elders. They had the ring of truth. The Indian Army behaved abominably. Soon afterwards, they were able to do what they liked with official sanction.

In 1955 the Assam Disturbed Areas Act allowed the Assam Rifles and Assam Armed Police to set about their campaign against Naga 'insurgents' without legal restraint. Entire age-old villages were burned to the ground during 1955–6, as many as 650 of them. Those spared the torch were uprooted and formed into easily guarded clusters; these were concentrations camps in all but name. Designed to divide villages from guerrilla armies, they also separated villagers from their fields and crops. Famine, starvation and disease were soon riding their apocalyptic horses up and down the Naga Hills.

To highlight the horror, the bodies of Naga 'rebels' Thepfucha, Purhielie and Llouphizhu were hung from poles in Chime market as a warning to would-be fellow insurgents. Rape was used almost systematically as a weapon against Naga women by Indian soldiers. The rape of men was something new, and abhorrent, to the Nagas. And so it went on.

The Nagas, of course, fought back. Records on both sides of the ensuing war are conflicting and confused. There is no official history. There is no doubt, however, that although atrocities were to be committed by both sides, somewhere between 100,000 and 200,000 Nagas, and very possibly more, died in clashes with Indian troops between 1952 and 1997. Because Nagaland was cut off to outsiders, it was all but impossible for foreign journalists to get inside the country to pursue some sort of truth. I do not doubt the gruesome tales I have heard in Nagaland of gratuitous killing, of rape, incarceration and torture. Little of this made news in Indian newspapers; virtually none of it was recorded elsewhere in the world. The Nagas were very much alone.

*

The High Command of the Indian Army had initially set out to win the hearts and minds of the Nagas. In 1955, the Chief of the Army Staff issued instructions to troops moving into the hills: 'You must remember that all people in the area in which you are operating are fellow Indians . . . some of these people are misguided and have taken to arms against their own people. You are to protect the mass of the people from these disruptive elements . . . you must therefore do everything possible to win their confidence and respect; and help them feel they belong to India.'

'But', as Lt General N. S. Narahari, an expert in the area who fought in the north-east between the 1960s and 1980s, has written, 'at the functional level, these teachings are somehow overlooked under stress'. According to Narahari, 'both the initial actions by the Army and the reaction of the rebel Nagas were extremely violent. While the former indulged in indiscriminate arrests, beatings to extract information, killings of innocent people and a burning of villages, the latter indulged in damaging bridges and roads, kidnappings for extortion, killing moderates and loyalists, forcible collection of "taxes" and food grains for building up their forces. They had a reasonable stock of Second World War, left-over, weapons.'

'There can be no denying', writes Nari Rustomji in *Imperilled Frontiers* (1983), 'that for a period of two to three years commencing from 1955, the military applied themselves with full blooded vigour to the business of "softening up" the recalcitrant Nagas. Soon there was retaliation from Phizo's army, and it was not long before it was a matter of who was softening up whom.'

Undoubtedly, the Indian Army had the upper hand in terms of manpower and firepower, yet anyone who has trekked the Naga Hills and met the Nagas themselves will know, only too well, just how alien and difficult the landscape of this part of the world would have been to inexperienced young Indian soldiers, and how very effective Nagas can be as guerrilla soldiers. The jungles here can be full of strange shrieks and cries. In the monsoon, the whole of Nagaland appears to turn into a sort of shifting swamp. In the winter, the highlands can be bitterly cold. Insects with powerful bites abound. Valleys are deeply shadowed. For regular army soldiers, there were to be no 'front lines' in Nagaland. Those I have met over the years in India who have been posted to 'keep the peace' in Nagaland have always been very glad indeed to get away from these wild places. But as to what actually happened, day to day, in those early stages of the Naga insurgency, or war of independence, few can say with any degree of accuracy today.

Most of the atrocities committed by the Indian armed forces in Nagaland over the decades have been by the highly controversial Assam Rifles. With its headquarters in Shillong, the motto of this long-standing force, thirty-one battalions and some 30,000 troops strong under the control of the Indian Ministry of Home Affairs, is 'Friends of the Hill People', a sign you see, often hand-painted, on the gates of forts dotted through Nagaland. The Assam Rifles know their patch rather well, as they should do, for the force was first formed, as the Cachar Levy, as long ago as 1835. This 750-strong troop, composed mostly of poorly paid Bengalis, was ordered to protect British and Indian settlements, particularly tea plantations, against raids by tribesmen, including the Nagas. In 1883 the Cachar Levy, merged with other local militia, became the Frontier Police, and was renamed the Assam Military Police in 1891. In 1920, eight years after the creation of the new province of Assam, and in honour of the force's very effective fighting in various theatres of the First World War, it was renamed the Assam Rifles. The newly named force did much useful work in the Second World War, helping to organise the flow of refugees fleeing Burma at the time of the Japanese advance into that country, and in doing much to organise the V (for 'Victor') force unit aimed at undermining Japanese communications. The

Assam Rifles also served with distinction during the Battle of Kohima.

After independence, the Assam Rifles were heavily involved in riot control in various parts of northern India, especially at the time of 'partition', when, horribly and violently, India tore itself apart as Muslims and Hindus divided their lives between the new republics of India and East and West Pakistan. The Rifles, by now composed of recruits from across northern India, and indeed other parts of the country, were the front-line troops at the time of the Chinese march into the North-East Frontier Agency and other points along the Indian border in 1962. Something went wrong, however, in Nagaland. Although the Assam Rifles have indeed helped with reconstruction work, medical aid, communications and even education in remote hill areas, they have also behaved brutally behind the closed borders of Nagaland. And here the Indian government must take the rap. Whenever a people, or a land, is cut off from the rest of the world, terrible things seem to happen. Law and order become a question of brute power and ruthless control. This was especially true not just in Nagaland but in other parts of the north-east when the highly controversial Armed Forces (Special Powers) Act was passed into the statute books in 1958. Under the articles of the Act, all security forces operating in an officially declared 'disturbed area' were given blanket permission to carry out their missions as they saw fit. This gave the Assam Rifles a mandate to stop, search, arrest and kill as necessary. Even a private soldier was now able to shoot to kill on the mere suspicion that such action was necessary to 'maintain public order'.

Nagaland had been declared a 'disturbed area' in 1956. Atrocities on a large scale were committed with the de facto backing of the law well into the 1990s. But, even today, cases of rape, torture and unjustifiable killing are reported by local people, peace campaigners and the national press. Some even lead to legal action. Because Nagaland is so very hard to reach and to travel through, news from the state has often been confused, contrary and clouded in a fog of claims and counter-claims by the military, paramilitary, police, independence armies, human rights activists and local people.

At the time of the first military actions taken against Naga rebels, leading to the destruction of entire villages, the establishment of concentration camps (a good old British invention dating from the Boer War), arbitrary arrests and the savage treatment of suspect rebels, many of the soldiers serving with both the Indian Army and the Assam Rifles were wholly ignorant of the areas they were torching and humiliating. This is less true today, but ordinary soldiers I have spoken to in villages and at bus stops and railway stations are still often confused about who exactly the Nagas are and why they have struggled so very long, one way or the other, for independence from India.

Kanwar Randip Singh, an Indian officer who served in the Naga Hills from 1953 to 1957, wrote a fascinating account of his experience and perceptions of the Nagas and their relationship with the Indian armed forces; in *The Nagas of Nagaland: Desperadoes and Heroes of Peace*, he observes, 'None of the officers from Assam stayed for any long period with Nagas as they considered it as a punishment posting. They naturally were always keen to get out and often managed it through contacts. The question of studying the Naga way of life, mixing with them, knowing them and their customs etc. therefore did not arise with them. In fact, they considered these people as subhuman, filthy and not worth mixing [with]. Therefore, naturally a big gap was created between the Nagas and the government after the British left.'

It is certainly true that, sections of the Assam Rifles aside, very few regular Indian soldiers and indeed only a tiny minority of Indian people had any idea about the life and lands of the Nagas. They might have been Aztecs, Hottentots, Masais or Eskimos to the denizens of Delhi. In 1954, John Bosco Jasokie, the public secretary of the Naga National Council and future chief minister of Nagaland, wrote a report on this very subject:

They [the plains people of Hindustan] believe that their way of life is the right way, but such a way of life horrifies us . . . they are not prepared to accept us as human beings and, therefore, it is easier for them to go out of all human decency in their dealings with us. I say this not to agitate the emotional feelings of our people, but that they have such an attitude towards our people is an undeniable fact . . . they think that by harassing the people they have done a great service to India, but actually India lost the friendship of the people.

There are many decent, cultured and highly educated Indian officers who have come to terms with Naga culture over the years. In all too many cases, however, an appreciation of the Nagas and their way of life was to be a slow learning curve. In his 1987 study of the Pakoi Nagas, Major General S. C. Sardespande came to the conclusion that 'Nagas are magnificent. You have to see and live amidst them to believe this simple statement. A very large majority of us know little about them. The little that we know is about their nakedness, headhunting and anti-national, hostile, underground, insurgent activity for the last thirty years . . . by nature they are suspicious, sensitive, wary, distrustful, inward looking, volatile and very proud.' If this is beginning to sound a little stereotypical and negative, Sardespande continues, 'There cannot be a better friend than the Naga once he identifies his friend; there cannot be a worse foe than the Naga once he feels deceived or let down. Deep inside his inscrutable interior and penetrating eyes there is a tremendous warmth, great geniality, sharp intellect and immense good will.'

This might sound belittling, yet the important point is that these observations were made twenty years ago at a time when Nagaland was completely cut off from the rest of the world, as from England, as from India. Imagine for a moment what it must have felt like for a young soldier brought up in the certainties of a 'Hindustani' city to have been packed off to the remote Naga Hills, where the naked natives would cut off your head with a gleaming dao and have the rest of you served for lunch as soon as look at your cap-badge, polished boots and carefully oiled .303 Lee-Enfield.

The only reliable first-hand reports by outsiders I can find of conflict in Nagaland in the period from 1956 to, well, very many years later, were by the *Observer*'s Gavin Young, who was to become a distinguished war correspondent and travel writer. Young had been to meet Phizo in London. As a result he was able to slip quietly into Nagaland in early 1961 without permission from the Indian authorities. Phizo had given Young detailed lists of atrocities committed by the Assam Armed Police, the Assam Rifles and the regular Indian Army. Although Delhi refuted each and every claim, even the Indian press admitted twenty-two atrocities involving torture, rape, massacres and the torching or bombing of entire villages; almost always, though, it justified such actions by claiming that Naga belligerence was to blame.

Young recalled his experiences in *The Nagas: An Unknown War.* Often under the cover of dark, he had been led by Naga guides for five days, walking ten to twelve hours a day, to a safe house some 8,000ft up in the hills, where 'giant haunches of buffalo meat and sides of pork hung from hooks in the ceiling' and where 'a monstrous cauldron of tea had been put to boil'. A smartly uniformed twenty-two-year-old Naga lieutenant, armed with a Sten gun, Webley pistol and a brace of hand grenades, had arrived shortly before him. The officer told Young that he had signed up with the 'Home Front' after his father was bayoneted to death by the Assam Rifles in 1956 and his mother was jailed. He had been a student then, and at the time when the Indians organised Naga students into compulsory labour squads. Instead of studying, many were forced to work as coolies.

Before Young set off on his next march to the Home Guards headquarters, he was surprised to see the platoon of soldiers assigned to accompany him kneeling down to pray: a 'Cromwellian ingredient in the Naga struggle'. The Nagas are certainly not puritans, but, yes, their religion is a part and parcel of their everyday lives. They are not, however, fighting a 'holy war'. Despite the fact that Christianity was brought to the Naga Hills by zealous missionaries, Nagas themselves have no interest in trying to convert others. They have nothing against Hinduism; their battle is purely for independence from India. When Young reached General Kaito Sukhai's Home Front headquarters, hidden from the air, and Indian Air Force fighter-bombers, by a great canopy of interweaving sixty-foot trees, he found a pristine camp complete with offices equipped with typewriters, radios, filing cabinets and paperwork, a spotless cookhouse, a badminton court, and a tidy officers' mess; over the table a sign read 'Praise God from whom all blessings flow, Praise him all creatures here below.'

All this was unexpected. It was even more unexpected to the captured Indian Air Force crew Young met. Although thin and bearded, the men had clearly been looked after well. The pilot of the DC-3 shot down by the Naga army was Flight Lieutenant Anand Singha. He told Young that he and his crew had known nothing about the Nagas except for the 'facts' that they were (a) rebels and (b) headhunting cannibals. 'When we climbed out of the aircraft, we didn't know how we would be received. I believed we might be eaten.' Singha's Naga guards found this very funny. Their cookhouse was well stocked with monkey meat, but not, as it proved, a single human head, whether pickled, stuffed, shrunken, sliced or otherwise. The rattle of typewriters, the sound of shuttlecocks and the soothing tones of the BBC World Service were not things Indian soldiers expected to find high in the Naga Hills.

Out on patrol, though, old habits died hard. Naga soldiers called to one another in whoops and cries all but indistinguishable from the birds and monkeys around them. They could move through the jungle – they still can – with the stealth of a panther. In some ways, I have learned to pity Indian recruits from faraway cities in the plains posted here. If you can remember pictures taken in 1982 of hapless teenage Argentinian soldiers from sunny Latin American towns and cities looking miserably out of place in the wind-blasted Falkland Islands you will be able to imagine something of the plight of Indian Army soldiers in Nagaland. They simply do not belong here. Nor do their methods.

'The tenor of Naga civilian complaints of Indian injustice was unvarying,' Young reported. 'Villagers jostled their way forward to describe personal sufferings in vivid detail. The stories of burned rice-stores and houses seemed endless. Individuals told how they had been beaten and tied up for hours without water; how they had been bound and hung head downwards from beams to be flogged; how sons, brothers and fathers had been bayoneted to death.'

Perhaps, most sadly of all, Young was asked, 'the Nagas served the British in both [world] wars. The British know what we're like, and our character hasn't changed. Why can't they speak up for us?' That was Phizo's big question five thousand miles to the west in London. It is the question Gurkhas treated poorly by the Britain they have served so bravely, and recently championed by the actress Joanna Lumley, have continued to ask. It is the big question that has hung over the dead and dying of Rwanda, Darfur and Zimbabwe. The British have done nothing for Nagaland, or almost anywhere else they once ruled, since they abandoned their empire. Britain doesn't like to offend sovereign governments, no matter how cruel or uncaring they are of those under their leaden feet. Young had no answer then, and I have no answer now. I have spoken to several British ministers from governments left and right, Tory and Labour over the past twenty years; most have never heard of Nagaland. And though we have a terrific store of knowledge about the Nagas, most of this is squirrelled away in silent archives in the Pitt-Rivers Museum in Oxford, at the School of Oriental and African Studies in London or in the fading memories of very old colonial hands, diplomats, adventurers and Second World War soldiers.

I noted that one private British soldier who had died at Kohima lived in my small Suffolk town. I went to find his house to see if anyone might remember him. I was sure they would. I looked up and down the narrow street and puzzled; his house number was 84. Here were 82 and 86, but where was 84? It turned out that it had been demolished years ago and replaced by a garage set behind a blank rendered wall. I couldn't help but feel that Britain was trying to erase the memory not only of the Nagas, but also of its own people who had helped shore up its version of civilisation in the steaming heat and driving rains of the Naga Hills.

Events in Nagaland, meanwhile, raced ahead of Phizo even as he tried to interest the British and US governments in the fate of his people and to demand that an inquiry be made into Indian atrocities. In 1960 a new body of moderate, or acquiescent, Nagas, the Naga People's Council (NPC), agreed to sit down with Delhi politicians and hammer out details of a new Naga state within the Indian union. That state, Nagaland, came into being on 1 December 1963. Immediately it divided the Nagas into two camps; those in the Indian circle, and those without who would continue to fight for freedom and who refused to recognise the state of Nagaland.

The NPC's victory had, at best, been a hollow one. It opened up the doors for a wave of Indian immigration into Nagaland, and most noticeably bureaucrats, politicians and administrators who would try, as they continue to try, to transform Nagaland into India. At the same time, it is the government of Nagaland that runs websites today celebrating a make-believe land of happy, exotically dressed dancing natives. Gavin Young's Nagas danced to American jive, played badminton, toted Bren guns and listened in to the BBC World Service. Mine sport AK-47s, satellite mobile phones and degrees from some of the best universities. Again, Phizo's address to his people made in 1951 matters. Not only have the Nagas lost and failed to regain their freedom, they are also presented to the world as an entertaining tourist attraction. They truly love their tribal costumes and their music and dances, but their lives also embrace many aspects of the modern world and have done so for a number of years. Young, online Nagas send their songs and accompanying videos to YouTube. They engage in worldwide debates on the internet and encounter vicious messages from mainland Indians. They might also go up-country and join in a snake ritual or eat monkey stew around a camp-fire. But, whoever they are, they are not living tourist-attraction tableaux. The few tourists who come this way, though, are largely unaware of the exceptional violence that reigned in Nagaland for more than forty years.

8

Nagaland Divided

The first ceasefire in this bloody conflict was proposed by a Baptist convention led by the peacenik Michael Scott, and signed, after six rounds of talks between the NNC and the Indian government, in September 1964. It didn't last long. Despite the truce, Naga aggression continued, and in 1969 Delhi, its patience exhausted, effectively tore up the treaty. Over the next six years, fighting was often intense. A number of military setbacks, combined with a real fear that communist Chinese involvement on their side would result in exchanging one oppressor for another, led to the NNC signing the Shillong Accord on 11 November 1975. The NNC leader at the time was Kevi Yalley, younger brother of A. Z. Phizo. Officially, at least, the Nagas had accepted the Indian constitution, although those who signed the Accord had not consulted Phizo.

The Nagas' mistrust of the Chinese, meanwhile, proved to be all too well founded. Even as the Shillong Accord was being signed in Assam, a party of some 150 soldiers under Isak Chisi Swu, a senior NNC minister, and Thuingaleng Muivah, the NNC general secretary, had recently been to China on a 'goodwill mission' together with Khaplang, a Burmese Naga and president of the Eastern Nagaland Revolutionary Council, a wing of the NNC formed to protect Naga interests in Burma.

They denounced the Accord, declared Phizo and the NNC traitors and, over the next five years, established the National Socialist Council of Nagaland (NSCN). The formation of the

NSCN was announced on 31 January 1980. Its manifesto was brief and to the point. Well, five points, to be exact:

1. Unquestionable rights of the Naga people over every inch of Nagaland.
2. Dictatorship of the people through the NSCN and practice of democracy as long as it is deemed necessary.
3. Faith in God and salvation of mankind through Jesus Christ.
4. Socialism and economic systems for the removal of exploitation and ensuring fair equality to all the people.
5. Rules out saving of Nagaland through peaceful means and pins its faith on arms to save the Nation and to ensure freedom to its people.

Try reading these five points again. The issue of freedom and the independence of the Naga people aside, here is a complex and contradictory mix of Naga nationalism, Maoist political and economic thinking, Christian worship – 'Nagaland for Christ' – and a commitment to democracy only as a stepping stone to the dictatorship of the people by the NSCN. This succinct and contradictory document sums up the strangeness of Naga politics. It illustrates the very different forces that have been at work on Naga society over the past century. And it shows why bringing peace to Nagaland was never going to be an easy task. The Indian government might promise democracy, and yet this was, for all too many years, democracy at the end of a rifle barrel, imposed on a people who, for the most part, never wanted to be Indians in the first place.

The NSCN had grander aspirations for Nagaland than Phizo. It believed from the start in a Greater Nagaland, or Nagalim, embracing the tribes of Arunachal Pradesh, Manipur and Burma, and its mission was internationalist from the word go. It quickly established a Government of the People's Republic of Nagaland in exile, which, following several later splits and mutations, continues to lobby for support for the Naga cause in various parts of the world.

In 1988, just eight years after its inception, the NSCN split into two rival groups along tribal lines: the NSCN (I-M) and NSCN (K). The former, led by Isak Chisi Swu and Thuingaleng Muivah (respectively, the 'I' and the 'M'), a politics graduate from St Anthony's College, Shillong, was made up primarily of Tangkhul Nagas; the latter, under S. S. Khaplang, largely comprised Hemi and Konyak Nagas. The NSCN (K) was essentially a male-dominated peasant army while the NSCN (I-M) was more attractive to educated Nagas, particularly to those with a real interest in radical politics; its ranks include highly competent women officers. Because of its more intellectual approach to the purpose of conflict, and its Christian-Maoist thinking, the NSCN (I-M) has often been a baffling presence to eastern Nagas who are first and foremost hunter-gathering farmers (happily defying neat anthropological classifications) and animists to boot. They are not persuaded by Maoism nor Christianity, nor by a curious alliance between the two.

The two groups, both based in Burma, were soon at one another's throats. On 30 April 1988, the NSCN (K) led an assault, backed by Burmese troops, against the NSCN (I-M), killing up to 140 men. Over the following nine years the two factions fought one another, while Phizo's National Government of Nagaland (NFG) occasionally waded in on the side of the NSCN (K). This, too, seems odd, but it has to be remembered that Nagaland remains a deeply tribal society and it is not all that long since warriors were raiding the village over the next hill and bringing back severed heads as trophies.

When I first tried to make sense of these divides, I have to confess that I was reminded of Monty Python's *Life of Brian*, the blessedly funny comedy in which the rival Judaean People's Liberation Front fight their hated enemy, the People's Liberation Front of Judea, while losing all sense that their common enemy is the legionary might of Rome. Equally, though, I can remember as a child guests from Muslim countries trying to understand why Irish Christians were killing one another in Ulster, even though Sunni and Shia Muslims have long been at one another's throats in the Middle East and elsewhere. And it was a Jewish friend who told us what has become a hoary old joke: a wandering Rabbi is held up by gunmen in Belfast during the Troubles. 'Are you a Protestant or a Catholic?' they demand. 'I'm a Jew,' replies the Rabbi. The gunmen bark back, 'Are you a Protestant Jew, or a Catholic Jew?'

*

In 1968, many Sema Nagas had made the first break from Phizo when the self-styled 'General Kaito' formed his Revolutionary Government of Nagaland (RGN); in 1973, the RGN's General Zuheto Swu went over to the Indian side completely, taking his army into the fold of the Border Security Force. In 1990, Phizo's NNC was split into an official group led by his daughter, Adino, and an unofficial faction championed by Khadao Youthan, a former associate of Phizo. To add to the confusion, in 1993 a savage war erupted across the Burmese and Nagaland borders between the NSCN (I-M) and the Kuki National Army (KNA) and Kuki Security Force (KSF). Representing a majority of the Kuki people, spread through Burma, Manipur, the Chittagong Hill tracts of Bangladesh and Nagaland, the KNA and KSF were fighting primarily over the issue of enforced local taxation of Kukis by the NSCN (I-M), who, by the way and to add to the confusion, were supported by some Kuki tribes. Whatever the politics, some 900 Kukis died and the Naga cause splintered into ever more warring factions.

The situation the Kukis found themselves in reflects the unclear nature of nations and states in north-east India and Burma. Like the much better-known stateless Kurds of Turkey, Iran, Syria and Iraq, the Kukis in India and Burma justifiably believe that, from a historical, cultural and even geographic point of view, they have nothing in common with either of the countries they have been governed by since the British packed up their kitbags and went home. The British, with no particular interest in Kuki territory, had left the Kukis to get on with their own lives, although, inevitably, there had been frictions. The worst of these erupted during the First World War, for reasons, as far as I can make out, to do with conscription of local men for service in the Labour Corps in France and Belgium, various local taxation issues and a British ban on Kukis carrying firearms. Such was the threat of the Kuki rebellion of 1917–19, or the 'Kuki War of Independence', that a British force of 2,600 Assam Rifles and 600 Burma Military Police under the command of Colonel L. W. Shakespear was needed to assume control. The task took two years and led to the arrest and imprisonment of eleven Kuki leaders.

Such tribal divisions, and the area's complex and often poorly documented history, have always made it difficult for outsiders to help when help was needed most. What had really happened where? Whose truth could any outsider believe? I was in Nagaland a year before the NSCN split, at the time of the infamous Operation Bluebird. This was, perhaps, the first time in recent history that enough foreign observers from human rights and other organisations were on the ground to witness the aftermath of a particularly savage assault by Indian troops on Naga civilians. On 9 July 1987 NSCN troops raided the 3rd Assam Rifles post at Oinam in the Shepoumaramth district of Manipur, part of what Naga rebels see as Greater Nagaland. They reportedly captured 90 self-loading rifles, 22 Sten guns, 10 hand-held rocket launchers, 60 mortar bombs, 396 hand-grenades and up to 34,000 rounds of ammunition, and killed nine or ten soldiers. Whatever the exact numbers, it had been an audacious and successful attack on a confident enemy.

With official approval, the Assam Rifles replied two days later with Operation Bluebird. Many of the soldiers involved in it were eventually to stand trial on charges of murder, rape, looting, illegal detention, the imposition of forced labour, the dismantling and desecration of churches, the destruction of homes and schools and arson.

What happened? Troops surrounded and sealed off thirty villages. Curfews were imposed and villagers were not allowed to tend their land. Concentration camps were set up. The local deputy commissioner and superintendent of police were prevented from discharging their duties. Having imposed a virtual lockdown, the Assam Rifles then went on a four-month killing and torture spree. The details beggar belief. In Oinam village alone, Sanlong, the village chief, was shot dead, as were the village teachers, Lash and Ring. Two women, Khola and Lomana, were forced to give birth in the open surrounded by jeering soldiers. Sixty-five houses were smashed down and two burned to the ground. One villager, Loathe, was buried alive; one favourite practice of Indian soldiers was to bury Nagas up to the neck and then kick their heads into pulp with their boots. Four villagers – three men and one teenage girl – died later of starvation in the local concentration camp.

Such atrocities were nothing new, but this time local and international human rights organisations were on hand to record them in detail. Despite intimidation by the Assam Rifles and their lawyers, local organisations, including the Naga People's Movement for Human Rights, the United Naga Council, the Manipur Baptist Convention Women's Union, the All-Naga Students Association and the Naga Doctors Forum on Human Rights, banded together to form the Co-ordination Committee on the Oinam Issue. When connections were made with Amnesty International, the case was given global prominence. In 1988 Amnesty International issued a statement to the 45th United Nations Commission on Human Rights:

In some countries, serious machinery for independent judicial investigation may be in place but its efforts to investigate human rights may be sabotaged. A court in India has been investigating allegations of reprisal killing and torture of villagers by the Assam Rifles in Manipur State. It is reported that members of the Assam Rifles have tried to intimidate witnesses, even resorting again to torture, and also to intimidate one of the lawyers by invading her lodging and threatening to use force against her. The government of India has regrettably not responded to Amnesty International's request to observe the proceedings.

Although the Assam Rifles ultimately got away with murder – the Guwahati High Court where the trials took place 'reserved judgement indefinitely' – it was now clear to India and the world, or at least to anyone who was listening in 1988, that the Nagas really were suffering and that theirs had been a largely lost voice. Operation Bluebird convinced very many Nagas that the armed struggle against India had to continue. Violations of human rights are still swept under the carpet throughout the Indian north-east. Generals smile and say, in effect, that in the heat of battle soldiers can be naughty boys, but that proven bad behaviour will be met with little more than a ticking off or, even in the very worst cases, dismissal. Unsurprisingly, attacks by Naga fighters on the Assam Rifles spiralled in the early and mid-1990s.

*

In 1991 two young British human rights activists, David Ward and Steve Hillman, smuggled their way into Nagaland posing as BBC cameramen and interviewed the inhabitants of thirty villages on camera. Here was graphic, and moving, evidence of the atrocities committed over the past few years, by the Assam Rifles in particular. In sixty hours of videotape, villagers tell their stories and show their obvious and horrible wounds. Here is a man whose teeth were pulled out one by one with pliers. Another, blind, had nails driven into his eyes. Mass rape, meanwhile, was a common weapon of humiliation and terror used by Indian soldiers against men and women; bored with conventional rape, soldiers would hang villagers upside down and insert chilli peppers into their anuses and vaginas.

At the time, there were up to 150,000 Indian soldiers in Nagaland fighting some 3,000 insurgents. Until Ward and Hillman were captured, and tortured, by Indian government agents there was no coverage of this assault on the people of Nagaland in either the Indian or the international press. Naga Vigil, the human rights body Ward had set up in England in 1989, campaigned effectively for the release of the two men, held for a year without trial at Naini Central Jail, Allahabad. The two men were finally flown back to England in 1993, some months after their case had been raised by John Major, Britain's Conservative prime minister, during an official visit he made to Delhi in 1992.

Ward, determined to do some good for the tribespeople he had come to know, was rearrested some two years after his return to Nagaland, again without the necessary permits and visas, at Noklak, some two hundred miles south of Dimapur. His case is an object lesson in just how tricky, and downright dangerous, Naga politics had become by the last years of the twentieth century. His story is also, by any standards, intriguing and controversial. Born in 1962 at Digboi, an oil town in Upper Assam, into a well-off family of Irish-Scottish tea planters, Ward was packed off at the age of seven with his younger brother, Michael, to the Benedictine school at Carlekemp Priory in North Berwick on the Lothian coast south-east of Edinburgh. He was not exactly happy in the care of the Benedictines, finding their rule too harsh – he was beaten often, and sometimes savagely so – and, in any case, he must have missed his carefree life scampering about in Assam. Young David ran away several times from school and was eventually expelled.

After a stint with the Royal Army Medical Corps, a job as a dispatch clerk with the Scotch House shop in Oxford Street, and spells as a swimming instructor for people with Down's syndrome and as an adventure-playground supervisor on the Rockingham

Estate, near the Elephant and Castle, Ward fell in with criminal gangs. Arrested for robbery at a petrol station in the Old Kent Road, he landed up in borstal (as young offender institutions were then known).

Prison is, as Ward insists, a school for crime. He graduated as a gangland villain. Arrested and sentenced to five years for a number of break-ins, he was eventually shipped off to HMP Parkhurst on the Isle of Wight, where he mucked in with the likes of gang boss Reggie Kray, the Brinks Mat bullion thieves, IRA prisoners including 'Brighton Bomber' Patrick McGee, and Harry Roberts, a south-London gangster and former soldier who had served in Malaya during the Emergency of 1948–60. Roberts was serving a life term for gunning down two of the three police officers shot in East Acton in 1966 during what became known as the Massacre of Braybrook Street. When Reggie Kray was 'recategorised', he gave Ward his prison vegetable garden to tend. His was, I suppose, a classic case of a rebel without a cause.

It was while he was in prison, though, that Ward began writing poetry and studying anthropology. He came across references to the Naga struggle for independence, and then stories of atrocities committed by the Indian military in Nagaland. This brought back what were clearly powerful childhood memories, especially those of Naga tribespeople dressed in black kilts, red shawls and white-feathered headdresses who came down from the hills from time to time to work on the family tea plantation in Assam. Despite living next door to the newly created state of Nagaland as a boy, and despite his father's visit to his old comrades' graves in Kohima, Ward realised that he had known nothing of the Nagas' struggle for independence.

Shocked by what he discovered about how badly Nagas had been treated by the Indian military over the years, Ward set up Naga Vigil while still in prison. He was moved to HMP Gartree, Leicestershire, where he attended a course in education run by Ben Howe, who had won the Military Cross at the Battle of

Kohima. Howe took Ward to see an exhibition of Naga culture that had been organised by Professor Alan Macfarlane at the department of Social Science and Anthropology at Cambridge. Macfarlane had also been born into a tea-planter's family in Assam.

In 1991, soon after his release, and having managed to get some training from the BBC *Video Diaries* team on how to use the latest hand-held camera, Ward set off for Nagaland with human rights activist and former fellow inmate Stephen Hillman. Neither man, of course, had the necessary visas. What must have seemed a well-intentioned, undeniably brave yet quixotic adventure ended when, having made their way through great tracts of western Nagaland, visiting thirty-two villages, the pair were stopped at an Assam Rifles road block while trying to move on to Burmese-occupied eastern Nagaland. Their driver, the Naga federal MP, Neipielie Chucha, was shot in the back. They managed to escape but were arrested while attempting to break through a second road block.

Still rare today, foreigners were hardly ever to be found in Nagaland a decade ago. The very few that made it to the Naga Hills were viewed with the utmost suspicion by Indian authorities, who assumed they must be gun-runners or drug-traffickers. In turn, Nagas often imagined them to be spies for the Indian government.

Ward returned to Nagaland around 2001 – again unofficially, of course; he was unlikely to have been welcomed by the authorities – hoping, it seems, to build a hospital and launch a malaria control programme while monitoring human rights abuses. Somehow or other, though, Ward became entangled in a particularly sticky web of Naga intrigue. He also became a soldier.

Ward was accused of sedition, working with terrorist groups and drug trafficking by the Indian authorities and of being an enemy, and an interfering busybody, by the NSCN (I-M) because of his apparent dealings, whatever these were, with the rival

NSCN (K). Anyone managing to travel off-piste in Nagaland must remember not to take sides and not to become embroiled in extremely complex cross-tribal politics which can never truly be understood by outsiders, no matter how well-meaning or keen to do so. Sympathising with the Nagas and their quest for freedom is one thing; getting bogged down in the unfathomable detail of modern-day Naga politics quite another. And, because the Indian authorities have shown themselves to be very touchy indeed over the issue of Nagaland, it can be hard for a foreigner to explain that a fascination for Nagaland and a concern for her people somehow cancels out a love for India herself.

*

The Far Pavilions is one of the great, passionate modern novels concerning the relationship between Britain and India. Published in 1978, it was written, mostly in Farnham, Surrey, by M. M. Kaye. Set between the Indian Mutiny, or First War of Independence, of 1857 and the massacre of the British at Kabul in 1879 during the Second Afghan War, it tells the story of the deeply moving, if illicit, love affair between an Indian princess and a British army officer. It took fifteen years to write and has sold more than fifteen million copies. It has been made into a popular film and, in 2004, made its debut in London's West End as a musical. The producer was Michael Ward, brother of David.

Michael Ward's career, following successful stints at Carlekemp Priory school and Edinburgh University, has been very different from his elder brother's. And yet, like his brother, like M. M. Kaye (who was born in Simla and left India 'very unwillingly' in 1947), and like me, the love of India ingrained from birth was never to leave him. After producing *The Far Pavilions*, Michael Ward went to live in Mumbai and set up his own film-production company. As for Mollie Kaye, she travelled around the world with her Anglo-Irish husband, Goff Hamilton, an Indian Army officer who later served with the British army, rising to the rank of major general. *The Far Pavilions* is, above all, a love letter to India.

The Ward brothers were born in Assam and clearly love India. But such love affairs can be hurtful, complex, dangerous and even fatal. For David Ward, a desire, however expressed, to return to the India he had loved as a child and to do some good there led to a second term of imprisonment in 2003. Refusing to admit to trumped-up claims that he had been drug trafficking, he went on a near-starvation diet while held for a year without trial in the maximum security wing of Delhi's Tihar jail. All serious charges against him were eventually dropped and he was deported for entering Nagaland without proper papers. A trial would not have been in India's interests; it would have drawn international press attention to Nagaland, whereas, to date, the world's press has kept well away from a story that, sixty years old, is very much past its sell-by date as far as most newspaper editors are concerned. In any case, Ward insists that he is 'not anti-Indian' and there is no reason to disbelieve him. He even hopes to go back to work on humanitarian projects in Nagaland, although not, rather sadly, with Atulu Dozo, the Naga woman he married on one of his early trips to the state; wanting a quieter life than her husband's, she has since asked for a divorce.

Ward was living quietly in Edinburgh when I spoke to him, happily reconciled with the daughter of his first marriage and trying to decide what to do next. For him the Nagas had become a love affair and a truly dangerous fixation, the good he intended to do there undermined mostly by tragic internecine politics. Having given eighteen years of a life lived passionately, and very bravely, to the cause of Naga freedom, and especially to those tribes that seem to exist in another time, another dimension, in eastern Nagalim, he has now withdrawn from Naga Vigil. He needs to live his own life, and he does not deserve the scorn that Naga factions he has unwittingly crossed continue to hurl after his name. His journeys, what he saw, the people he met, and what happened to him are the stuff of an extraordinary 200,000-word manuscript entitled 'Behind the Bamboo Curtain', written since returning from India in 2004. One day soon it will make a great book and perhaps the basis for a moving film that could shine a global spotlight on the story and continuing plight of the Nagas.

In early 2001 the NSCN (K), the faction Ward had most dealings with, announced a formal ceasefire, theoretically putting an end to armed conflict in Nagaland. Some hope. In April 2001 alone, fighting between the (K) and (I-M) factions resulted in forty-five deaths, while some 4,500 people were forced to flee from fifteen villages in the Mon district. To complicate matters, Thuingaleng Muivah had been arrested in Thailand in January, travelling on a forged South Korean passport at the time he should have been at a negotiating table with Indian federal and Naga state officials. He was released only after a widespread appeal from a wide circle of interested parties in September 2001. Travel for those perceived by India as insurgents is obviously tricky; so much so that neither Thuingaleng Muivah nor Isak Chisi Swu had, as far as I can ascertain, even been in Nagaland between 1966 and 1999, when they attended an official meeting regarding the extension of a ceasefire to include all areas of Nagalim.

Since I first went there in the footsteps of my father and grandfather in the early 1980s, violence between the Indian Army and Naga rebels has become, by and large, a thing of the dim and brutal past. Nowadays the Indian Army and the Assam Rifles barely need to take up arms. Sadly, this is because the Nagas have been doing the job for them, tearing themselves apart. Today there exists a political and military stalemate of sorts among the various Naga factions. A rain-forest limbo. What violence remains in Nagaland is almost entirely internecine, while independence seems as far off as ever it did.

*

While Nagas have been fighting Nagas, the development of the state by Delhi has been rapidly changing Nagaland's ethnic mix. As central government funding has increased, so has the number of outsiders. The population increase between 1981 and 1991 alone was an astonishing 50 per cent. Many of the newcomers are Hindus working in government departments, business and academia. Manual work such as road building and rickshaw pulling is largely in the gnarled hands of poor Muslims from Bangladesh. The latter, often marrying Sema Naga women in the Dimapur area, have sired a new generation of Muslims, many of whom have been radicalised in recent years. Any appeal for independence today relying on more than a blunt call to arms in the hills needs to take into account this fast-changing demographic.

The Naga cause has long had an international dimension, of course. Soon after Indian independence it became clear that China and Pakistan were keen to use the Naga struggle as a means of needling and even threatening the new republic. A. Z. Phizo visited Karachi in 1962 to discuss mutual collaboration, and Pakistan has armed and most probably trained Naga soldiers, especially in the former East Pakistan (Bangladesh since 1971) over several decades. Specifically, Pakistan has used the Naga fight for independence as one way of drawing Indian troops away from the disputed Kashmiri border. In fact, by covertly supporting rival Naga factions over the years, Pakistan has tried, though with very mixed results, to create a hydra-headed enemy for the Indian Army in the Naga Hills and Manipur. To the same end the Maoist (although Christian) and Chinese-backed NSCN began to arm, train, finance and generally encourage a large number of guerrilla armies in other of the Seven Sister states of north-east India to make life ever more difficult for Delhi and its armed forces.

As an American Baptist minister told me one day in 1993, looking out from the porch of his Mopochuket mission church into the rain-soaked hills beyond Dimapur:

it's a bit like the way Latin American revolutionaries bated the US in the sixties. You'd never know when another guerrilla army backed by the Cubans, or whoever, would pop up in the jungles of Bolivia or Colombia or the Dominican Republic and act as if they were taking on the whole armed might of the United States. Remember Che Guevara? He gave a speech at the UN in '64, I think, in which he called for revolutionaries around the world to create a shed-load of Vietnams to taunt, and, I guess, ultimately to bring down the United States, taunting us like a bear in a pit. That's been going on here, which is why your train [from Calcutta to Dimapur] was halted in Assam; those rebs weren't Nagas; probably Garo insurgents [from the Garo Hills in Meghalaya, formerly part of Assam, and even wetter than Nagaland], paid for by the NSCN and, through them, Beijing.

Leaders of the NSCN (I-M) have certainly talked about a 'United Front', and although, as we will see in the last chapter of the book, they now appear to be growing softer in their approach to India – and, indeed the whole notion of independence – they were indeed promoting and arming other insurgent groups in the Seven Sisters between the 1960s and the early 2000s.

While nominally supporting such major revolutionary groups in Kashmir, Jammu and the Punjab, all a long way from the Naga Hills, the NSCN (I-M) was very active in the creation of a number of regional guerrilla bands. When my train to Dimapur was held up in 1993, the young masked men, armed with an impressive array of rapid-fire Chinese guns, were indeed, as my Baptist minister friend suggested, disaffected Garo tribesmen. I had no idea then that their guerrilla group, the A'Chik Liberation Matgrik Army (ALMA), had been formed just two years earlier, and that it was to surrender, lock, stock and AK-47, in October 1994 to the Indian Army. The short-lived ALMA was more an expression of frustration among Garo youngsters, I think, than the product of a seasoned, and reasoned, struggle against a specific enemy. When my train was held up, it was for effect and for a little loot. The young men seemed a little like the gentlemen highwaymen of English yore. Although they would not say where they were from, they were trying, I thought, a little too hard not to smile when engaged in conversation.

I have since been told, by an Indian army officer in Shillong who knows the Garo Hills well, that, although trained by NSCN (I-M) soldiers, ALMA was only really active in hold-ups and bank robberies and these for the purpose of funding the NSCN (I-M). 'It seemed like easy money to these young men,' said Colonel Mahi, 'but, they were not hardened to life as guerrilla fighters, and, in the end, I think they were most happy to give themselves in. They were, though, a sign of what we faced increasingly in the Seven Sisters: insurgent groups funded and trained by Naga rebels.' Who, in turn, were funded by governments and other interested parties beyond India's borders.

The NSCN (I-M) has also supported, if not always kick-started, insurgent groups in the North Cachar Hills of Assam, in Mizoram and in Meghalaya. It has also encouraged the Muslim United Liberation Tigers of Assam and the Zomi Revolutionary Army (ZRA), groups that have been involved in a number of cases of violent kidnappings and other attacks in central Manipur.

The formation of a United Liberation Front of the Seven Sisters in 1993 by the leaders of the NSCM (I-M) was the last truly ambitious attempt by Naga rebels to extend their fight against India throughout the region. The aim was, ultimately, to free Nagaland and to create not just a Greater Nagaland, but very possibly an independent state encompassing this entire region.

This, of course, would have been a very appealing idea not just to the Nagas, but to Pakistan, China, Burma and, perhaps, to the United States too, although no one in Washington would have admitted to such a sentiment either at the time or now. And, yet, the idea of an independent state of Bengal, taking in the whole of the Seven Sisters, had been hatched by the British at the end of the Second World War. The idea was obvious: to maintain a British, and thus Western, presence in the region once India had become independent; a Bengal independent of India would have acted as a buffer state between China and India. In the event, the Chinese did indeed attempt to invade India and Beijing has long believed that parts of what are northern India today remain, in theory, Chinese territory. India's borders have never been as clear as they appear on globes and in atlases, while in the north-east they are tenuous and hard to believe in.

If the British had played with the idea of an independent state of Bengal, loyal to Westminster, so had Washington. Until the early 1970s – and this is hazy territory – it seems that the United States had backed Naga insurgency with supplies of arms from Thailand. CIA agents, easily mistaken for missionaries, had been active in the Naga Hills in the 1950s. Certainly the idea of an independent Bengal had been doing the rounds in Washington as it had in London. Although the Americans, unlike the British, had few sentimental reasons to care about the region, they were deeply concerned with Chinese ambition in the area. The domino theory, dreamed up in far-distant Washington, was very much current. First China had turned communist; Vietnam would soon be all Red. It was only a matter of time before the whole of South-East Asia went the same way, and who knew which countries were in danger after that: Australia? India? So, it must have seemed a good idea at the time to set about creating an independent Bengal loyal to Washington.

Even then, the story is more complex, as it always is with Nagaland and India's troubled north-east. At the time of Indian independence, the Americans, seeing that British influence was on the wane both in the subcontinent and in South-East Asia generally, were keen to undermine further the position of their former wartime allies. In the early 1950s, when CIA operatives were active in the Naga Hills, Britain was still a force to be reckoned with both militarily and in terms of the development and sales of its often ingenious military hardware. Westminster had yet to become Washington's compliant poodle; as far as the CIA, at least, was concerned, Britain needed taking down a step or three. Political and quasi-military involvement in north-east India was one way of undermining the British while attempting to establish some sort of regional base loyal to the US in the face of the perceived communist expansion in South-East Asia.

The US was certainly right to worry about Chinese involvement. A former colleague of General Kaito Sema showed me creased colour photographs of himself and fellow Naga activists standing in front of various Chinese tourist attractions, taken sometime in the early 1970s. This is them inside the Forbidden City. Now they're in front of the Temple of Heaven. This one must be somewhere in the grounds of the Summer Palace. Oh, and here they are, leaning against the infinite parapets of the Great Wall of China.

Delhi, too, has long had every reason to fear Chinese ambition in Nagaland and the north-east. On 10 October 1962 after a prolonged and heated historical dispute over the sovereignty of the Aksai Chin region, a desert land the size of Switzerland set improbably high above Ladakh between the twin Chinese-administered areas of Tibet and Xinjiang and the equally inhospitable state of Arunachal Pradesh, known to the British as the North-East Frontier Agency, the Chinese effectively invaded India.

The Chinese appeared to have had no difficulty in penetrating either Aksai Chin or Arunachal Pradesh, despite the terrific heights of the mountains – up to 22,000ft – and the terrifyingly cold weather that winter. My own memories of a brief journey through Aksai Chin are painful to recall: a cold winter sun created the setting for potentially fine photographs of the great lakes and salt plains there, but it was so cold, even at midday, that all I wanted to do was to curl into my fur-lined sleeping bag and reach for my hip-flask and its fast-disappearing reserves of

Irish whiskey. The area is all but uninhabited, and those who do eke out a living here are clearly Tibetans with absolutely no connection whatsoever to India or its way of life; what poor villages there are have little to offer in the way of meals beyond bowls of greasy noodles. Many troops on either side were to die from exposure and frostbite here, their hands frozen to their weapons. By the time a ceasefire was declared on 21 November 1962, the Fourth Front Red Army, led by Zhang Guotao, had successfully occupied both this disputed territory and, further east, Arunachal Pradesh, another European country-sized state.

This Sino-Indian war, however brief, was a stark reminder to politicians in Delhi, and perhaps to the Indian people in general, that their long northern borders are both uncertain and permeable and that the peoples living along them have no especial loyalty to India. It was an even starker reminder that the country's north-eastern neighbour was not be underestimated. Just as the British had failed to understand how powerful the Japanese military had become on the eve of the fall of Singapore, so senior Indian military officers were convinced that the Chinese would run away as soon as a shot was fired in their direction. The People's Revolutionary Army, however, was no paper tiger.

In the course of this short but bloody war the Chinese army pushed deep into Assam, prompting Nehru to call for US support. Washington responded by ordering an aircraft carrier to the Bay of Bengal, but before it arrived the shooting had stopped. The Chinese marched out of Arunachal Pradesh to the lines they had held before hostilities began, but retained Aksai Chin, through which they have since built a reliable road. Ever since – occasional skirmishes aside – a precarious peace has existed between the two sides. The Nagas, of course, were intrigued to see how easily the Chinese had moved into the north-east. Equally, though, those independent of Chinese backing and ideology recall the Japanese invasion of 1944; the support of an outside Asian superpower might seem appealing in theory, yet in reality the Naga cause has not been best served by governments with ambitions on a global rather than a regional or local scale.

It remains difficult to gauge the extent to which the Chinese, at the time of the Sino-Indian War and in the following years, saw the Nagas as a way of distracting the Indian Army and drawing it ever deeper into a futile battle against guerrilla armies. According to the 9 August 1968 issue of *Time* magazine, 'Mao Tse-tung, true to his own policy of supporting "wars of national liberation", has lately taken to supplying the arts and tools of subversion to the Nagas.' The report continued, 'More than 1,000 Nagas are known to have trekked 300 miles through Burma to China's Yunnan province for arms, indoctrination and training. Another 1,000 have been intercepted by Indian troops and turned back. Friendly Nagas in Burma sometimes aid would-be rebels travelling to China, but others have beheaded at least three Naga rebels and presented their severed heads to Indian officials as signs of good will.' The report is vague and clearly not first hand, yet gives some idea of Chinese ambition in Nagaland in the 1960s, and of how, as ever, Nagas were divided among themselves.

Time is, of course, an American magazine, and the US was very much worried by Chinese military ambitions in the sixties. Rather comically, the Indians were concerned about US involvement in Nagaland not because of arms but because of religion. Commentators in the mainstream Indian press continue to assert that Naga insurgents are funded, in part, by the Baptist Church.

'That's so much hooey', says my American missionary acquaintance in Mopochuket:

It's true that today about 80 per cent of Nagas are Baptists and, sure, this is the most Baptist state in the world. I think the Indians got a little hot under the collar, especially about the time Billy Graham led a three-day crusade in Nagaland in 1972. Something like half a million, or half the total number of people living here, came out to see him and hear him preach. I guess this was problematical for Hindus. Nagas aren't just Christians; they're English speakers, they write in Roman script, they've fought the Indian Army for decades . . . perhaps it can look as if foreigners are behind all of this.

Involvement with international politics at this level, however, encouraged the NSCN (I-M) to take its fight beyond that of arms alone to one of intelligent propaganda on a world stage. With its goodwill links with such bodies as the UN Human Rights Organisation in Geneva, the Unrepresented Nations People's Organisation in The Hague and the UN Working Group on Indigenous Peoples, the NSCN (I-M) has spread its gospel far and wide. And even if Nagaland itself has very largely been cut off from the rest of the world since the early 1960s, and in all practical terms since about 1890, the NSCN (I-M) has done much to ensure that the Naga people, and their long struggle with Delhi, are not entirely forgotten. Now, with the internet at its disposal, this most effective of the Naga independence groups has been increasingly able to get its message out to the world beyond encircling Indian soldiery and daunting mountain ranges.

That this message has sometimes been less than convincing is due to two damaging factors – damaging, that is, to the NSCN (I-M). First, it is widely believed, although certainly not proven, that the movement and its army are to some extent funded by drug money. Very sadly, Nagaland has become a drug-trafficking route from Thailand through Asia, and somehow from there to Europe. According to its enemies, the NSCN (I-M) earns substantial sums through this dismal trade. Second, the NSCN (I-M), although it is not alone in this among rebel groups in Nagaland, extorts 'taxes' from local people and businesses to pay for arms, training and who knows what. Villagers in northern Nagaland have told me that if they refuse to pay, they are in danger of being shot dead. 'They shout "Nagaland for Christ" as they pull the trigger.'

The conflation of extreme religious beliefs and violence is not, nor has it ever been, uncommon. Like holy warriors elsewhere in the world and at other times in history, Naga soldiers carry both a gun and a sacred book, the Bible in their case. A command headquarters in the highest northern hills is divided into fortified areas named after chapters in the Old Testament. And, just as Cromwell's soldiers during the English Civil War often bore names taken at random from the Good Book, so Naga soldiers I've met have adopted noms-de-guerre from the Bible. That eight out of ten Nagas have been baptised into a version of Christ's message moulded and nurtured in the United States is a curious accident of history rather than an indication that the US has a vested interest in challenging the Indian government through the wrong end of the Bible.

*

There is, meanwhile, at least one obvious reason for a number of world powers, including the United States, to retain more than a vestigial interest in Nagaland. Oil. Oil was discovered in the Wokha district of Nagaland, some sixty miles from Kohima, in 1973. From 1981 to 1994 oil wells at Changpang, owned by the state-run Oil and Natural Gas Corporation, produced something like 250 tons of crude oil a day. Disruption caused by Naga rebels ended operations. Today, there is a renewed interest in oil production. If the oil flows again, as it might yet do, expect a sudden worldwide interest in Nagaland from government officials, business executives and the military. You can also expect attacks on a revived oil industry there. Although many mainland Indians believe that trade, industry and economic prosperity are the key ways to pacify Nagaland, many, indeed perhaps the majority of Nagas have precious little interest in becoming members of some kind of tribal bourgeoisie. In an age when money, and money culture, is king, queen and all princes from Seattle to Sydney via Stuttgart and Shanghai, who now believes there are peoples in the world who don't really care much about being rich?

But I have met A. Z. Phizo, who clearly had no interest in money, and several latter-day Naga leaders who, again, have no obvious aspiration to financial gain. Few seem actively interested in exploiting Nagaland's wealth of natural resources; aside from oil, the hills and lowlands of the state are laced with gold, uranium, chromide, coal, jade and other precious stones, as well as poppies long cultivated for the opium trade that, much to its credit, the original NSCN did much to halt (as they did with headhunting). True, there has been much exploitation of the land in recent years, and I have seen many great gashes in the landscape and some horribly primitive mines, but this has largely been the work of companies with little or no interest in conservation or local culture barging their way in from mainland India.

I have never met the reclusive Thuingaleng Muivah or Isak Chisi Swu, but I somehow doubt that what they secretly crave is the life of a successful Indian entrepreneur. Both men are in their seventies now. Perhaps they are seeking a comfortable life, if not a wealthy one. Certainly, both men seem more or less committed to bringing peace to Nagaland. A younger generation, however, believes this to be a cop-out by their elders; there is no guarantee that Nagaland will become a quiescent part of the Republic of India in years to come.

The dream of a ceasefire has, in reality, often been more of a nightmare. Clashes between Naga independence groups were not going to be stopped by treaties signed by politicians. On a trip to Nagaland in 2002 I sat drinking tea with lorry drivers beside the road from Imphal to Dimapur. They told me that they were effectively on strike. How could they do their job when they never knew when members of the NSCN (I-M) would demand goods and 'taxes' from them at gunpoint? I noted these random incidents, officially reported, that year alone:

18 January:	Six NSCN (K) members killed by NSCN (I-M) gunmen at Tenyiphe, near Dimapur.
23 August:	A group of thirty or forty armed NSCN-IM members attack an unauthorised NSCN (K) camp hosting around forty insurgents, killing three NSCN (K) activists, at New Chumukedima in the Dimapur district.
23 August:	An NSCN (I-M) insurgent is killed at Suruhoto in the Zunheboto district during an attack by NSCN (K) members.
4 September:	Two NSCN (I-M) members killed by NSCN (K) at Cheteba town in the Phek district.
8 September:	NSCN (I-M) insurgents killed two leaders of Khaplang faction, including a captain and the Angami region's finance secretary.
12 October:	Members of the NSCN (I-M) shot dead a Khaplang insurgent at Rusoma village, Kohima district.
13 October:	Three NSCN (K) members killed in an attack by NSCN (I-M) insurgents at Yoruba gate, Phek district.
3 November:	NSCN (K) insurgents killed two NNC members in Zunheboto town.
4 December:	NSCN (I-M) members killed two NNC members during an attack on the outfit's camp at Mowu, Phek district.

All this had happened while the Nagaland state government and, to an extent, the mainland press seemed to be saying that all was sweetness and light in the Naga Hills. What had certainly changed by the beginning of the twentieth century was the role of the Indian Army. Its soldiers were now behaving remarkably well, for the most part, after decades of often brutal oppression that had only intensified and spread support for the Nagas' fight for independence.

The army was confident enough in 2002 to issue orders to the effect that soldiers of all insurgent groups should be issued with photo-ID cards and return to designated bases. The orders were not exactly complied with, while ID cards, here as elsewhere in the world, are a bit of a joke. Most mainland Indians would be unable to tell a Naga from someone from Borneo, Tibet or the Bolivian highlands. Indeed, when Phizo escaped to London, he arrived in England on a fake Peruvian passport. He might easily have been a descendant of the Incas as far as a 1960s British passport official was concerned. In any case, as young men and women in a Dimapur cyber-cafe have told me, even the hopelessly complex and imprudently costly British identity cards championed by the New Labour governments of Tony Blair and Gordon Brown would have been tapped into and subverted in no time at all by clever teenage computer whizzes anywhere in the world. They are pleased, though, as most Nagas would be, that normal decent British citizens would sooner go to jail than carry such symbols of government paranoia and control in their pockets. 'We will come and fight with you,' they say, laughing.

Back in 2002, however, the NSCN (K), concerned with the number of immigrants pouring into Nagaland from Bangladesh, issued its own ID cards to Muslims living in Naga areas. At the same time, it called for non-recognition of marriages between Nagas and Muslims, a limit on the number of Muslims living in any one 'sector', or tribal area, to 2,500 and a ban on the use of loud-speakers at mosques. Nagas are keen on the idea of freedom, but by the first years of the twenty-first century they were having to face up to the fact that even their remote and seemingly forgotten corner of the world was becoming, in its own particular way, globalised. As Delhi attempted to 'normalise' life in Nagaland by gradually increasing economic aid to the state, so people far poorer than the Nagas themselves began to see this as a land of relative prosperity. 'Our land is our heritage. To none shall it be surrendered,' thundered Phizo when the sun set on the British Raj sixty years ago. To none, except economic migrants from India and Bangladesh, Indian Hindus and Muslims, various business corporations, US interests vaguely covered by the parasol of the Baptist Church, a smattering of tourists in and around Dimapur and Kohima, and to the encroaching power of money, ideas and values spread so easily, so alluringly, by the internet and the World Wide Web.

9

Kuknalim!

In the story of all this bloodshed and political intrigue, it is important to remember just how beautiful Nagaland is. I need to walk back in my mind's eye to those seemingly infinite folds of blue hills, to deep-down green valleys hiding rivers where rare fishing cats (*Prionailurus viverrinus*) can be found patiently hunting their prey. There are, I've been told, more than three hundred varieties of orchid in Nagaland. I like the way, if you're feeling strong, you can walk in a single day from dense rainforest and its snakes, turtles, tree frogs and clumps of tall, wavering bamboo, up through prodigious rhododendron plantations and fields crowned with princely orchids, up again through slopes adorned with chestnut, oak, birch, cherry, maple, laurel, fig and magnolia, to alpine pastures laced and dotted with flowers that you might mistake for the edelweiss and gentian of a Swiss summer. And, if you're quiet, and well away from soldiery and the clash of arms, you'll come across shy and happily unfamiliar animals.

I have crossed paths with sun bears, the smallest of the bear family, and even met a pair kept as pets. I have seen dense choirs of pig-tailed macaques chattering in transepts of trees. A Naga farmer showed me his tamed band of these monkeys; they fetch coconuts for him from the tallest trees. Of birds, I'm pleased to have had the rare Blyth's tragopan, a handsome red-throated pheasant, pointed out to me and to have watched the heavy flight of increasingly rare wreathed hornbills, whose feathers are prized by the Nagas for their headdresses. I've enjoyed being teased by curious whistling mynahs and, my patience rewarded, watched sparrow-sized orange-rumped honeyguides settle on the branches of trees busy with intersections of marching insects. Jackals, gibbons and barking deer are never far away.

Unlike my father, I have never seen a tiger or snow leopard in the Naga Hills. Elephants, yes, on the lower slopes leading down to the tea plantations and paddy fields of Assam, and one on a hilltop well to the north of Kohima, but of the most burning bright of the big cats, not even an uncertain shadow of a striped tail shimmering through the sundown rainforests. Tigers are still hunted in Nagaland, where, at the last official count some ten years ago, about eighty were said to survive.

Sadly, Nagaland's abundant treasury of wildlife has long been under threat. For all their beauty, many breeds of animal have been hunted promiscuously for food, fur, feathers and, increasingly today, dubious potions that can be sold across the Chinese border to keep vain old men supposedly horny. (Can't they buy Viagra?) If tigers are rare, wild dogs appear to have vanished entirely; most have ended up in the cooking pot. Today, dog fur, once popular in a number of traditional Naga costumes, like bear fur, is hard to get. Spiders, bats, grubs, frogs and turtles, meanwhile, are all snared and boiled and served with rice for supper. The acreage of virgin rainforest is falling year by year. At one time this loss, at a more or less sustainable rate, resulted from the Nagas' traditional slash-and-burn farming methods; today it is caused by logging on an industrial scale and by the search for and extraction of raw materials. In the sidings at Dimapur station long, low trains loaded with logs sit patiently waiting for their dispatch to mainland India.

Even so, a special natural beauty parades through the Naga Hills, rising above ramshackle marketplaces and smoking hearths. Here is a landscape that has been pushed by three mountain ranges at the south-eastern tip of the Himalayas into a petrified seascape of intermittent sunlit and shaded hillsides and sudden, plunging valleys; in some lights, the hills resemble the creation of a particularly imaginative artist. I have to remember all this and play it back in my mind like a film, especially because so much of Nagaland's recent history has been so dominated by warfare and vicious internal politics that the land itself can seem unimportant in the telling of human stories, or else simply exists as a sort of soft-focus backdrop. Yet this intensely coloured, deliciously scented, saw-toothed landscape has determined to a great degree the life and character of many Naga tribes.

Sitting on a fine evening looking down on a traditional highland village with its shaggy coat of generously thatched roofs gathered haphazardly around the village's communal morung, its door flanked by the horns of oxen, is to enjoy a view and a sense of place all but unchanged for hundreds of years. For all the shiny appeal of modern technology and what we call 'lifestyles', it is not hard to see why, if you lived here, you would fight to preserve such a way of life.

Looking out to just such a view not so long ago, while the sun set, monkeys whooped, and an electric chorus of insects charged the warm air, I thought of men like my father and grandfather, and great-uncles and distant cousins, who loved this land for its hills, its flora and fauna, its distinctive peoples and its sheer beauty. They came to map, build schools, offer medical help and sometimes, yes, to 'maintain order'; but they sketched what they saw, noted what they heard, and when they retired or were asked to leave India, they would sit in clubs or at home with curry and rice for supper, and still see blue-tinted shadows of the Naga Hills as the sun set and gin bottles were cracked open while tonic fizzed. (No ice, of course. Not done.) Now, the few visitors who trek off the state's newly smoothed, if limited and carefully patrolled, tourist track are seen, even by Nagas themselves, as objects of suspicion. The landscapes of Nagaland are beautiful, but have lost whatever innocence they once enjoyed.

My friend Grace, an Ao Naga with an MSc in Zoology and Botany from the University of Calcutta, sat with me one evening in her tribal village of Chungtia and, over mugs of red tea and ginger biscuits, we discussed this idea of 'innocence'. 'There are virtually no written records of Naga life before the arrival of the British,' she said, 'so we can only listen to folk songs and stories handed down from generation to generation to get a picture of what life was life before guns and machines. But, if you watch the Chungtia war dance – it's very famous in Nagaland – you get some idea of how aggressive the tribes must have been when they wanted to be. You love the beauty of Nagaland, and you believe in freedom, but I think yours is a romantic view. Didn't we all lose our innocence when Adam and Eve were expelled from Paradise?'

Grace is an example of how Nagaland, or at least a part of Nagaland, has been changing, in the twenty-first century. Well educated, energetic and wise, her circle of Naga friends are increasingly flying the nest and studying not just in mainland India, but across the world. She, at least, came back, and to a village where a communal standpipe for drinking water and washing her veils of jet-black hair are not exactly a match for power-showers in smart Sydney bathrooms or bottles of chilled mineral water in gleaming seafront bars. 'Oh, yes; I mean, many of us do,' she says. 'We love these hills, too! I had the good fortune to travel to Australia on a scholarship. I loved being there, but one weekend I was taken up into the Blue Mountains outside Sydney, and I began to cry; it was very beautiful, but it reminded me of our own blue hills. And there's so much for my generation to do. We don't want to fight for factions, we want to work for all our people.'

I have been impressed by the ways in which young people like Grace have been looking ahead to see how Naga traditions and ways of life, Naga song, dance, energy, ceremony, craft and story telling, can yet be woven into the workings of the encroaching global economy. Equally, there is an ever-increasing number of Nagas who live and work, usually successfully, in various parts of the world. The more, in fact, that Nagas take part in the modern world, the more absurd the infighting in Nagaland itself will seem. The more Nagas tell their own story to the rest of the world, the less chance India will have of keeping a lid on the state they imposed on the Naga Hills in 1963.

'These people are cannibals, yes cannibals,' a perfectly charming engine driver told me as his locomotive – an oily black WP Pacific studded with decorative silver stars – was being watered at the end of a platform at Old Delhi station some twenty years ago. 'Very savage, and, I tell you, too much trouble. I cannot understand why you want to go there. Leave them to the Assam Rifles. They know how to deal with these people.'

As Nagas take up professorships in European, North American and Australasian universities, racist jibes from mainland Indians will sound increasingly hollow. As long as Naga culture can be allowed to thrive in an increasingly globalised economy, it might just be possible for the Naga people to rescue themselves from their state of bullied isolation. Whether or not Delhi will relax its draconian grip on Nagaland is another question, and one that desperately needs to be answered if Nagaland is to open up to the world and to develop, in Nehru's words, along the lines of its own genius, or guiding spirit.

Responding to the news of yet more killings between members of rival NSCN factions in the summer and autumn of 2007, Dr Paul Pimomo, Naga born Professor of English Literature at Central Washington University, wrote a powerful essay comparing the folly of division among warring groups with the disastrous effects of the Irish Civil War and the present struggle in Palestine on the futures of these two troubled countries. Pimomo makes the point that although NSCN activists had set out with the best intentions, they were now seen by a younger generation of Nagas as out of date and even absurd:

It is as though they were saying, 'Let's kill each other, destroy each other's property and reputation and, in the process, create fear and insecurity among the Nagas because we are

217

Naga patriots who love our homeland.' This statement makes no sense, of course, and it is not what (I-M) or (K) have set out to do for themselves or for the Naga people. But, intended or not, the effect of their actions on the public in Nagaland, as well as the perception they create in people's minds, is real. Both (I-M) and (K) need to recognise this reality about themselves and deal with the situation in a hurry.

In June 2007, armed clashes between NSCN (I-M) and (K) factions had taken place under the nose of the Assam Rifles in the strategically important town of Tizit in the Mon district. Machine guns, grenades and mortars were fired in broad daylight as terrified civilians fled their homes. After the attack, an NSCN (I-M) leader, R. H. Raising, explained that 'the Assam Rifles have been collaborating with the Khaplang group by providing its arms, ammunition, transport and other logistical support to target us'; so, clearly, the rival group had to be punished. But an official statement from the NSCN (K) said of the same incident, 'The NSCN (I-M) is a gang of terrorists and has been openly violating the [2001] ceasefire ground rules.' So, they needed punishing, too.

Drawing comparisons with the Irish experience, Pimomo suggests that 'what is going on in Nagaland today between the two factions of the NSCN parallels the deadly rivalry between the supporters of the Irish Free State Treaty led by Michael Collins and the anti-Treaty Republican group under Eamon de Valera. The Irish are still paying for those leaders' lack of vision at the momentous crossroads in their struggle for a united Irish nation.'

Coming up to date, Pimomo cites the bitter clash between the Fatah party and Hamas in Palestine: 'What Hamas and Fatah are doing to themselves has derailed the Palestinian people's dream for a homeland. Palestinians have never been farther from realising their goal since 1948 than they are today thanks to the Fatah–Hamas rivalry.'

Calling for unity among Naga factions, Pimomo ends his essay with another reference to Ireland:

But even more telling and relevant for Nagas is the story of an Irish soldier in 'The Sniper', written by Liam O'Flaherty who fought on the Republican side against the Free Staters during the civil war. The story is set at dusk in Dublin with the sound of heavy guns in the background and with rifle snipers from rival armies hiding, dodging and hunting each other in the streets. After an intense and intricate angling for the enemy, the adept sniper in the story guns down a soldier on the roof of a building across the street. He watches the enemy fall to the ground, and shudders; the lust of battle suddenly dies in him; he is struck with remorse; he curses the war, curses himself, curses everybody. He becomes curious about the identity of the enemy he has killed, so sneaks over to where the body fell, dodging a hail of bullets. Then throwing himself face down beside the corpse, 'The sniper turned over the dead body and looked into his brother's face.'

Was anyone in Nagaland listening to the wisdom of the professor writing thousands of miles away on the Pacific coast of the United States? Clearly not. A week after the bloody episode in Tizit, the NSCN (I-M) launched an attack on the Khaplang group camp there, killing Tahjen Konyak from Lohko village and injuring others. Brigadier Phunthing Shimrang of the NSCN (I-M) said that his army would not allow their rivals to set up camp in or around Tizit as the area had been under NSCN (I-M) command for many years.

The Assam Rifles, meanwhile, do not always stand by while rival Naga factions assault one another. In July 2006, six badly injured villagers from Noney in the Tamenglong district of Manipur, including five teenage schoolgirls, still in their uniforms, were taken to hospital in Imphal after a confrontation with the Indian military force. Some five hundred villagers had demonstrated outside the Assam Rifles camp, demanding the release of twenty-two-year-old Simeon Kabui of Tousang village, said by the Assam Rifles to be an NSCN (I-M) member. The soldiers claimed that stones had been thrown at them, so, naturally, they defended themselves, in the way armed soldiers do.

The fighting between Naga factions only encourages the majority of Indians, or at least those who are aware of conflict in the north-east, to believe that Nagas are responsible for anything bad that happens along the Brahmaputra. In October 2004 two bombs exploded one morning in Dimapur, one at the railway station, the other at the town's crowded Hong Kong market; twenty-eight people were killed and more than a hundred injured. Everyone I spoke to pointed the finger at the NSCN, some saying it was the (I-M) group out to get the (K) tendency, others the exact opposite. Quite why either group would attack Dimapur station or the Hong Kong market seemed to bother few people, Indian or Naga. The BBC's correspondent Subir Bhaumik reported the attack as very probably the work of the National Democratic Front of Bodoland (NDFB), a guerrilla group admittedly with links to NSCN (I-M), but bombing central Dimapur would surely be something no mainstream Naga activist could or would condone. Or might they? No matter what, the Naga groups were blamed by many who would have been hard pressed in any case to explain the difference between the many liberation armies in the Indian north-east, or tell you which were in action and which in abeyance, depending on who had signed a ceasefire with Delhi and for how long.

The NSCN (K) and (I-M) continue to attack and taunt one another. The (I-M) sits in Delhi meeting rooms, looking for some long-term solution to the question of Naga independence, while the (K) faction stands back, refusing to cooperate. Kughalu Mulatonu, a (K) leader, has said that 'the . . . talks between I-M and the Indian government have made the I-M group a stooge in the hands of the Indian government. In some years [time], these people will start singing "Vande Mataram".'

This is a stinging accusation. 'Vande Mataram' is the Indian national anthem. But, just to demonstrate how factional and problematic politics, and differences in cultural and religious beliefs, can be in the subcontinent, the 'Vande Mataram' remains a source of controversy in India. Written in 1876 by Bankim Chandra Chatterjee (or Chattopadhyay), a nineteenth-century Indian poet, journalist and civil servant, the anthem goes something like this in English:

> Mother, I salute thee!
> Rich with thy hurrying streams,
> Bright with orchard gleams,
> Cool with thy winds of delight,
> Green fields waving, Mother of might,
> Mother free!

Or, perhaps, like this:

> I bow to thee, Mother,
> Richly watered, richly fruited
> Cool with the winds of the south,
> Dark with the crops of the harvests,
> The Mother!

Because some Muslims are unsure whether the opening words imply worshipping Mother India rather than simply saluting her, they refuse to sing their own national anthem. Although this seems like an unnecessarily pedantic game of semantics, this curious state of affairs underlines the extraordinary complexity of Indian life. Nothing is ever simple; factionalism is rife. But who knows who might yet be singing the 'Vande Mataram'? For the main body of the Indian Army, the days of the killing fields of Nagaland are largely over, if not forgotten. The army's

Operation Good Samaritan has been creating roads, sports grounds and water supplies. They have been trying hard to win hearts and minds among the lowland Nagas, at least, and to an extent they may have succeeded. As for local state politicians, according to David Ward, 'They run with both the fox and the hounds . . . thinking nothing of shouting "Jai Hind!" [Long live India!] whilst pilfering the pockets of their benefactors in New Delhi, and "Kuknalim!" [Victory!] after crossing the Nagaland Gate in Dimapur to appease the nationalists with a few crumbs that fall from their table.'

Thuingaleng Muivah, meanwhile, gave an interview to Delhi-based news agency Asia News International at the end of October 2007 saying that a decade of peace talks with Delhi are coming to an end. Muivah said that if talks broke down again, the NSCN (I-M) cadres 'would be forced back into the jungle'. 'For the last ten years,' he continued, 'we have been talking and talking. They [India] are giving arms and ammunition to the (K) group and (K) is fighting with us . . . if the jungle is better, we have to go. You can't afford to be seen to be bearing with the Indian insult. We have had enough patience . . . cease-fire is in crisis.' Some Nagas, especially those with government jobs, might be doing well today, but the Naga nationalist armies are still very much on the march, even though their aims seem more confused than ever.

Muivah and NSCN (I-M) chairman Isak Chisi Swu appear to be saying that they are now happy for Nagaland to be a part of an Indian federation, although by 'Nagaland' they mean Nagalim, or Greater Nagaland. And even if all Nagas living in the Indian part of Nagalim, which includes sections of Manipur, Arunachal Pradesh and Assam, were to agree with Muivah and Chisi Swu, it's unlikely that any of these states would abandon even an acre of its territory for the sake of creating Greater Nagaland. And Burma certainly wouldn't. Check mate, then. Or stalemate, at best.

*

While the ageing leaders of the long-divided Naga national movement consider a return to full-time fighting, Nagaland itself continues to change. Take, for example, the Miss Nagaland 2007 beauty contest, organised by the Beauty and Aesthetics Society of Nagaland and held at the State Academy Hall, Kohima, on 1 December that year. The winner was pretty Miss Imsulemla (Miss Mokokchung 2007), who won a cash prize of Rs50,000 (about £625 at the time), along with 'gifts and hampers'. In her gracious acceptance speech, Miss Imsulemla said that she hoped to become an air-hostess. Other awards that evening were for Miss Perfect '10', Miss Photogenic, Miss Beautiful Skin and Miss Congeniality. At the end of the show, Master Seyiekhrietho, a local *Kids for Fame* TV talent-show finalist, brought the house down with a lively rendition of 'Hound Dog', the rock 'n' roll hit recorded by Elvis Presley in 1956 as Nagaland went up in flames.

The Miss Nagaland contest was designed to coincide with the opening of the 2007 Hornbill Festival, an official seven-day event and now by far the largest of its kind in the state. It was opened by Kateekal Sankaranarayanan, the new governor of both Nagaland and Arunachal Pradesh. He announced that along with the Hornbill Motor Rally that had been added to the festival in recent years, there would now be a Hornbill National Rock Contest. 'We can make Nagaland a hub of Western music,' said the less than hip seventy-four-year-old governor, 'not only in India but in the whole of South-East Asia.'

The festival closed with a 'Celebration of Naga Colours and Rhythm' attended by Her Majesty's Deputy High Commissioner for Eastern India, Mr Simon Wilson. Did Mr Wilson wear a feathered hat with plumes? Probably not. Even so, this might have been 1937, except for the rock music.

More significantly, the governor also announced the first new internal flights in Nagaland since 1989, although these were to be (a) by helicopter only and (b) largely for the use of politicians, VIPs, corporate executives and tourists. Nevertheless, the skies were becoming safer. A speech given by Jairam Ramesh, Union Minister for Commerce, at the Naga Heritage Complex in Kisama on the second day of the Hornbill Festival was more direct. He told his audience that Nagaland would change greatly in the next five years. The state is rich in natural resources and these would be explored (and no doubt exploited, although he did not use the word). There would be drilling for oil as well as the commercial growing of new crops such as citronella, eucalyptus and ginseng.

At much the same time Neiphiu Rio, Nagaland's chief minister, announced the floating of a new joint-venture infrastructure company, IDCON (Infrastructure Development Corporation of Nagaland), that would create a 'special economic zone' in which industrial parks, power plants and the service sector, especially hotels, would thrive. This programme, said Mr Rio, was a part of Nagaland state's Vision 2020 initiative. 'It is our strategy,' he said, 'to become a developed and industrial state by 2020.' But what about violence in Nagaland? What about the NSCN? Mr Rio told reporters that issues concerning law and order and insurgency were no reasons for development in Nagaland to be held back, citing the example of Israel: 'The violence and tensions under which the [Israeli] society exists is known to all of us. However, its economy is developing in an amazing manner. In fact, it is becoming the world leader in many technologies, specially in the fields of agriculture and water management.'

These events and speeches are significant, though at the same time funny and a little sad. Perhaps Nagaland is indeed about to reap some benefit from modernisation, globalism, the shining example of the Indian government's Look East policy. Yet, to me, it all seems just a little patronising. Here, it seems, is the imperial Roman policy of 'bread and circuses' at work. Give the people cheap food and free entertainment, the more colourful the better, and they will in all likelihood abstain from real politics and refrain from rebellious behaviour.

Modern development in Nagaland is decidedly patchy. A fundamentalist form of Christianity, although very much alive, can be censorious. The Nagaland Baptist Church Council heartily approved of, and perhaps even promoted, the Nagaland government's decision to ban Dan Brown's best-selling novel *The Da Vinci Code* (2003) and to advise Naga interests not to distribute or screen the 2006 film of the book. The Revd L. Kari Longchar made the point that if Danish cartoons of the prophet Mohammed could offend Muslims, then a story that distorted the history of Christianity would cause even greater damage to the sentiments of Naga Christians. Such nannying, though, treats the Naga faithful like children. Just as no Christian sure in their beliefs could have been offended by Monty Python's hilariously irreverent *Life of Brian*, surely no Naga should mistake Brown's fiction for anything other than an entertaining romp.

Far more questionable is the political and economic basis of the 'bread and circuses' policy aimed at encouraging Nagas to be somehow content, and protest free, as the region is transformed into modern India's North-Eastern Tiger. The Look East policy was first formulated in 1992, following hard on the collapse of the Soviet Union, one of India's most important trading partners. Delhi's new policy was aimed at tying India's fortunes to those of the economic 'tigers' of South-East Asia. In 1997 India became a member of ASEAN, the Association of South-East Asian Nations. At the ASEAN summit held in Bali in October 2003, the Indian prime minister Atal Bihari Vajpayee announced ambitious initiatives for economic cooperation. Free-trade links throughout the region would be matched by new road and rail links from India to Burma, Thailand and China. Old regional ties based on an anti-colonial brotherhood had now given way to ones based on trade and economic development. All this was particularly satisfying to India because such development would pass through Naga territory in Nagaland, Arunachal Pradesh and Burma. Even better, although China would still be competing for the same South-East Asian markets as India, the two Asian superpowers could forge an unprecedented alliance in the face of what they saw as US plans for world domination, economically, culturally and militarily.

There proved to be, though, a rather large stumbling block in the way of these roller-coaster plans: Nagaland. Apparently, politicians in Delhi know precious little about the geography of Nagaland and its sister states. A railway from Dimapur to Kohima and further south to Imphal in the next few years? Have they ever seen this landscape? Do they know about the disruption caused by Naga liberationists in the area?

As for a highway stretching from Guwahati to Beijing – now that really would be a wonder of the modern world. Anyone who has driven National Highway 39 from Imphal to Dimapur will know how difficult getting anything done quickly will be. The existing road is in a rough and not always ready state of repair. A tragicomedy ensued when, in November 2004, the current Indian prime minister Manmohan Singh, the first Sikh to hold the office, flagged off the inaugural India-ASEAN car rally from Guwahati, with cars racing away on an incredible 8,000-kilometre adventure to Indonesia, taking in Nagaland and Burma on the way. Expensive-looking media folk and nattily dressed VIPs from the mainland clapped each other on the back as they revelled in the festivities. This was an enjoyable way to nurture Look East.

Pretty much everyone from west of Guwahati, however, appeared to have little knowledge of local roads. Competitors were shocked by the state of NH39, and NH39 is Nagaland's very best. To keep the rally going, the road was closed to all other traffic while heavily armed military convoys escorted the visitors in case of attack from Naga insurrectionists. Here is a highway split into sections by the Naga armies who demand tolls, usually of around Rs2,000 a vehicle at each checkpoint. Drivers used to the comforts of mainland India were shocked by the complete lack of roadside infrastructure. (On the plus side, conditions became even worse as they headed into Burma.)

If all this was a rude awakening, making Look East appear premature, matters were hardly helped when in December 2007 the NSCN (I-M) issued a statement to the effect that no road or other major construction would be carried out in Naga areas without its permission. As for the rail link that might yet connect isolated Manipur and its Nagas to the rest of India, the NSCN (I-M) made it clear that construction materials for such a line would be destroyed, labourers arrested and 'taxes' demanded from contractors.

All this is naturally frustrating to Indian federal politicians hoping to solve the problem of Nagaland and the north-east with transnational economic development. What should it do? If, as some have suggested, the new roads and rail links were instead built through northern Bangladesh, how would this help development in the troubled, and poor, Naga Hills? Why, in any case, would India throw in its lot with Bangladesh, a country increasingly moving away from its status as a secular state, and thus a worry to many in India? There is also talk of laying a pipeline from offshore Burmese oil plants, across Naga territory in Burma and across Bangladesh to India. India desperately needs more fuel to nurture its economic growth, and it seeks conventional ways to garner such energy. New gas fields discovered in Arunachal Pradesh would also mean pipelines running through Naga territory. But unless the Naga armies can be either crushed, starved of support or persuaded to play ball, such supplies can never be guaranteed.

Certainly there are plenty of voices in Delhi and elsewhere in India suggesting that what is needed, above all, is close cooperation between the Burmese and Indian military to flush out the Naga insurgents once and for all. This, though, is more easily said than done. In parts of northern Burma, the military is in cahoots with the NSCN (I-M). The landscape beyond the modestly developed lowlands is almost impossible for any army without expert local knowledge to force its way through. And, surely, India cannot go back to the bad old days of burning villages, destroying churches, rushing up concentration camps and torturing and raping local people, can it?

*

'Do you remember Khalistan?' asked one of my fellow passengers, a Hindu sales manager representing a pharmaceuticals company, on board the Kamrup Express one day.

'Khalistan, the Sikh republic-that-never-was in the Punjab?' I said.

'Yes. Well, the government took firm action, and not a moment too soon, and we have no more of breakaway Khalistan now, isn't it?'

But, we do, or India does. The Punjab separatist movement that dreamed of creating an independent Sikh state, Khalistan, was kicked very hard indeed by the Indian military on 5 June 1984 when, in an attempt to arrest the Khalistan movement leader, Jarnail Singh Bhindranwale, the army assaulted the Darbar Sahib (Abode of God), or Golden Temple, at Amritsar. This is the Sikh religion's holiest shrine. No one knows for sure how many innocent people died, but Amnesty International believes that 2,000 civilians were killed in the attack.

The result was far from being the end of Khalistan. That October the Indian prime minister, Indira Gandhi, was assassinated by two of her Sikh bodyguards, Beant Singh and Satwant Singh. Others killed in this reprisal for the assault on the Golden Temple included several high-ranking Indian officers, the army chief General Arun Shridhar Vaidya among them. An ensuing riot in Delhi witnessed the deaths of 4,000 Sikhs. Despite so much blood being needlessly spilt, Sikhs, notably those living beyond the Indian borders, continue to campaign for the establishment of Khalistan.

The Khalistan experience is a reminder, if any were needed, that the Republic of India is a very complex entity, a vast country embracing very different peoples with very different aspirations.

Not all the Girls Aloud CDs, cable TV channels, baseball caps, digital gizmos and cans of Coke in the world have the power to answer the separate demands of all these peoples. But to assault them is very probably the most short-sighted and ultimately ineffective policy of all.

Nagaland, though, is a difficult nut for mainstream Indian politicians to crack. Force has been abusive and, ultimately, all but useless. Vast sums of official money poured into Nagaland over the past decade have been wasted. Just where have all those rupees gone? Into the pockets of state politicians, officials and dodgy business enterprises, say the NSCN, its (I-M) and (K) factions for once in agreement. David Ward, many missionaries and representatives of the few charities penetrating far in Nagaland believe the same. It would certainly be interesting to see the state's finances audited by a team of disinterested accountants from Canada or Finland. The books could never, ever balance. Above all, there are very few politicians with credibility in both mainland India and in Nagaland. That small number includes Sanayangba Chubatoshi Jamir, governor of Maharashtra from 2008, who also served as governor of Nagaland between 1980 and 1983. Since 1979 Jamir has been a member of India's dominant Congress Party. Although popular in many parts of Nagaland, and respected in Delhi, he is portrayed by certain NSCN factions as a traitor to his own people, even though he has been deliberately excluded from some of the peace talks between the Indian federal and state authorities and the NSCN.

Such depth of feeling was demonstrated when this charming, highly educated Ao Naga made a visit to Nagaland in November 2007 and an attempt was made on his life near Changki village as he journeyed to Dimapur from his home town of Mokokchung in the northern hills. Taking as few risks as possible, Mr Jamir had been travelling in a thirty-vehicle convoy when mortar shells suddenly rained down from the hills. Fortunately, Jamir was unhurt. The NSCN (I-M), which had made three earlier attempts

229

to assassinate Jamir, denied responsibility for the attack; instead, it claimed that Jamir had stage-managed the whole event in a bid to discredit (I-M).

What is certain is that the NSCN (I-M), and doubtless other Naga factions too, had been very much concerned about the upcoming spring 2008 elections in Nagaland. If Jamir were to stand successfully for his home town of Mokokchung on a Congress Party ticket, he would increase the share of the Congress vote in Nagaland, undermining the authority, the power and certainly the credibility of the NSCN as he did so. As it happened, I had been sent a number of glowing reports from Indian sources and mainland publications on the health and welfare of Mokokchung as the town celebrated its Golden Jubilee in 2007. This made sense. Jamir plus a healthy report on the progress of Mokokchung equals votes in favour of the Congress Party and Delhi. If Mokokchung, the third of Nagaland's major towns after Dimapur and Kohima, could be shown to be prospering, and in a popular and democratically approved fashion, then the rest of Nagaland might begin to fall in line.

Mokokchung is certainly an interesting place. Set towards the north of the state at an elevation of some 4,500ft, from a distance it might almost be mistaken for an Italian hill town. Close up, it boasts big, modern concrete buildings – Baptist church, government office, even hotels (although the design of the Inigo clearly owes little to Jones, and the Igloo is not exactly chilly) – and is busy with cars and even commuters. Unlike other major Naga settlements where most people tend to live and cluster in the centre of town, Mokokchung is surrounded by an ever-growing suburban sprawl, or, more accurately, a cluster of satellite villages that have been drawn closer, year by year, into its orbit. Isn't this where Yimyu village once stood? Could this be the site of Marepkong? Villages that existed as distinct entities in the early 1990s seem to have vanished into the spreading waistline of Mokokchung. The population is about 60,000. Could this be a model for future development in Nagaland?

Certainly, Mokokchung has long been a centre of Western influence in the Naga Hills. The British set up one of their first bases here, while it was to Mokokchung that the first US Baptist missionaries came in 1872. This is where the first Christian Naga marriages were made, and this is where most of the first generation of modern Nagaland's politicians and civil servants was educated. And, although Mokokchung is a traditional gathering point for Naga national rebels, neither of the principal NSCN factions has been able to get a grip on the town. Set between the tea plantations of Upper Assam and potentially rich oilfields, Mokokchung is a natural economic or trading bridge between India and South-East Asia. The Indian government has invested heavily in a revived paper mill in the district, while promoting the growth of the local, and undeveloped, spice trade.

As Kuholi Chishi, vice-principal of Mokokchung's Fazl Ali College, the oldest in Nagaland, told reporters on the occasion of the golden jubilee of Mokokchung district in 2007, 'Young people in Mokokchung, or for that matter in the entire state, are no longer influenced or attracted by insurgency. Instead they are more futuristic and practical today, looking at building careers by acquiring good education. The mindset of the younger generation is different, and Mokokchung has already seen a new set of Naga entrepreneurs emerging, as the gun culture is beginning to fade out.'

Mokokchung has certainly changed from the first time I went there, and not least because the town I first saw was largely burned to the ground in December 1994 by Indian armed forces in retaliation for the death of a colonel. By Naga standards, the town is prosperous. There are plenty of baseball caps on show, during the day at least, and the town has even been host to *Naga Idol*, the ubiquitous talent-spotting TV-show franchise having penetrated even to this remote corner of the world. Still, some of the music is good, while the show does much to promote awareness of safe sex. (Aids has become a major problem in Nagaland in recent years, not least because the number of Nagas 'chasing the dragon' has been on the rise, too, their use of shared needles helping to spread the HIV virus.)

Prosperity, though, is an elastic concept. Although the town is busy during the day, a self-imposed curfew seems to come down on Mokokchung all too early. If you want to eat out, you need to do so by five p.m.; on most nights the town is battened down by seven. Water is at a premium while, like Nagaland as a whole, Mokokchung is officially 'dry', so it is hard to find much else to drink. Fear of the factional terrors the dark might bring is the reason Naga towns shut down and lock up for the night at sunset. If you want to be able to drink a (rice) beer or chat over a fire into the evening, you need to head for the distant hills, to the traditional villages, where there might be very little money and no cars, TVs or telephones, but where there will be life and soul and even parties.

Mokokchung provided a significant number of those Naga politicians involved in brokering the deal that led to the formation of Nagaland state in 1963. Unsurprisingly, then, it has long been a centre of Congress Party influence; thus, despite its faults, it gets a good press, especially from journalists who have never set foot there.

As for Jamir, he is clearly a remarkable fellow. A Christian, born in Ungma village, near Mokokchung in 1931, he studied law in Calcutta and Allahabad. He returned to the blue hills to become one of the architects of the sixteenth Indian state. As an MP, the first from Nagaland, he served in Delhi as a deputy minister in a variety of federal departments and was at one point parliamentary secretary to Nehru – no friend, of course, to the great majority of Nagas. Eventually he was elected chief minister of Nagaland, not once but four times. As well as the 2007 attempt on his life by Naga rebels, he has survived five more. The first was made in February 1990, when his car was ambushed by insurgents in Kohima. Jamir's driver and bodyguard were killed and his wife injured. In November 1992 Jamir was shot three times in the upper abdomen by Naga rebels at Nagaland

House, New Delhi. His survival was considered miraculous. Pipe bombs were planted to coincide with his arrival in Chumukedima in March 1994; these were detected in the nick of time. An ambush was made on his motorcade at the same location in November 1996. A fifth attempt on Jamir's life was made in November 1999, when his motorcade came under fire near Phepima and two of his security guards were killed.

The manner in which Jamir shrugged off these assassination attempts has impressed everyone; well, everyone except his key enemies in Nagaland. He has publicly forgiven them all. During his last term as governor of Nagaland he went even further, understandably calling on the army to tighten security measures but at the same time extending a hand in welcome to human rights organisations working in the state. Their role, he recognised, was as important in nurturing reconciliation between rival Naga factions as that played by any well-intended politician.

Despite such gestures, the mistrust continues. Jamir might have tried his very best over the years, but he is seen by those determined to create an independent Nagalim as a Delhi man, a Naga who is too close to India and its central government for comfort. Equally, the NSCN (I-M) and all those striving towards Nagalim dispute the assertion by Jamir and many Delhi politicians that the best route to a peaceful Nagaland is via economic development. While a number of lowland Nagas living in the former British 'administered areas', i.e. the lowlands, are doing a little bit better than they did before, those in the northern hills, and especially the *kingphi-kan* ('people from behind the mountain') in the Burmese part of the tribal areas, are living lives of poverty. For those across the border, there is little that Delhi can to do to ameliorate the situation, for demands on the military government in Rangoon are unlikely to be well received.

The NSCN (I-M), meanwhile, argues that for Nagalim to go it alone as an independent country would be best all round. Not only would violence end once Nagalim was free from India, but the new country would have generous friends, such as China, which would help it find its economic feet without demanding political control. An independent Nagalim might well be able to make it on its own, but whether violence within the country would stop, and whether this would occur sooner or later, is something very much harder to predict. Sectional violence tends to breed ever more splintered sectional violence, with violence itself becoming a way of life (and death). Given its new-found status in the early twenty-first century as a world superpower, a status achieved more by trade and international cooperation than by sheer military muscle and threats, China is unlikely to want to invest in a land riven with internal conflict.

When the latest attempt on Jamir's life was made in autumn 2007, and with state elections due in February 2008, a number of Indian reporters feared the onset of a fresh 'killing season' in Nagaland. One can only dream of a day when Naga will sit down peacefully with Naga in a Nagalim that might or might not include tribal territories outside the borders of Nagaland state and which might or might not be independent from India. Looking at the long list of violent incidents and intimidation that took place in Nagaland in just one year – 2007 – it is, it must be said, difficult to see such a happy dawn ever breaking over these troubled blue hills. Among the many killings of activists and civilians alike by rival NSCN factions, on 14 January the NSCN (K) asked Khekiho Zhimomi, Nagaland's Industries and Commerce minister, to submit Rs9.5m to its 'finance ministry' before 20 January. Or else. On 18 January Nagaland police arrested ten NSCN (K) militants, including its 'finance secretary' Inaka Swu, at 'an unspecified place between Officers Hill colony and Paramedical colony in the Kohima District'.

The following day a crowd some 10,000 strong marched to the office of the deputy commissioner in Phek, demanding that something should be done to rid the town of the presence of the NSCN, both (K) and (I-M), and the Naga National Council. On 28 January the NSCN (K) reiterated a previously issued 'quit' notice, advising Tangkhuls, the tribespeople who form the bulk of the NSCN (I-M), to leave Nagaland before 5 February, otherwise 'if anything happens to any Tangkhul be he/she a government servant or a businessman or a student or terrorist, it will be taken as self-inflicted punishment and no Naga organisation can be blamed'. This is like Lancastrians ordering all Yorkshire folk out of northern England within a week on pain of death, a stark illustration of the tragic absurdity of internecine strife in Nagaland.

That was just January. Edited highlights, as it were, of the rest of the year, included a major operation in February against the NSCN (K) and the United Liberation Front of Asom in Burma by the Myanmar armed forces, during which at least a hundred rebels were killed; a claim by the NSCN (K) that it had received financial support from the Congress Party; the lynching of three NSCN (I-M) members by civilians in Tuensang; the torching of hundreds of homes along with granaries and churches at Inavi village in the Peren district by the NSCN (I-M); and, just before Christmas, an attempt by Nagaland's chief minister, Neiphiu Rio, to negotiate a ceasefire between the Burmese army and the NSCN (K) because 'peace in the Naga areas of Myanmar is essential to develop trade with Myanmar through Nagaland'.

I should add just one more of the officially catalogued events of 2007. On 24 June, two brand-new excavators sent from Guwahati to Imphal were hijacked on the road south from Kohima by four unidentified gunmen. I mention this to show how talk of 'visionary' economic development in Nagaland is very hard to follow up in practice. Equipment, funds and personnel simply vanish into the jungle.

The other incidents I have chosen more or less at random to stress how strange Nagaland will seem to outsiders, and how violent it remains, even if sporadically so. As a foreigner with a love for India and a fascination for its remote borders, but supporting no side, belonging to no faction, no party (as in England, as away from home), I am hardly in a position to offer a solution for the political problems of Nagaland, nor, I know, would such suggestions be well received. None the less, sixty years of strife is sixty years too long.

That strife has affected every part of Naga culture. True, there may be a new generation of Nagas who simply want to enjoy life and to get away from the politics, the violence and the descent into warring factions, but, sadly, they cannot escape those sixty years of fighting and cruelty. The very first published volume of poetry by a single Naga voice, *Kelhoukevira* (1982), by Easterine Kire Iralu, is much concerned with the effect of the deaths of warriors, including those of three of her uncles, victims of the Indo-Naga conflict. Iralu has also written the first Naga novel in English, *A Naga Village Remembered* (2003), which is not quite the same as Ronald Blythe's *Akenfield* (1969) or Flora Thompson's trilogy *Lark Rise to Candleford* (1939–43), two of the twentieth-century works of fiction through which Britons map and treasure a passing English countryside and rural way of life. *A Naga Village Remembered* is rooted in the story of the suppression of Khonoma by the British in 1879.

Iralu's first reliable memory is as a five-year-old lying flat on a cold cement floor with her younger brother while shots reverberated around her neighbourhood in Kohima. Her father was shot at. A school friend was killed. When she was sixteen, she witnessed a military convoy shell houses at random in Kohima, killing and maiming many people, including small children. Between 2000 and 2005, because of the political writings of her husband, she lived in fear of gunmen, sitting up at nights, a double-barrelled shotgun in her hands in case of attack. Her son was kidnapped and imprisoned for three days. One of her daughters, held up in an ambush, watched as one of her party was shot dead by her attackers. Easterine Kire Iralu, like many Naga refugees caught up in the death-dealing of factional politics, wants to do something for her people. It's best she writes and gets her work as widely published as possible, for it is only, as she says herself, by understanding Nagaland that one might begin to unravel its politics and to address its future.

Back in Nagaland, there are many struggling to find a way forward from violence, and, yes, there is, in the lowlands at least, an up-and-coming young generation of Nagas expressing their concerns in music, writing, fashion and academia rather than through the brutal logic of the gun. However, there has yet to emerge a modern Naga culture that can surmount, or even balance, the weight of mainland Indian, Western and global culture seeping into the lowlands and the western and northern, if not, as yet, the eastern hills of Nagaland. I wish it would. If only, for example, Naga architecture could challenge the lumpen new concrete buildings that have begun to dominate and even to characterise the larger Naga towns and villages. The traditional buildings of Nagaland offer many clues for a way forward to a new local architecture, one with its own character and panache.

I thought of this particularly one day when I walked past the site of the old governor's house in Kohima and discovered only a hole in the ground. I was told by workmen on site that a modern 'luxury villa' was to be built in its place. The photographs I have since been sent show a building that might be found lounging on the fringes of practically every town and city in mainland India. The old governor's house, last rebuilt in 1957 on Garrison Hill, had been a modest affair, a construction of timber, bamboo and concrete-rendered walls. It was charm exemplified, but obviously not good enough for visiting VIPs from the mainland, and there was much tut-tutting over the state of the accommodation during the visits of the president in 2002 and the prime minister the following year. So, in 2004, the old building was demolished and a new design prepared by a Guwahati planning consortium. The house was completed in January 2006 and inaugurated by Nagaland's chief minister, Shri Neiphiu Rio, the following month. It looks to me rather like a downmarket hotel or upmarket bordello, but this is in the nature of the aesthetic of such 'modern' Indian homes, which are every bit as banal as those being rushed up in Britain today in executive cul-de-sacs the length and breadth of the country. No one expects a talent like that of

237

Edwin Lutyens or Sri Lanka's Geoffrey Bawa to emerge overnight in Kohima, capable of fusing traditional and modern design and raising architecture into the realms of artistry, but it does seem a shame that Nagaland has yet to find a way of representing itself architecturally when so many buildings are rising, partly as the fruit of Delhi's Look East policy. Until Nagas band together to forge a powerful modern culture, such developments remain unlikely, and buildings, as with so much else in terms of infrastructure, goods and culture, will continue to be shipped in from abroad. The fighting needs to stop first.

And yet, as one Naga chief, who wisely asked to remain anonymous, told an Indian news agency recently, 'My blood is Naga. That is God's decision. That does not mean that India is bad, but we are different. In 1956 our parents would say freedom first and peace second. Now, peace and unity are the first priorities. But, if the rebels were united, I would fight for them tomorrow.'

Epilogue

Moments before he died on 27 October 2006, Baba Lal Ji Maharaj, a 125-year-old sadhu, or Hindu holy man, who lived in Saiji village in the Ashok Nagar district of Madhya Pradesh in central India, announced that he was, in fact, Subhas Chandra Bose. At last, the case of the mysterious fate of the controversial Indian nationalist who had sought Hitler's help and fought with the Japanese to rid India of the British had been solved. For decades conspiracy theories concerning the fate of the supreme commander of the Indian National Army had been rife in India. Did Bose really die in an air crash at the Matsuyama airbase in northern Formosa on 18 August 1945, or had this all been a ploy to cover his disappearance either underground or to the USSR? Whatever the truth, and despite exhaustive inquiries by official Indian commissions, Bose's afterlife here on earth has clearly been a long one.

I was tickled at first, and then rather moved, and even slightly jolted by the story of Baba Lal Ji Maharaj's revelatory death. I revelled in the details. Not only was the sadhu's house in a village ashram a rich source of newspaper cuttings, photographs and travel tickets relating to the life and times of Bose, but the holy man had pointed to deep scars on his body that he said were the marks of wounds received when he 'fell from a plane' at the time of that fateful Formosa air crash more than sixty years ago.

As Kavindra Pal Singh Chouhan, a local policeman, went to gather evidence at the sadhu's house, crowds began to gather. This was not something that could simply be brushed off. Baba

Lal Ji Maharaj was, after all, a holy man and he had often spoken of Bose. The police officer told news reporters arriving on the scene, 'If the need arises, his body will be exhumed to confirm the claims.'

If Sherlock Holmes had been on the spot, he might have quickly deduced, by means of elementary arithmetic, that if the Baba Lal Ji Maharaj was 125 years old, he would have been born in 1881, sixteen years before Bose. It is possible that, after many years smoking sacred ganja, the Baba might have been mixing up his dates and may have been a mere 109 years old at the time of his death. It is also true that there is a long tradition of divine madness in Hinduism. And, yet, although the sadhu's story might seem on the lanky side of tall, the fact that it aroused widespread interest says much about certain aspects of life in India, and, to me, about the strange and almost inevitably distant relationship between India and Nagaland.

India is a predominantly Hindu country, and for all its immense wealth and, equally, its numbing and ineffable poverty, Hinduism both underpins and illuminates, in very bright colours indeed, much of its everyday life. Somewhere between four and five million sadhus live in India. Some are considered to be saintly gurus while there are those, well known to tourists, who are nothing more than gaily painted actors playing up to the gullibility of foreigners with generous purses who feel they ought to give alms to a holy man.

The sadhus are very much at the centre of the mind-boggling Kumbh Mela, the great Festival of the Pot of Nectar of Immortality that takes place every three years, rotating among four holy cities along the Ganges. In Hindu creation myths the gods once fought a fierce battle over a *kumbh* (pitcher) that contained the nectar of immortality. In the clash, four drops fell to earth in the towns of Allahabad, Haridwar, Nasik and Ujjain. These are the host cities for the greatest of Hindu festivals. I joined in the Kumbh Mela at Allahabad in January 2001. Gathered together to bathe in the confluence of the Ganges and

Yamuna, the River of Enlightenment, were between seventy and one hundred million pilgrims – yes, really, that many – in the company of what certainly looked to be every last sadhu in the subcontinent. All devoted Hindus aim to bathe here at least once in their lives. And what a time to do so, for among religious festivals this must be one of the most colourful, moving and overwhelming.

At these great festivals, sadhus are sought out as gurus. Here, if anywhere, they are not the mere beggars or colourful ascetics tourists might easily mistake them for, but the living embodiment of the divine. When they die, sadhus go to live on the foothills of Vishnu's sacred mountain at the source of the Ganges, where they glory in a state of enlightenment. It is easy to be sceptical if you find the gloriously complex ways of Hinduism too different from that of your own experience, and too difficult to come to terms with. But the point here is that, when he died and told a local policeman his 'secret', Baba Lal Ji Maharaj was saying that Bose himself was divine.

For separatist Nagas I have spoken to about the incident in Madhya Pradesh, the story of Baba Lal Ji Maharaj is significant in that it underlines their feeling that India, or 'Hindustan', has an almost divine mission to impress its values, its politics and its alien way of life on the Nagas, if not its religious beliefs; Hinduism itself is happy for any number of faiths to bloom, while 'Hindu fundamentalism' is a very recent phenomenon best explained, perhaps, as a counterbalance to the rise of intolerant Christian and Islamic fundamentalism. Certainly, many Nagas believe that their hills are being colonised by India, or that they are being patronised by mainland Indians who are really interested in Nagaland for only two reasons: its strategic role as a buffer state between India and China and its largely unexploited mineral wealth.

Clearly, there have been many misunderstandings between Naga tribespeople and Indian officials. Many of these may well stem from the simple fact that as you trek through Nagaland you rarely meet Indians. Soldiers, yes, along with a few logging contractors, helicopter pilots and well-meaning conservationists, but the ever-growing group of civil servants and politicians waxing fat on 'infrastructure' subsidies channelled into Nagaland might as well be invisible. When officials head into the smaller towns and hill villages of Nagaland it is usually by helicopter or else in convoys of cars provided with military escorts. Of course, they have every reason to fear ambush and even sudden death. Yet the more remote the new rulers of Nagaland appear to be, the greater the suspicion will grow that Nagas are second-class citizens, naked, singing, dancing cannibals to be looked down upon.

*

Pihota is a Naga doctor who walks from village to village with essential medical supplies, and to vaccinate children against disease. As we strolled together through a village north of Mon, I asked what she thought about the Raj:

> I am not standing up for the British Empire, but what my father and grandfather and many uncles say is that they did meet British officers even in villages in the non-administered areas. They didn't drive or fly then. They walked, and I think that by walking and meeting villagers face-to-face and drinking tea and beer with them, they came to know quite a bit about us, and even came to admire our people. I am not saying that bad things didn't happen between our people and the British, although no one in India would agree with this, I think that somehow things were a little better in the old days before India took over. I'm not talking about money and the modern way of life in the lowlands, but of the way people were looked on.

Perhaps she was just being kind to me. A part of what the British had learned about the running of an empire was unconsciously modelled on the tradition of both the Romans and the Mongols, whose own empire stretched from Hungary to Vietnam; both realised that if they left local people to their own devices and cultures, and allowed them a certain degree of freedom of control in areas of everyday life, then they would be more or less willing to cede political control in order to preserve their identity. Britain ruled India and Burma through a host of local princes and tribal chiefs, but ultimately the boot was on the imperial foot.

My impression, though, is that Nagas are either looked down upon by many contemporary Indian officials, or else feel that they are being looked down upon. Either way, this is not a happy situation. Early in 2009 the National Archives of India was asked to help with the loss of the state map submitted to the Home Ministry in Delhi in 1979. The map had been an important document aimed, in part, at settling border disputes with Assam. It had been handed over to officials in Assam that year and, rather conveniently, went missing. There were no copies. The loss of such a key document shows just how casually Nagas, and Nagaland, are treated. Here was a state without a map to call its own. From an official point of view it might as well not exist. What a clever way to get rid of troublesome Nagaland once and for fall. Erase it from the maps of India.

Intriguingly, work on redrawing the map began with the help of the National Archives. Fifty-three old maps drawn up by British colonial officers and district officers were dusted down and opened up into the service of Nagaland.

What I can't help sensing from stories like this and many others is that, the actions of Naga independence armies aside, until the development of Nagaland reflects true Naga sentiments, values, beliefs, culture and aesthetics, and until these are accepted by the Indian government, the Nagas will continue to feel as if they are part of a colonial system. Unless India does more than try to pump government money into Nagaland that, in any case, all too often ends up in the hands of the wrong people, the Nagas will not simply continue to fight for their independence, but may yet turn increasingly to other powers, notably China, for assistance, friendship and development. This would make sense in several ways. With the British Empire long gone, and US influence on the wane, China is fast becoming not only the new political and economic superpower but also the hub around which global markets turn. Anyone who has witnessed the Chinese at work, not just in boardrooms and government offices but in the factories and fields of Africa, the West Indies and various quarters of Latin America, will know how very effectively, whatever their motive, they are contributing to the development of the world's poor and ramshackle countries. Given the fact the Nagas themselves may have originated in south-west China, they might well find themselves shaking hands and drinking beer with a race they feel they have more in common with than the Hindu plainspeople of India – or, of course, the British of long ago.

The fact that Nagas tend to speak English and have historical cultural links with the Chinese should, in theory, put in them in a favourable position in terms of global economic development. And, yet, they remain landlocked, effectively cut off from the rest of the world and divided among themselves by sixty years of war. Some of the best minds, the best-educated people in Nagaland, are members of the NSCN and particularly the NSCN (I-M), which in large parts of the state, and beyond its 1963 borders, effectively acts as a second or overlapping government, complete with its own ministers and ministries. India's Look East policy is a way of trying to bring Nagaland and the other 'sister' states of the north-east into the modern world while broadening and deepening its trade links with South-East Asia, partly to counterbalance Chinese domination of the global economy. Ideally, this policy will gradually nurture an educated middle class in Nagaland that will want, soon enough, to be a fully paid-up member of the *Economist*-reading, internationally minded bourgeoisie.

I like to read *The Economist* on long-haul flights. Its soothing world view, rooted in the liberal economics of Adam Smith and in the comfortable arms of liberal democracy, the rule of law, prudence and common sense, makes all seem somehow well with the world. Every article is meticulously written, yet unashamedly edited into a smooth and seamless philosophy. Balanced. Measured. Passions calmed. Sure of itself, and ever so slightly smug. Its adverts offer jobs bedecked with entertainingly pompous titles – 'Global Chief Executive, Corporate Operations', that kind of thing – demanding degrees from business schools and offering salaries that would keep 2,500 families in Nagaland sheltered, fed and clothed for a year. But this supremely rational, cat-got-the-cream world view fails, albeit with perfectly good grace, to take into account tribal loyalties, desires for independence, or myriad other factors that matter most to many people. Although the business community the world over will disagree, there is just a slim chance that the global economy could yet allow many differences to blossom and thrive and that some of us do not want to be Club Class business executives or politicians in natty suits flying around the world to attend important PowerPoint presentation conferences.

It is easy to label anyone who seeks out and encourages difference as a romantic, a latter-day Don Quixote tilting at windmills. Yet I think it is important for peoples in the world who feel themselves to be unheard, misunderstood or otherwise pushed into a dark and uncomfortable corner where no foreign light shines, to have their story told, and for them to feel that they do not have to move forward into the modern world in step with everyone else. So many of today's problems are caused by the most powerful governments believing that their ways are the right ones – 'All ways are my ways', as the Queen of Hearts said to Alice – and that they somehow have a right to impose their values, their political and economic systems, their financial institutions and even their holier-than-thou, and sometimes explosive, religions on the rest of the world.

Even the UN and the various aid and peacekeeping NGOs (non-governmental organisations) that accompany it around the world are not always looked on benignly, or as appropriate saviours, by those living in some of the poorest and most battered corners of the planet. Not long ago, while making a BBC radio programme on Asmara, the extraordinary and rather beautiful Italian-fascist-style capital of Eritrea on the east coast of Africa, I was a touch surprised to see ranks of brand-new off-road vehicles, all gleaming white and emblazoned with big black UN initials, lined up outside the country's one modern air-conditioned five-star hotel, the Intercontinental Asmara, set well out of town, and away from local people, on the road to the airport. This was the lodging house of power-showered UN and NGO folk. A party of groomed Italian UN soldiers seemed to spend their time either larking about in the hotel's outdoor swimming pool or at the tables of the restaurant-bar in the company of astonishingly beautiful local girls wearing so few clothes that Christoph von Fürer-Haimendorf could only ever have labelled them 'Naked Eritreans'. UN and NGO folk, many of them good and committed people doing their best, are called 'men in Jeeps' here, as in many other poor countries where those charged with providing outside aid and security seem like colonial police and officials, especially to those eking out a living in far-flung villages without running water, much less electricity or phones or radio or TV.

The example of David Ward, the Naga Vigil human rights activist, serves as a good example of how the best intentions of an independently minded foreigner, even one with a big-hearted, highly personal and intelligently empathetic belief in the cause of a particular people, can be misunderstood by all sides in a country at war with itself. Ward's mistake – the word sounds a little unkind – in Nagaland was to side, more by accident than design, with one political, and thus tribal, faction. In doing so, he found himself hunted by both Indian security forces and rival Naga factions. He is now viewed by many Nagas as, at best, an interfering busybody and at worst an enemy, and this despite the many genuine benefits he has brought to some of the very poorest villages in Nagalim.

My own feeling is that the best way for me to help Nagaland is to bring its story to the attention of the world, in the hope that its plight might be discussed openly and intelligently. If India were to open the borders of Nagaland to foreigners, it would very probably be for the better rather for the worse. There will never be a flood of tourists to this difficult if bewitching terrain, and yet an exchange of ideas, dreams, values, medical aid and joint-venture projects between Nagas and people from different corners of the world could well enable it to feel less persecuted, less suspicious of outside influences, and even allow it to flourish.

*

Many foreigners have tried to liberate the isolated and oppressed in recent history. Despite their best intentions, the results of their actions have often been mixed, confused and misunderstood. T. E. Lawrence has probably had the greatest influence on successive waves of romantic travellers longing to encounter and share the life of wild and distant people, and even to do some good. Lawrence's dream of a liberated and independent Arabia was, as is well known, cruelly shattered by the political connivance of the British and French who had, all along, planned to divide the desert sands into a number of artificial kingdoms under their protection and influence, not least because these ancient and yet to be developed lands were already known to be rich in oil. Lawrence's fate, despite his fame, was to be derided by the majority of British politicians and officials as a romantic and unreliable adventurer while being despised by the very Arabs he had fought with for being a British officer in the service of a duplicitous and greedy empire. No wonder that, having written his biblical-style epic *Seven Pillars of Wisdom* (1922), Lawrence shied away from the fame he won among popular audiences as the white-robed, messianic and impossibly heroic 'Lawrence of Arabia'; he sought refuge as a common soldier in the army and the RAF and died in a motorcycle accident in the lanes of Dorset, a corner of south-west England that is culturally as far, I think, as it is possible to be from the burning Arabian sands.

As for David Ward, now living quietly in Scotland, his love for the Naga people he knows so well has not diminished, but he has had to come to terms with the fact that foreigners can never really 'win' in countries torn apart by internal factions.

By the time I came to Nagaland, following my own star and to an extent in the footsteps of my father, grandfather and other relatives burning bright in old and curling family photographs, who became involved in east and north-east India via medicine, soldiery, tea, ships and railways, I wished to be no more than an observer in a world that I so much wanted to be so very special. When I finally identified an opportunity to reach Nagaland via a long trek down from the foothills of the Himalayas, all I wanted to do was to walk, talk and look. I had no interest in any form of interference, nor did I even plan to write this or any other book about the blue hills east of Assam.

Since childhood, I have been an avid reader of classic travel books by enticing British writers like Richard Burton, Charles Doughty, Harry St John Philby, T. E. Lawrence, Robert Byron, Wilfred Thesiger, Jan Morris, Eric Newby, Colin Thubron and Bruce Chatwin. And, yet, I suppose I wanted Nagaland, my Nagaland, to be a private hideaway, my Secret Garden, my Lost World, my Shangri-La. This was partly because it was forbidden in terms of visa restrictions, but more because it represented the veiled world of an India, and lands beyond, that I had dreamed of visiting from a very young age (although, at the time, in a manner and style befitting a grandchild, as it were, of the British Empire).

It seems odd, and even rather funny, to me that the Nagaland now presented for the delight of Indian and international tourists on official state websites is an even more naive and *Boy's Own*-style land than that of my childhood imagination. No mention is made of politics, war, or even the true beauty of the Naga Hills, much less the complex nature and culture of its many peoples.

I had fallen in love with India, as so many others have, at first sight and smell. How could I not have? From watching a roseate sun rise over Mount Everest as I first stood on Tiger Hill, a short trek from Ghum station on the 'Toy Train' railway up to Darjeeling, to the sight of girls in saris at Calcutta bus-stops weaving headily scented fresh flowers into one another's glistening palm-oiled hair, India held me in her voluptuous embrace. And, yet, Nagaland, those distant, sealed-off Naga Hills, seemed to belong, if they existed at all, in another world and one that might not have changed, for all I knew, since the days of British colonial officers in sola topees and long khaki shorts.

In this spirit, here is J. P. Mills, again, writing to Mrs Pamela Mills in Assam, from 'Camp Phire-Ahire' on 14 November 1936:

We had our bellyful of hills today, not a hundred yards level in 10 miles. First we dropped 2,000 ft. to a stream and climbed 1,500 ft. to Thungare, then down another 1,500 ft. to a stream which is the frontier, and up about 3,000 ft. to our camp, a fine spacious one.

We were all pretty cooked, a change into a dry shirt and rest, sandwiches, and the Baron [Christoph von Fürer-Haimendorf] and I went to look at the village. Every one is so friendly that we did not take an escort into the village, where the Gaonbura gave us an exhibition with a crossbow, the popular weapon in this part of the world.

Then I came back, found my tent up, took off my boots and slept like the dead till tea. I think tea is the best meal of the day on these shows, and there is no doubt it does cheer one up.

We gather every evening before dinner. Williams is pretty tired, I fancy. I heard his call for the Hospital Orderly to massage him. The Baron lay down and went to sleep the moment he had finished his sandwiches, just where he was sitting! Smith is fairly cooked, I fancy, but he bustles round far more than he need. Your tough Philip [Mills] is going very strong, thank you, though he is a good deal older than anyone else in the whole outfit. We sat over drinks till 9.15, a very cheerful party – soup, fish, barking deer and dried fruit. We are very short of vegetables, Smith having arrived in Mokokchung too late to have any ready yet. So we had a tin of Baked Beans!

We've got a short march tomorrow. The Column goes down a valley and up the other side. The Baron and I are going round through some villages, a little longer but less steep.

Short of a lot of detailed information on the notional geography, wildlife, flora, fauna and even the wild edible mushrooms of Nagaland, this Boy Scout world, so far from Calcutta, Tiger Hill, Rajastan, the Punjab or Delhi, was pretty much all I had to go on. Even then, Mills's letter is not all it seems. It was written, along with many more, on a 'punitive expedition' made by the district officer, together with a company of soldiers into the eastern hills and across the border into Burma – a part of the British Empire, too, at the time. The expedition was fired on by Naga tribes, and fired back. In an interview made on video by Alan Macfarlane, Professor of Social Anthropology at Cambridge University, an elderly von Fürer-Haimendorf spoke of the party having to flee attacking tribesmen, of the British soldiers gunning five of them down, and also of the party's burning of houses in badly behaved villages. It took some while for me to piece together anything like a true picture of Nagaland, then, as now. I hope that what you might see in this book is how a child of his times in one part of the world grew up to meet a land and a people that could not be contained in a childhood dream or within the walls of a secret, and very hilly, garden. And why this author, having kept this story to himself for so long, has thought it best to tell it in the hope that the Nagas will get a fair hearing from beyond the fortress of their stunningly beautiful hills.

I cannot say, nor am I qualified to do so, what exactly will happen to the Nagas. Will they become a part of the modern world of getting and spending, prowling aimlessly around air-conditioned shopping malls? Will the gunmen of Nagalim's warring factions put down their weapons and lock them away? Will the veterans of the NSCN seem like political dinosaurs to younger generations desiring peace and economic development? In their case, and to borrow from the words of the Irish poet W. B. Yeats, who knew the effect of factional violence all too well, 'too long a sacrifice can make a stone of the heart'. And might the Indian government finally tell its army that one day soon it will no longer have the right of unfettered arrest in Nagaland?

Understandably mistrustful of India, Nagas cling to their quest for sovereignty as if to a totem pole, as Lt General N. S. Narahari underlines in his thoughtful analysis of the state in his book *Security Threats to North-East India*; yet tribalism and factional war have made independence all but impossible to achieve. Although Narahari acknowledges the Naga claim that the tribes have never been subjugated to be a myth of their own making, he does point out that the great strength of Naga society was its 'village level democratic method of organisation'. This, though, as he says, has been undermined, not least by the proliferation of corrupt layers of bureaucracy.

Here is a land that could be both beautiful and productive, abundant in hydro-electricity, wildlife sanctuaries, coffee plantations, the manufacture of beautifully designed and crafted goods, well-tended farms and villages that could retain their character even as water flows, clinics open and schools teach. A tropical Switzerland? Not exactly, but somewhere more akin to one than the poor and policed Indian colony it is at present. Here, after all, is a land that for all its isolation has been connected to some of the great events, global languages and world leaders of the past decades. The curious case of Baba Lal Ji Maharaj reminded me of the extraordinary cast of characters who have played a role in the making of Nagaland. Who would ever have thought that the hill paths of Nagaland could take us to the offices of Adolf Hitler and Emperor Hirohito? And, yet, just as

251

the Battle of Kohima, one of the most important of the Second World War, is largely unknown or forgotten, so Nagaland and the story of the Nagas remains walled in, a land where you walk above the clouds but which has very nearly been wiped clean off the Atlas. I have tried my flawed best to colour it back in.

*

I put the finishing touches to this book in the study of a Georgian rectory facing an old Suffolk walled garden. On most days, the garden was alive with birds. One frosty, wind-whipped morning, when the sea, not far away, had brought a flock of marauding seagulls this way, I watched with interest their effect on the pecking order inside these secret walls. As usual, the small birds – sparrows, robins, finches – squabbled over the sunflower seeds on offer in a feeder hanging from an apple tree. There were more than enough seeds for all of them, yet how they fluttered and fought to stop one another feeding. But they all scattered when the gulls dived in, wary of landing in such an unfamiliar and closely defined space, so scavenging little while causing the maximum disruption to the local birds, scared of their Gothic beaks and powerful wings. So much on offer, I thought, and such a lovely place to be, and yet so much conflict to the detriment of all.

Or, not quite all. Between skirmishes, doves would flutter down from the roof of the coach house overlooking the garden and eat all the seed that had spilt, untaken, onto the grass, and look cooingly content. I looked up over the garden walls to the distant frosty hills and thought again of Nagaland, and of how, from J. P. Mills and Christoph von Fürer-Haimendorf, from A. Z. Phizo and Jawaharlal Nehru, Subhas Chandra Bose and British officers of my father's generation, to the Naga cadres of the NSCN (K) and NSCN (I-M), we are all creatures of our own walled gardens. And, even when we lift ourselves up above the hills in order to see the bigger picture, how disinterested, detached and lonely our view must seem to those fighting, however messily, for survival and freedom below.

Selected Bibliography

Anand, Colonel V. K., *Nagaland in Transition*, Associated Publishing House, 1967
— *Conflict in Nagaland: A Study of Insurgency and Counter-insurgency*, Chanakaya, 1980
Ao, Alemchiba, *The Arts and Crafts of Nagaland*, Naga Institute of Culture, 1968
— *A Brief Historical Account of Nagaland*, Naga Institute of Culture, 1970
Ao, Tajenyuba, *History of Anglo-Naga Affairs*, Gauhati, 1958
— *British Occupation of Naga Country*, Naga Literature Society, 1993
Arya, Aditya and Joshi, Vibha, *The Land of the Nagas*, Mapin Publishing, 2004
Barpujari, S. K., *The American Missionaries and Northeast India: A Documentary Study, Christianity and its Impact on the Nagas*, Spectrum, 1986
Bayly, Christopher and Harper, Tim, *Forgotten Armies: Britain's Asian Empire and War with Japan*, Allen Lane, 2004
Boruah, B. K., *Nagamese: The Language of Nagaland*, Mittal, 1993
Chasie, Charles, *The Naga Imbroglio*, United Publishers, 1999
Daili-Mao, Ashikho, *Nagas: Problems and Politics*, Ashish Publishing House, 1992
Elwin, Verrier, *The Nagas in the Nineteenth Century*, Oxford University Press, 1969
Gangmumei, Kamei, *Jadonang: A Mystic Naga Rebel*, privately published, 1997; Lamyanba Printers, 2002
Ghosh, B. B., *History of Nagaland*, S. Chand, 1982
Graham Bower, Ursula, *Naga Path*, Faber and Faber, 1952
— *The Hidden Land*, John Murray, 1953
Guha, Ramachandra, *India after Gandhi: The History of the World's Largest Democracy*, Macmillan, 2007
Gundevi, Y. D., *War and Peace in Nagaland*, Palit and Palit, 1975
Hargovind, Joshi, *Nagaland, Past and Present*, Akansha, 2001
Horam M., *Nagas: Old Ways and New Trends*, Cosmo, 1988
Hutton, J. H., 'Tour Diaries in Unadministered Areas', School of African and Oriental Studies archive, 1918
— *The Sema Nagas*, Macmillan, 1921

—— *The Angami Nagas, With Some Notes on Neighbouring Tribes*, Macmillan, 1921

Iralu, Easterine Kire, *Kelhoukevira [Land of My Dreams]*, J. B. Lama, 1982

—— *A Naga Village Remembered*, Kali for Women, 2003

Jacobs, Julian, *The Nagas: Hill Peoples of North East India*, Thames and Hudson, 1990

—— *The Nagas: Society, Culture and Colonial Encounters*, River Books, 1990

Jacobs, Julian, et al., *The Nagas*, Thames & Hudson, 1990

Johnstone, Sir James, *My Experiences in Manipur and the Naga Hills*, Sampson Low Marston and Co., 1896

Luithui, Luingam and Haksar, Nandita, *Nagaland File: A Question of Human Rights*, Lancer, 1985

Mills, J. P., *The Lhota Nagas*, Macmillan, 1922

—— *The Ao Nagas*, Macmillan, 1926

—— *The Rengma Nagas*, Macmillan, 1937

Mitra, Subhaadra, *Nagaland, Contemporary Ethnography*, Cosmo, 1999

Narahari, Lt Gen. N. S., *Security Threats to North-East India: The Socio-Economic Tensions*, Manas Publications, 2002

Nibedion, Nirmal, *Nagaland: The Night of the Guerrillas*, Spantech & Lancer, 1998

Patterson, George M., *Peking versus Delhi*, Faber and Faber, 1963

Puthenpurakal, Joseph, *Baptist Missions in Nagaland*, South Asia Books, 1984

Reid, Sir Robert, *History of Frontier Areas Bordering Assam from 1833–1941*, Shillong, 1948

Richards, Louanne, *Journey into Nagaland*, Abzu, 1995

Sanyu, Visier, *History of Nagas and Nagaland: Dynamics of Oral Tradition in Village Formation*, Firma KLM, 1997

Sema, Piketo, *British Policy and Administration in Nagaland, 1881–1947*, Scholar, 1991

Sen, Spira, *Tribes of Nagaland*, Mittal, 1987

Shakespear, L. W., *History of the Assam Rifles*, Spectrum, 1929 (republished 1980)

Shanker, Kiran, *Naga Folk Tales*, Maitra/Mittal Publications, 1990

Sharma S. H. and Sharma, Usha (eds.), *Discovery of North-East India: Geography, History, Culture, Religion, Politics, Sociology, Science, Education and Economy*, Vol. IX: *Nagaland*, Mittal, 2005

Shimray, R. R., *Origin and Culture of Nagas*, Samsok, 1985

Singh, Chandrika, *Political Evolution of Nagaland*, Lancers, 1981

Singh, Kanwar Randeep, *The Nagas of Nagaland: Desperadoes and Heroes of Peace*, Deep and Deep, 1987

Singh, K. S., *People of India*, Vol. III: *Nagaland*, Seagull Books, 1995

Singh, Longjam Randeep, *National Security Problem in India: A Case Study of the Insurgency Problem in Nagaland and Manipur*, Ashish Publishing House, 2000

Singh, Prakash, *Nagaland*, National Book Trust (India), 1977

Slim, Field Marshal William, *Defeat into Victory: Battling Japan in Burma and India, 1942–1945*, Cassell, 1956

Smith, John Butler, *Travels and Adventures in the Province of Assam during the Residence of Fourteen Years*, Elder and Co., 1855

Stirn, Aglaja and Van Ham, Peter, *The Hidden World of the Naga: Living Traditions in Northeast India and Burma*, Prestel, 2003

Steyn, Peter, *Zapuphizo, Voice of the Nagas*, Kegan Paul International/ Whitaker, 2002

Stracey, P. D., *Nagaland Nightmare*, Allied Publishers, 1968

Thompson, Julian, *Behind Enemy Lines*, Sidgwick & Jackson, 2007

van Eekelen, W. F., *Indian Foreign Policy and the Border Dispute with China*, Martinus Nijhoff, 1964

van Ham, Peter and Stirn, Aglaja, *Seven Sisters of India: Tribal Worlds between Tibet and Burma*, Prestel, 2001

van Ham, Peter and Saul, Jamie, *Expedition Naga, Diaries from the Hills in Northeast India 1921–37, 2002–2006*, ACC Editions, 2008

Verrier, Elwin (ed.), *Nagaland*, Spectrum, 1997

von Fürer-Haimendorf, Christoph, *The Naked Nagas, Headhunters of Assam in Peace and War*, Methuen, 1939

—— *Return to the Naked Nagas*, John Murray, 1952

—— *The Sherpas of Nepal*, John Murray, 1964

—— *The Tribes of India: Struggle for Survival*, University of California Press, 1982

Ward, David, 'Behind the Bamboo Curtain', unpublished manuscript

Woodthorpe, Robert Gosset, *The Lushai Expedition, 1871–2*, Hurst & Blackett, 1873

Yonuo Asoso, *The Rising Nagas: A Historical and Political Study*, Manas Publications, 1974

Young, Gavin, *The Nagas: An Unknown War*, National Naga Council, 1962

Zehol, Lucy, *Woman in Naga Society*, Regency, 1998

Zhimoni, Kuhoi K., *Politics and Militancy in Nagaland*, Deep and Deep, 1003

There is also in existence, although hidden away until the dust in Nagaland and Nagalim settles, a Naga national archive containing many more books than those mentioned in the text or listed above. The archive also includes films, maps, audio cassettes, diaries and some 12,000 letters and other documents concerning Naga culture, politics and history.

Index